HARCOURT BRACE & COMPANY · 1919–1994 · SEVENTY-FIVE YEARS ·

Innocents in Africa

DRURY PIFER

Innocents

AN AMERICAN FAMILY'S STORY

in Africa

Harcourt Brace & Company

New York   San Diego   London

Requests for permission to make copies of any part
of the work should be mailed to:
Permissions Department, Harcourt Brace & Company,
6277 Sea Harbor Drive, Orlando, Florida 32887-6777.

Library of Congress Cataloging-in-Publication Data
Pifer, Drury L.
Innocents in Africa: an American family's story/by Drury
Pifer.—1st ed.
p.   cm.
ISBN 0-15-107564-6
1. Pifer, Drury L.   2. Americans—South Africa—
Biography.   3. South Africa—Biography.   I. Title.
DT1768.A62P54   1994
968'.00413'092—dc20   93-22926

Designed by Lori J. McThomas
Printed in the United States of America
First edition

A B C D E

To the memory of my mother and father,
and in memory of my daughter Kimberley.

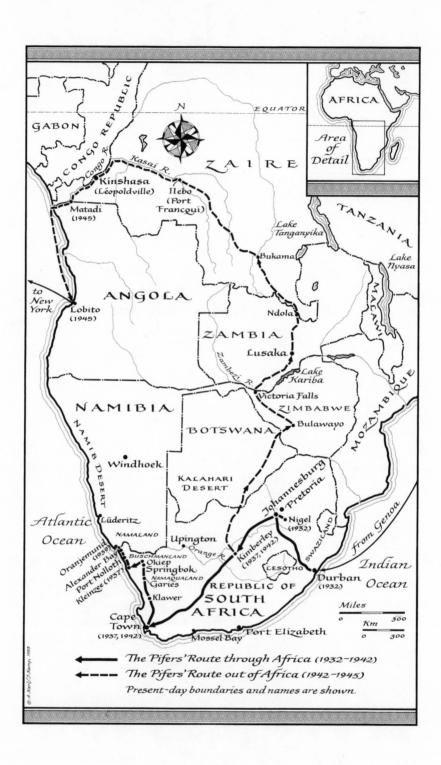

AFRICA

Area of Detail

EQUATOR

GABON

CONGO REPUBLIC

Congo R.

Kasai R.

Kinshasa
(Léopoldville)

Ilebo
(Port
Francqui)

Matadi
(1945)

ZAIRE

TANZANIA

Lake
Tanganyika

Lake
Nyasa

Bukama

to
New
York

Lobito
(1945)

ANGOLA

Ndola

ZAMBIA

Lusaka

Zambezi R.

Lake
Kariba

MALAWI

Victoria Falls

ZIMBABWE

MOZAMBIQUE

NAMIBIA

BOTSWANA

Bulawayo

NAMIB DESERT

Windhoek

KALAHARI
DESERT

Johannesburg
Pretoria

*Atlantic
Ocean*

Lüderitz

NAMALAND

Upington

Orange R.

Nigel
(1932)

Kimberley
(1937, 1942)

SWAZILAND

From Genoa

Oranjemund (1939)
Alexander Bay
Port Nolloth
Kleinzee (1937)

BUSCHMANLAND

Okiep
Springbok
NAMAQUALAND
Garies

LESOTHO

Durban
(1932)

*Indian
Ocean*

Klawer

REPUBLIC OF
SOUTH
AFRICA

Cape
Town
(1937, 1942)

Mossel Bay

Port Elizabeth

Miles
0   300
Km
0   300

⬅ The Pifers' Route through Africa (1932–1942)
⬅- - The Pifers' Route out of Africa (1942–1945)
Present-day boundaries and names are shown.

© A. Karl/J. Kemp, 1995

Contents

Contents

Acknowledgments

THIS MEMOIR COULD NOT HAVE BEEN WRITTEN IF MY GRAND-mother, Elizabeth Tarrent Newman, had not saved the letters our family mailed her every week for thirteen years from the African continent.

The book was begun at the suggestion of my friend, Tracy Johnston, whose encouragement and practical advice were crucial. I particularly wish to thank my uncle, Emil Martin, for detailed information about our family's early days; my sister, Patricia Pifer, for the extended loan of that old photo album which revived so many memories; and my cousin, Joan Woodard, for all she told me about the last days of our uncle Nick. I am also grateful to my agent, Gloria Loomis, and my editor, Pat Strachan, for their enthusiasm and patience.

Last but always first, love and gratitude to my wife, Ellen, who so often kept me from losing track in the thickets of my syntax.

Innocents in Africa was written with the partial aid of a grant from the Delaware State Arts Council.

Innocents in Africa

1

Another Africa

OUR FOUR-ROOM HOUSE IN THE NAMAQUALAND DESERT WAS HEDGED from the shifting sands by a corrugated iron fence. The wind singing in the electric wires is a sound I knew before I became conscious of myself. The afternoon wind was always there at the windows, rattling their frames, restless under the roof. At night the stars were so brilliant they seemed closer than the flat hills to the east. The village was called Oranjemund because it had been thrown up near the mud-choked mouth of the Orange River, but no orange trees grew on its banks. Dust coated the crockery, dust impregnated the curtains and sifted through my sister's hair, dust floated on the surface of my milk. When you think of South-West Africa, think of flies and wind and dust.

I used to climb up on the tin outhouse roof so that the driving sand wouldn't lash my face. On the horizon, I could almost see the ocean. The Atlantic is cold off Oranjemund. The waves are steep

and businesslike as they stride toward shore. Strange to think that
now, as I write, green waves are rolling out of a black sea across
those cold beaches, washing along that wind-battered shore exactly
as they did then. Though I have changed out of all recognition and
my parents are no longer alive, still the same waves come sweeping
in to the foot of those same bleached and desolate towns—Lüderitz,
Port Nolloth, Walvis Bay. The names on the map are the same too;
villages inhabited by poor Africans, bored bureaucrats, glum police
officers, and dusty Boers who come off their farms looking more like
golems than men.

By the time my father made it out to that godforsaken coast, the
desert looked like heaven to him. He had escaped the gold mines on
the Rand where a man named Fleisher was trying to destroy him. My
mother would have preferred New York or Paris, but remote landscapes attracted my father, wastelands where the rocks promised trea-
sures—copper, gold, diamonds.

Tall, immensely kind, and seldom impatient, he had the awkward-
ness of an original, the look of a solitary who never feels entirely at
his ease unless he's solving a problem. He was a mining engineer the
way other men are composers, or inventors, or mystics. In time, we
came to misunderstand each other perfectly. I read literature; he read
landscapes. He was at home with heavy machinery; I was attracted
to aircraft. As a young man, he went to Alaska to work underground.
As a young man, I went there to fly geologists over the mountains.
His handwriting was wonderfully precise, leaning exactly fifteen degrees to the right; mine leans where it likes and exhibits the scrawl
of a will at cross-purposes. Above all things, I love music and hate
noise. He was tone-deaf, at home with giant jackhammers and expert
in the use of high explosives.

We were always pleased to see other other, but our common
ground contained a bottomless pit. I could never quite reach him (a
common failing among sons and fathers), and he never could quite
make me out. It was not easy to connect with a male child attracted
to Emily Dickinson and blind to core samples. All of the offices he

inhabited were crowded with rocks and mineral samples—stalactites, crystals, diorite. When we moved (and we moved often) his heavy box of specimens moved with us. They lay in glass cabinets, or crept quietly out across chairs and desks. My interest in the Arts (with a big A) seemed to him fatuous and impractical. He occasionally detected signs that I was not entirely an idiot, but my future worried him. He suspected I might not have one.

I imagined that the gray distance in the landscape of the Pacific Northwest had penetrated his heart and stuck there like a speck of glass. I experienced a dreamlike frustration whenever I went hunting for his soul in whatever remote Alaska he kept it buried. We talked about fishing or Red China or the fate of the universe. To him I must have seemed confused, soft, unfocused—a poor candidate for manhood.

Having endured the slavery of the gold mines, he'd gone out into the Namaqualand to sift through millions of tons of sand and stone for diamonds and was immediately at home in the desert. Cities were full of middlemen. Types. That was his view. Real work was done in the earth, plowing it or going underground.

My cities were constructed from images I picked up in the *Arabian Nights*, from Hans Christian Andersen or Charles Dickens. Surrounded by dunes that might appear or disappear in an afternoon, my imagination had few fetters. The ghostly double in my mind ran down twisting streets, through secret doorways into gardens with red brick walls. In the desert, the imagination is watered by literature and the horizon. It was always a city I saw rising up in the desert haze—clock towers, flying buttresses of watery stone set in a blue lake, unreal. When I was a child I would set out for the mirage knowing the thing was an illusion but unable to believe it was nothing at all. Trudging through the hot sand, I saw the white and blue domes waver and retreat. If I had a future I knew it was there, written in those watery forms, no matter the whole thing was an apparition, an atmospheric trick.

A *fata morgana*, my mother once called it—an expression I found lovely and frightening. (Soon, a handful of idiotic ideas would reduce Europe to rubble and a few more years erase my indestructible parents from this rickety world—demonstrating how our apparently solid planet is a kind of apparition, a temporary configuration of words and dust.)

How can anyone appreciate a city until his car breaks down in the desert? You must leave Lüderitz and bump along ragged roads to Cape Town. The track is composed of shifting sand. The luggage is piled on the roof; the trunk is stuffed with tins of gasoline. You must travel in a new Lincoln Zephyr that overheats every half hour, and then, seventy miles from the nearest town, explodes in a tower of steam. You must walk through the freezing night, shivering until the sun rises and 120 degree heat turns the sand into a stove top that blisters your feet through the soles of your city shoes. You must see fifty pale blue Camelots rise before you, glittering in the heat haze and humming with human voices that resolve into the whispering of a morning wind. If you limp far enough you find what you are looking for— a battered Shell Petrol sign and a small, toothless garage mechanic, dressed in khaki shorts three sizes too large. Pascal talks about his terror of infinite space. You don't have to fly to the moon to find it. Leave the city and go far enough and it's all around you. I feel little inclination to return.

In the mines, my father was kindly but formidable; at home, he was the man with all the answers and the family clown. Unlike the humorless Afrikaner men and the pompous Germans, he didn't mind playing the fool. And there was nothing my mother loved more than a good laugh. Once, when the tide was high off Kleinzee and the water too deep for my father to wade out to his favorite fishing rock, he stripped naked and swam out wearing only a hat. He emerged with the aplomb of a British diplomat, pale buttocks gleaming, and I remember my mother rolling about on her beach blanket, helpless with laughter.

She was the clairvoyant one and had the intuitive edge over him.

Mad about music and painting, she was gifted with the greater personal force, so the last word was usually hers. Science was my father's guide and it provided him with every answer except how to live his life. He and my mother had both experienced childhood as a kind of prison. Both came from extremely poor homes. Her stepfather had moved his family into a chicken coop soon after arriving in Seattle. His mother set up in a one-room apartment in Seattle after her divorce. My mother's stepfather was violent. My father's father was a drunk. So both of my parents craved order. He came to trust in reason. He was drawn to things, while she was interested in people. Both of them had tremendous faith in hard work—somewhat misplaced as it turned out.

My parents lacked fathers because their mothers had very bad luck with men. My father took his father (Drury Fair Pifer of Charleston, South Carolina) as an object lesson in failure. Drury Fair had done things so terrible that my grandmother, Elizabeth Chalmers Tarrent, would never speak of them. A kind of spectral silence had swallowed up any mention of Drury Fair. So we knew never to ask about the old boy. I don't recall Bess ever pronouncing his name aloud. Of course we imagined the worse—hard whiskey, vomity afternoons in filthy brothels among plump, naked women. Whatever he did, Bess had run from him like a wounded thing, getting out of Charleston and going as far away as the train would take her.

Drury Fair had caused Bess so much pain that she felt extreme discomfort having to pronounce the word "Drury." Yet both her son and grandson were named Drury. This left her in a quandary, our names reflecting, as names often do, the betrayals and failures of a previous generation. Whenever she was in the room, people called my father Gus. She knew the moment she left everyone switched to Drury. But that was all right as long as she herself was never exposed to the contaminated syllables. For twelve years, I was to know her only through her letters and the lacy valentines and the books she sent into our remote desert. When I finally met her in Seattle's King Street Station one day in 1945 (clumpy shoes, black hat, white gloves, firm mouth) she did try out "Drury" on me. But the word stuck in her throat and she quickly reverted to Lou. So Lou I became whenever she was present, though the name (my middle name) disappeared when she died (December, 1960) and never saw service again.

The man Bess admired most was Drury Fair's father, Augustus Poindexter Pifer. He was always "Captain Pifer" to her. So I imagined him in a gray field uniform—floppy field hat, gray gloves, medals, and boots. My sister and I figured she fell in love with the captain and married the ne'er-do-well son by default. Captain Pifer was well regarded in South Carolina, having served as the officer in charge of General Robert E. Lee's personal bodyguard. Later he became president of two women's colleges (no one now remembers which ones). He died in 1907, and six years later Bess fled west with her nine-year-old son.

Bess kept Captain Pifer's obituary among her papers, and it was so curiously written that I made a copy for myself. The style is ornate, the sentiments tropical, but the gilded prose throws some light on the history that informed my father's childhood. Though he grew up in the remote Northwest, his mother dominated his childhood and the world she approved was the one reflected in Captain Pifer's obituary. The passage is long; this excerpt is brief:

Captain Pifer was first a gentleman. He was cast in the heroic mould, but he was as tender as a woman. . . . He realized the frailties and weaknesses of humanity, and for those who failed he had cheer and hope. . . . Personal letters to him after the war from General Lee showed in what esteem his old commander held him. And Captain Pifer loved General Lee, and he loved the South. He loved Southern traditions, he loved Southern people and he loved Southern soil. . . . He was always approachable and was frequently sought by those younger than himself . . . for he was deeply learned and widely read, and his discussion of men and measures was always interesting and entertaining. . . .

In the Charleston where Bess grew up, this kind of language flowered as naturally as the magnolias. But setting aside General Lee and the Southern soil, the ideals expressed here are the kind of thing Bess passed on to her boy. She found herself a single parent in 1913 and she managed to survive and eventually thrive in the social void of the Northwest by clinging to ornate old ideals. The useless Drury Fair never sent a dime. She never complained. She had broken Southern law (any woman who leaves her husband is lost), and she expected to be cast out. But these constraints imposed by her Southern past toughened her will. She survived.

Her powerful attraction to decorum was written all over my father though he kept some of its more flowery aspects to himself. This private side of his nature may be reflected in another passage from the captain's obituary.

When it was learned that he was dead, found dead in his bed, his features in as calm repose as though he were a child asleep after a day with its toys, one was reminded of the passing of Tennyson's Arthur, for Captain Pifer was as knightly and his passing as fitting. . . . It was as though Captain Pifer's funeral barge had been launched upon the great sea, gently floating beyond the horizon of mortal vision. . . . [And here a very long quote from Tennyson follows, depositing the Captain, finally, in the] "island valley of Avilion / where falls not hail, or rain, or any snow, / nor ever wind blows loudly . . ."

I am sure my father never read much Tennyson. Poetry baffled him. But poetry was a part of him nevertheless, and it set him in some measure against himself. Its power was reflected in the photographic prints he liked to make, in the films he shot, and in his attraction to the metallurgical process that transformed earth into concentrate and concentrate into a field of pretty stones where gold or diamonds lay glittering. But he suppressed this desire for beauty in himself, never allowing beauty to detach itself from science and technology.

Ten years after he had returned from Africa, when I was making one of my periodic visits to his corner office overlooking the University of Washington campus, he expressed scorn for Theodore Roethke, the poet, who happened to be a teacher of mine. Roethke sometimes suffered breakdowns in class and was removed, with a lot of uproar, by men in white suits. But I thought Roethke was the only person on campus worthy of the title teacher. Someone in the administration office told my father Roethke's madness was a publicity stunt—what writers do to attract the attention of a listless public.

I attacked my father for listening to gossip, and he was quite willing to hear me out. He often appeared abashed when confronted by passionate opinions. I remember the same look on his face when my mother went after him for some remark of his she disagreed with. "If you know Roethke, then you have reason for your opinion," he said.

While I was in college and still had all the answers, my father seemed to me naive, unable to deal with the slippery substance of his life. After our mother's death, my sister and I agreed he was being eaten alive in his second marriage. Dismayed and helpless, we watched him turn into what seemed to us the shadow of his former self. He would spend his final two decades floundering in a suburban existence that confined and diminished him.

When I visited him in his airy office at the university, my affection was undercut by frustration. I hardly knew what to say. He wanted his old life back. We all wanted the old life back. But it was buried with his wife, our mother. He and I never quite expressed what we had in common—that neither of us would accept the world on its own terms. I longed to advise him as my mother would have done. But I was only a callow son with a rubber backbone. My grades were on a roller coaster as I flopped from music to biology to history, tasting everything and mastering nothing—least of all myself. I spent hours in the library reading books unrelated to my courses or composing music that I seldom bothered to work out completely. He didn't tell me that I was lazy, badly misinformed, self-indulgent, and undisciplined. He was the least brutal of men.

If character is fate, then we were both fated to wrestle with ridiculous professions. I know he often cursed his work (as I sometimes curse mine). We were born into an age of middlemen, a time when miners, farmers, fishermen, and poets are socially invisible. Technology has transformed every perspective. Simone Weil remarks that social prestige accords honor to selected professions only. But "the often incredible heroism displayed by miners or fishermen barely awakes an echo among miners or fishermen themselves," she goes on. "And deprivation of honor attains an extreme degree in the total diminution of respect reserved for certain categories of human beings."

My father belonged, I now realize, to such a category. There were days when he looked back over his life and judged the whole thing a mistake, a disaster. Given his intelligence and energy, a dozen other professions would have made him more successful and well-off. Near the end of his life, he lost what money he had in an investment that in any other year would have made him rich.

Recently, I returned to the School of Mines and found the elegant old building transformed into a warren of tiny offices, airless offices. In each office sat a professor staring at a computer screen. The fine old watercolor landscapes in the lobby had been replaced by black-and-white photos of squeaky-clean miners operating beautiful new equipment in spacious underground caverns. My father's corner office had become inaccessible. It was blocked off by walls and locked doors. When I mentioned his name, expressions were blank. No one there had ever heard of him. The tenure of memory in university departments is very brief, and I stumbled out of the place like a man gratefully exiting a bad dream.

Was his life a mistake? a series of chances missed? Would his

young wife have lived to an old age had she never endured the dust-
storms in Namaqualand; the thin, frozen air of the Rand; the years
of witless gossip, the isolation, the exile? Did he blame himself for
her early death?

With so many new technologies blossoming, why choose mining? I
can only guess. Once, when I was reading aloud to him from Oswald
Spengler's evil *Decline of the West,* a certain paragraph arrested my
father's attention. He abruptly jumped up and, taking the volume
from my hands, went to copy down the words. This is the passage:

> The early artificers, in particular the metal smiths, appeared to those
> around them as somehow uncanny. It is the metals, above all, to
> whose sites in the earth primitive man is led by some mystical trait.
> Old trade routes lead to ore deposits that are kept secret. Through the
> life of the settled countryside and over distant seas travel tales and
> persistent legends of islands of tin, and lands of gold. The primary
> trade of all is the metal trade. On this foundation arises the technique
> of the higher Cultures. . . .

My father's life, and the way he seized on these obscure words,
makes me suspect he belonged to that mysterious race the Norsemen
called gnomes—creatures attracted to treasure, to minerals that run
like a network of metal nerves under the earth. And if this "uncan-
nily mystical trait" were not found in some people (the way musical
talent or legal genius is found in others), there would be no Bronze
Age, no Agamemnon's mask, no *Iliad,* no steam engine, no Golden
Gate Bridge.

My father himself would have explained it this way. The Africa of
1932 promised an outside chance to marginal people, those willing
to hock everything and borrow to pay their passage, those willing to
bet everything on a letter or a rumor. For outsiders like himself, to

journey so far from home might well gobble up a lifetime, but he couldn't know that.

Aged nineteen, my father had decided he might take advantage of his interest in geology and enter a basic industry where work would always be available. The world could not get on without minerals. So he put himself through school and graduated near the top of his class with two degrees. He then wrote over a hundred letters and mailed them to every mining company he could find an address for. It was the bottom of the depression. He got back only one reply from a manager of a gold mine on the Rand (a mining region on the Transvaal in South Africa). His name was Williamson and this Williamson was willing to try out an American who was not afraid to start at the bottom.

The trip from Seattle to Nigel, which was forty miles from Johannesburg, would take three months, and my mother wanted to make it into a poor person's grand tour. Her mother's family lived in the seaside village of Crikvenica in Croatia, overlooking the Adriatic Sea. She would, of course, stop there and hit every museum she could find. She wanted to see the Alps and Venice.

To make the trip they borrowed money. My parents got a loan from Louis Newman, a businessman who had married Bess Pifer the previous year. I doubt old Newman felt like forking over a thousand dollars in the worst year of the depression, but he owed my mother a lot. She had picked him up one afternoon in a downtown department store after overhearing his thick German accent. She told him she needed a native speaker to practice her German on, and he agreed to meet with her once a week. To pay for the lessons she would translate and type for him. She thought he might like to meet her mother-in-law, a Southern belle.

My father thought her plan to get old Newman together with his mother was ludicrous. Bess was suspicious and frosty. She did like to trot out her Southern charm occasionally, but she could be as blunt and tough as old shoe leather. A survivor first and a snob only when she had plenty of social elbowroom, she took her own sweet time to warm to a new face. Her new daughter-in-law had come from a doubtful environment—a violent stepfather, a mother with a thick accent. Once accepting, though, Bess was loyal to the grave. But, over the years, she had frozen herself into an apparently permanent independence, so my father was sure she would have nothing to do with Newman, encumbered by his thick accent and suspicious sisters.

Louis Newman was near seventy, very grave, and even more set in his ways than Bess. His sisters depended on him for their income and naturally regarded any romantic attachment as a direct threat to their welfare. It must have come as a terrible shock when their ancient brother told them he was marrying a superannuated Southern belle.

Whether Louis was swept off his feet or merely saw in Bess a good housekeeper and nurse, I don't know. But he married her within a year, and when my mother suggested the African loan he didn't hesitate. Louis would die long before my parents made it back from Africa, but Bess always remained their iron link with home. For thirteen years she was a solid rock in a sea of change, sending clothes, toys, books, valentines, and news of family disasters that everyone else tried to suppress.

After selling all their wedding presents and ignoring the advice of their friends, my parents left Seattle at twenty past one on the fifth of March 1932. The moment is faithfully recorded in my mother's little green diary. After a long farewell lunch with Louis and Bess, they drove away almost gaily, figuring they'd be back in three years at most.

It had rained steadily for sixteen weeks that spring. Rivers were flooding. Towns disappeared underwater. After logging 174 miles in a deluge, they parked for the night near the Oregon border, where they rented a cabin in a forest. My mother's first letter to Bess was written that night. (There would be hundreds more, and Bess would hand them all to me in 1960, a few months before she died, with the stern command, "I know you will write something!")

I see in my mother's first note a prophecy and an allegory. Not yet out of Washington State, she glimpsed "a man pushing his wife and child home in a rowboat" through the town of Kelso. The woman sheltered the child in her arms under an umbrella, "while her husband in hip boots pushed the boat like a Venetian gondolier right down the middle of the flooded main street. Only he wasn't singing." And she adds, "Scuse the awful writing. Done on the cracker box."

The picture of that family caught in a flood glitters in the mirror of my imagination as the real figures must have done in my mother's mind. Specters in a watery landscape—on closer inspection they turn into familiar doubles. The child is myself, born the following year. The flood is whatever adversity you please—the depression that set them in motion, the Namaqualand Desert that would burn up their youth, the European war that would keep them exiled. Starting out in a flood, the travelers soon found themselves in a parched land beneath an unrelenting sun, performing their transit from water to fire, innocence to experience.

I see my mother's familiar hand, still young, moving over the blue-and-white cracker box as she writes. Five hours into a thirteen-year journey, the smell of damp fire smoke and pine penetrates the cabin where she sits. The rain falls on the long deserted beaches that run along the gray Oregon coast, and on the coast of Africa the waves roll in at that moment as they roll in now as I write.

2

Arriving

THE FIRST STAGE OF THEIR JOURNEY CROSSED THE UNITED STATES and they calculated to hit every city where Bess had siblings. Scattered from Austin, Texas, to Charleston, South Carolina, were three sisters and a brother. The idea was to borrow money. My parents saw a lot of the South, but raised not a dime. Aunt Brantly in Austin was sympathetic but broke. Olive in New Orleans met them in a fur wrap and expressed surprise that her nephew's foreign wife spoke English without an accent. Whenever the subject of money came up she complained that her hearing was going. Robert Hayne, Bess's little brother, was the most beautiful member of the family, especially exquisite in 1932. There exists a snapshot of him in a white suit, fondling a short black cane as he lounges fabulously by a swimming pool. His mind was light as a feather, and after he had made his wonderful first impression there was little to be done with him. All of his disposable income went for fine cuisine and minstrel shows.

The long roundabout loop that took them from Seattle to New York by way of Texas and Louisiana cost a total of $154.36. San Francisco had no bridges then, and the air in Los Angeles was crystal clear. In the Southwest desert their car lost a generator (a portent of things to come in the Namaqualand Desert).

In New York, my parents sold the car for $40.00, which didn't cover the cost of ten days in a seedy room in Greenwich Village ($47.40). The ticket to France set them back $657.40. This figure indicates how expensive travel was back when a loaf of bread cost five cents. Multiply this by the cost of a loaf today and you end up with the passage costing something like $20,000 in contemporary dollars.

While waiting for their boat to embark, they lived on eggs, corn flakes, and cocoa for a week. On the day they left America, my mother notes, the film *Grand Hotel* opened in New York. It would catch up with them seven years later in Oranjemund. They were driven to the dock by Haroldine McLellan, my mother's loyal college friend, married to a geologist in New Jersey. In the last letter she wrote before her death in 1988, Haroldine described my parents' final day in the U.S.

"From their shabby room with its frugal amenities, we transported ourselves to the sunny, open deck of an ocean liner. There we were greeted by a smartly dressed young woman wearing a well tailored tan suit, high heels, and a fur jacket that may have been mink. Her name was Gladys Ratliff and she lived in Englewood across the Hudson." Gladys made it perfectly clear that she was my father's long-lost love and she hogged the conversation for an hour, pointedly ignoring his wife. According to Haroldine, this tickled my mother. "I could see that Pat was having trouble not to laugh out loud. It was just the sort of encounter she got a kick out of."

Gladys was saying good-bye to the man who represented her "wild youth." After the ship had sailed, she invited herself to lunch with Haroldine. "All she wanted to talk about was Drury. She was, I thought, the classic example of a girl who can't resist seeing again a boy she dated for pleasure. Seeing him about to embark on a great adventure, she would ever after wish she hadn't dropped him for the safe man she married."

This brief description of Gladys is as close as I will ever get to the mystery of my father's love life before he devoted himself entirely to Patricia Martincevic. It never occurred to my mother that Drury Augustus Poindexter Pifer was someone too dangerous to consider seriously as a husband. But I see now that Gladys Ratliff was right. My father was lucky to survive Africa, though he looked that day more like a physicist on his way to a conference than a man who would soon be working in poisonous water up to his waist. In a snapshot Haroldine took, he wears a suit and vest. The trousers badly need pressing. My mother has on a pleated skirt and well-worn cardigan. Her angora wool cap is firmly tied under her chin. A lock of her dark hair has escaped and flies straight up in the breeze.

From Cherbourg, where they landed, she mailed Bess their first hotel bill and reports that, including breakfast, dinner, and two taxi rides, they spent $3.15. In Germany and Italy, popular enthusiasm was growing for brutes with great faith in simple solutions. Hitler had found a way of inspiring hoodlums with a higher political purpose and, in the name of economic recovery, was preparing to put an end to European civilization. Mussolini had transformed hordes of laughing Italians into grim supermen who trotted through the streets in platoons, kicking up their knees like well-trained horses. In Genoa, my mother got her first glimpse of the fascism she would have to live with in South-West Africa seven years later. She wrote Bess that policemen infested every street, wearing "long olive green capes reaching to the knee and thrown across the chest up around the neck, and little Robin Hood hats with long turkey feathers. All they do is stand around and look important. Gus saw a picture he wanted and aimed the camera when a fierce-looking policeman on the train scowled and growled at him, telling him in no uncertain terms No Pictures!"

Before sailing from Genoa, they visited my mother's relatives on the Adriatic, who treated them "like visiting royalty and stuffed us to the gills." (During the war she would mail these same relatives a constant stream of clothes and food.)

When they picked up their steamer ticket to Durban, the clerk said South African Immigration required a three-hundred dollar cash deposit from all aliens entering the country. My father was forty dollars short, but figured the letter guaranteeing his job in Nigel would get him through. "No use worrying about it till we get there," my mother wrote Bess. (Not worrying until we got there was to become our way of life.)

Sailing the Red Sea—dead calm, enamel blue—my mother picked among the passengers for people she fancied. She made friends with a Romanian art dealer reading a book on diamond prospecting, a family of German Jews with every penny they had locked up in the rings they wore, and a Muslim couple who checked the ship's position before praying to Mecca. My father made friends with a student from Scotland. Trevor McGaffin was heading for Stanford University by way of Cape Town, Christchurch, and Honolulu.

The morning they arrived in Durban, my parents were told by immigration officials that there was no way they would be allowed off the ship. The letter guaranteeing work met none of the official criteria. The deposit required to visit South Africa was three hundred pounds sterling, not three hundred dollars, as they had been informed in Genoa. They were being asked for over fifteen hundred dollars.

My father said he had two degrees in mineral engineering and that a mine manager ("Phone him if you don't believe me") was waiting for him in Nigel. The officials said that if he set foot on South African soil he would be arrested and deported, after a healthy period of incarceration.

It had cost my parents $1,339 to get from Seattle to Durban. There was absolutely no way they could get back to the States on their remaining two hundred dollars. The ship's captain slipped them ashore that night so that my father might cable Williamson, the mine manager in Nigel. Williamson immediately cabled immigration, promising to sign anything. He told the officials the job was guaranteed once my father passed the physical exam.

This proviso raised fresh alarms in the minds of the authorities. New forms were typed up, appended, signed, stamped, and stapled. The question of my father's lungs and blood was now on the agenda.

A week passed. The ship was provisioned and prepared for sailing. The morning of its departure, the Americans were visited by a senior customs official "with cracked green teeth, bad breath and reeking of body odor." This gentleman had been flushed from his office by a telephone call from Williamson who was threatening to inform higher-ups in the mining industry and create a flap. The official told my parents that thousands of South Africans were out of work. What South Africa needed was American tourists, not American miners. Official doubt had been expressed concerning Mr. Pifer's motives. Foreigners often came to steal technical secrets. It seemed unlikely that a man with two university degrees in mining engineering would travel from one end of the earth to the other to work as a common miner. "No, my friend. Don't assume we South Africans are so simple-minded. We know all the tricks."

My father argued that no American spy would arrive in South Africa broke and unable to pay the immigration deposit. "You've seen my papers. You've spoken to Williamson. You know I can't afford a ticket home. What more do you want?"

"My good friend, we have no way of knowing what is your little game," said the grinning official with the bad teeth. "And I am very sorry we can do nothing for you. Good luck, eh?"

With the gift of hindsight, I see my young parents desperately striving to enter the country that would become their prison. I see the official with the green teeth as my ally. Had he sent them back to Europe, they would have made out somehow. My mother's health might never have been undermined by the high altitude of the Rand

and, later, the dust in the Namaqualand. Chance and biology would have guaranteed my nonexistence, but nonexistence is never a problem. In any case, fate, following its own obscure logic, took another tack.

The ship was set to depart in forty minutes. My parents had slipped into the somnambulant passivity that deadens the pain of complete defeat when Trevor McGaffin appeared, bobbing up the gangplank. He had been "doing a bit of thinking" and decided he would loan them the money they needed. He had sufficient funds for two years in California and figured they could pay back the loan in the meantime.

Speechless with gratitude, my parents stumbled ashore minutes before the ship's lines were cast off. They exchanged addresses with the young Scotsman. He had a train to catch and bounded into a taxi. They never saw him again.

The men at the Office of Immigration were not pleased. Money conjured out of thin air raised official hackles. Nor did they believe in the existence of Trevor McGaffin. Why had he disappeared? Notions of friendship and trust lay well outside their purview. Rummaging in their fat books of rules and regulations they came up with a new, higher figure and claimed that irregularities of an extremely technical nature led them to demand a guarantee of another £250.

For the moment, the unwanted Americans at least had a foothold on dry land while their ship back to nowhere was plowing through the Red Sea. Immigration detained them in a building downtown. Williamson, in a fury, came up with the money required. Cables were fired back and forth, and only after the Anglo American Mining Company had filed a registered document at the capital in Pretoria guaranteeing work for two years, were the Americans reluctantly released.

It was the middle of winter, a cold July. It got even colder on the train to Nigel, which climbed steadily through an altitude of 4,000 feet, traversing a dull, featureless plateau. My parents woke that first morning in a region of glittering white frost. There were no lions, no elephants, no antelope, no trees, no bushes—just the flat, unbroken circle of the horizon. It looked more like Siberia than Africa. But they were jubilant, free at last to get on with their lives.

The little town of Nigel, south of Johannesburg, imitated an English village—red brick houses, a touch of Tudor here and there, tiny lawns manicured by African men with hand clippers. Only the peppertrees, with their filigree leaves and wizened pepper pods were African. The mimosa, the acacia, the jacaranda, and the red weaver birds of summer were absent.

Contrary to everything Immigration had said, business was booming on the Rand as the price of gold rose every week. Hotels were packed. No houses, no rooms, not even a hovel was available for rent. Company houses were offered only to old hands or favorites. Vacancies came up only when a miner retired or was killed. However, accidents occurred often, so my parents were told that with luck they might get a company house in three years. They stuffed themselves meanwhile into a hotel room—no indoor toilets, no plumbing above the first floor. The menu was boiled meat, boiled potatoes, boiled carrots, boiled pudding, and on Sundays, burned joints of beef. There they camped for several weeks until my mother, studying bulletin boards and knocking on doors while my father was underground, found a back room in a tiny house owned by an English couple named Balham.

The Balhams were perpetually down on their luck, but relentlessly cheerful in the cockney manner. The rented room included meals, but was dark and small and, as I read the numbers, cost more than my father was making. How they survived their first months in Nigel, I simply do not know. The Balhams' was, however, a major improvement over the hotel with its hysterical clientele and occasional running water.

The Balhams' good cheer masked desperation and high anxiety. They always spent more than they had and were gradually hocking the furniture, the dishes, whatever would sell. Ida, their maid, was pregnant and spent hours sitting in a strip of sunlight in the back-yard, smoking cigars stolen from Mr. Balham (who stole them from someone at work). The house was ice cold, but the Balhams insisted that low temperatures kept you fit. They regarded shivering as a kind of exercise. Despite the freezing rooms and the bad food, their bank account was forever overdrawn. Mrs. Balham liked to say that God will provide, and Mr. Balham helped God along by quietly embez-zling money from the cartage firm where he worked.

Because the house was so cold, its inhabitants resembled human coatracks. Mrs. Balham padded about wrapped in a blanket over a sweater and coat. Books and newspapers were read in bed. My mother now understood why every woman in Nigel knitted con-stantly. She picked up the habit at once and began clicking away on her first pair of socks. "Not the Africa we imagined!" she wrote home. "We have never been so cold as we have been here! And the *food!*"

Cod fried in stale lard and weary vegetables cooked into a kind of beige sludge were prepared by Ida. ("I trained her myself!" chirped Mrs. Balham.) An obscure logic convinced the Balhams that the plenitude of fresh beef in South Africa made fresh greens unneces-sary. The rules of cockney cuisine dictate that salad greens should be served with cold pressed meat only. But cold pressed meat was unnec-essary in a land of abundant beef, so greens were no longer needed. Breakfast consisted of strong tea or weak coffee and stale bread toasted in an open flame on the end of a fork, provided the fork had not been hocked. The toast was improved by a powerful beef extract (Boveril) spread a quarter of an inch thick.

My father had lost fifteen pounds trying to save money on the trip to Africa. Underground now ten hours a day, his weight continued to drop, so my mother took charge of the kitchen. It was a primitive cave without ventilation, refrigerator, or electric stove. Food was locked in a pantry at the opposite end of the house. Mrs. Balham

kept the pantry key on her person and surrendered it only upon request. My mother was asked to bring it back immediately after re-
locking the pantry, just as Ida did. Any other arrangement, said Mrs.
Balham, would hurt Ida's feelings. Sugar, mealie meal (maize), tea,
and some coal were left out for Ida to "steal." This pilfering was
carefully factored in as part of the cost of keeping a servant. You
were then free to complain about the immorality of the natives.

When, after some months, my parents found a house to rent, the
Balhams were upset. Mr. Balham was hooked on American cooking
and suggested a lower rent if my mother continued in the kitchen.
The idea of going back to Ida's burned roasts, which resembled
shrunken human heads, was depressing. To convince them that moving was too expensive, Balham tried to sell them the furniture in
their room at double its value. This intricate but charmingly ineffec-
tive way of cheating them was characteristic of the cheerful Mr. Balham, who was arrested for embezzling and thrown into prison a few
weeks after they moved out. Plucky Mrs. Balham hired herself out as
a cook at one of the local hotels.

After an uncomfortable and boring first year in Nigel, my mother
began to dream of home. The new rented house was a tiny fake-
English cottage that looked across a limitless grassland (veld) where
oxen grazed. At night they could be heard outside the window,
gloomily chewing their cud. She compares these placid animals to
the women that formed her society during those first months. "I wish
you could get a peep at these vacuous and empty-headed women who
don't even read the paper, let alone a whole book! Some of these
teas I go to are enough to make me scream. The only topic of conversation is servants. Do you know that one woman I was talking to had
no idea who Mussolini was? Had never heard of him!"

Her main job was fighting homesickness and the feeling that she
had been dumped in a sort of purgatory where nothing of any significance would ever occur. It was clear that getting home might take
years longer than they had calculated.

"If I can get my manager's ticket early I will be home in five," my father wrote his mother. But that was assuming everything would go like clockwork. The depression would be replaced by a healthy economy. He would be promoted according to his ability. He would be elevated to management. His health would hold up. He would not be maimed. He would not be killed.

3

Self-destructing

During her first weeks on the Rand, my mother wrote Bess, "Gus says it makes him sick the way some of these Afrikaners kick and manhandle the natives. The blacks down here are most submissive and servile. They have been abused so much that they are afraid to look a white person in the face almost. But we think that blacks are a damned sight more decent than some of the whites. . . . They think Gus is just great because he treats them fairly. The black boys try to help him to learn the language too. Every day he comes home with some story about the natives and himself."

My father was sent underground as an "unofficial learner" at £1.50 per day (about eight dollars). South Africa advertised itself as a bilingual country, and every white school student learned both English and Afrikaans. But underground the miners spoke only Afrikaans or Zulu. Thus my father's first weeks in Africa were spent thousands of feet below the surface of the earth attempting to absorb instructions in gibberish.

He wrote Bess he was "feeling perfectly useless. . . . Most of the natives don't understand English at all and it is absolutely necessary to know their language. There is a lot of Dutch and English mixed in because there are no equivalents in the native tongue, and some native words cover a multitude of things—for instance *mtambu* means vine, rope, string, wire, cable, fuse." During his first year in South Africa, all his spare time was spent with his nose in a book, muttering Zulu and Afrikaans. After learning the basics, nights, weekends, and holidays were absorbed in the study of technical and legal information. A tangle of rules and regulations had grown up. The company had to contend with a vast undergrowth of conflicting cultures, class systems, languages, and tribal differences. My father planned to pass the series of tough exams that barred his way up the ladder as quickly as possible, in months instead of years. If he were more efficient than anyone else, he would soon be managing a mine and could then go home with the sort of experience he could sell to any mine in the United States.

In South Africa, his two American degrees in mining counted for nothing. He was required to labor a full year as a "learner" before they let him use the same pneumatic drill he had used for months in Alaska, where he had worked after graduation. A "Certificate of Competency" was required for each step on the way up. Then came the exams for shift boss, mine captain, and, finally, manager. Passing the exam didn't guarantee advancement, only made it possible.

Despite all, the job was exactly what he wanted. The work, he wrote home, "is never routine." To my mind, this is like Dante remarking that no two hours in hell are exactly alike. Consider that every eight hours, three thousand natives and several hundred whites were hurled underground, while another three thousand were shot up to the surface, in batches of one hundred, in triple-decker cages—

steel elevators with open sides. As this contraption picked up speed, the rock walls dissolved into a blur and the miners dropped straight down into the earth at a speed of two thousand feet per minute. (The effect on the eardrums is singular, especially if your sinuses are not in mint condition.)

Forced air was driven into the mine shafts by enormous ventilators, and the tunnels were forever being hosed down to control the fine silicate dust. But no miner's lungs were free of silt. Each year the workers were checked for the lung disease, phthisis, that eventually afflicted every old-timer. During blasting, the ventilation system was shut off and temperatures soared quickly to one hundred and fifty degrees. After dynamiting, the tunnel became a chaos of broken rock and choking dust that the miners rapidly washed down with fire hoses before too much of the stuff was inhaled. The ventilation lines were then reassembled, gas leaks checked out, ceilings propped up with timber, and underground springs blocked or diverted before the tunnel turned into an underground river.

The gold ran in threads through narrow layers called reefs. Crawl corridors called stopes were drilled alongside the gold reefs. They resembled the crawl corridors in Egyptian pyramids, and miners wriggled up and down these narrow tubes, breaking out the rock by drilling holes where they placed charges of dynamite.

The native workers wore heavy boots and shorts and gunnysacks slit for the arms and head to poke through. Many had tribal ornaments—brass rings around their bellies and calves, their faces carved and notched with the ornamental scars honored by their tribes. To reach the work site, the miners walked along an underground tunnel a mile long, descending a twenty-degree incline in ninety-degree heat. After the shift was over and they were exhausted, they came back out uphill.

To overcome the fatigue and the boredom the miners would sing. When I went underground with my father a few years later, I heard their voices echoing through the stone passages, glorious and doleful at the same time. It was as if the earth itself were singing, a male chorus rising out of the stone. Liberally translated, their song would run something like this:

Solo voice: *We go to break rock!* Chorus: *Damn the rock!*
Solo voice: *We go to sweat like oxen!* Chorus: *Damn the oxen!*
Solo voice: *We go to get rich!* Chorus: *Damn the rich!*
Solo voice: *We go to make old baas happy.* Chorus: *Damn old baas!*

At the end of their shift, as they climbed the steep incline to the cage station, their singing took on strange, tortured effects reminiscent of those Russian work songs in which excruciating effort is indicated by a formal groan:

Solo voice: *Do we love the rock?* Chorus: *(Groan) Yah.*
Solo voice: *Do we love the dust?* Chorus: *(Groan) Oh, yah.*
Solo voice: *Do we love the baas?* Chorus: *(Groan) Oh, yah.*

I remember the sinister smell of dynamited stone that pervaded the tunnels. And I thought of it again when the astronauts, returning from the first moon landing, described the moon-dead dust as having "the smell of blasted rock." The gold miners operated in an environment no less alien. But while the moon was sterile, the mine was not. Standing water underground was alive with a rich mix of bacterial and viral invaders. Any break in the skin was dangerous. My father suffered everything from mumps and measles and debilitating fevers to a major outbreak of boils and blood poisoning.

He describes the work this way: "The reef is six inches wide and flat, lying at an angle of fifteen degrees. To mine the reef a stope is dug which is twenty-four inches wide. The miner works all day long lying down. The place is too low to crawl in and the hanging wall (overhead) is sharp and bruises every time it hits the body. So we slide along on our seats and elbows wearing a rubber fabric pad over the seat of our pants and using a small stick or wedge to protect our forearms and elbows. You can imagine shoveling, cutting timber, carrying pneumatic drills, and building stone walls in a space two feet high. It's not so bad after one gets used to it, but work is very inefficient and adequate supervision of labor almost impossible."

Unable at first to understand what anyone was saying, it took him some weeks to perceive that the "stupidity" of the black miners was an act veiling sardonic resentment. "The Africans," my father noted, "have a secret name for every white man. I don't know what mine is yet, but I hope it isn't anything like the one the mine captain is favored with. He is commonly known as Monkey's Ass. Some time ago this chap was standing on the station as the cage load of blacks moved away and just then one of them yelled, 'Good-bye, Monkey's Ass!' So the captain rang the cage to a stop and pulled each man out and gave him a sock on the jaw and a kick in the pants and made all of them go to the end of the line. Just a good old South African custom. It's common policy down here to give a native a blow if he is slow or doesn't understand. A good slap settles everything to the white man's satisfaction."

He was astounded by the tribal hatreds that flared into fights among his work crews. During his first week on the job (soon he became so used to the violence that stories of tribal squabbling disappear from his letters), he wrote to his mother: "One of my machine boys is in the hospital now with a split stomach, stabbed going out Saturday night alone. Three of my men got to fighting underground the other day, two on one. So I gave the attackers a thrashing with a two-foot length of heavy water hose till they lay down, yelling. It's all peaceful now, but their victim thinks he's my pet and he's loafing. So now I have to deal with him somehow. All sounds pretty bloodthirsty and melodramatic, doesn't it? It's not so cruel as it sounds. Do you know what these blighters do for amusement on Sunday? They get pieces of bicycle chain, fasten them on the end of a short stick, and then with a second stick for defense, have a go at each other just for fun. They are devilishly cruel to each other. Now could you ever believe that I would turn out to be an African slave driver? Driver and driven. The way the bosses want things done with a minimum of help and material in the shortest time possible is a caution." He is writing to his mother and putting all of this in the most genteel language possible.

During his first months on the job, he assumed his Afrikaner instructors were right about the African miners. He wrote home: "The worst thing about working down here is having to depend on these savages to do civilized, skilled jobs. So few of them have any instinct for even simple machine work. I've seen natives who have been working with bolts and nuts for several months who seem unable to learn to put the nut in and turn it in the right direction. They simply go on twisting it to the left."

This apparent lack of "instinct for even simple machine work" changed after the natives got to know him better. And when Williamson put him in charge of drilling efficiency, he set about changing the way the Africans were trained and handled. "The white miners are afraid of new ideas or methods. They fight against them at every turn. So I have to work through the natives until I can convince the white miners that new methods work. I have about one hundred and fifty stopes to regulate with forty-five to fifty white miners, each with three machine drill boys. I was on a development for a few weeks last month in a certain area and before I left there wasn't a machine boy there who would do what the miner told him if it disagreed with any of my instructions. There is nothing like getting some understanding with the natives for getting a job done."

Contract miners who had broken 276 feet of rock within a month received a bonus of five shillings (about $1.50) for every foot thereafter. By working double shifts, my father averaged 325 feet a month. I calculate he made a twelve or thirteen pound bonus each month (about $65). Most of this money was mailed to Trevor McGaffin in California.

It's not clear from my parent's letters how long it took them to clear up the McGaffin debt. They treated the family debt to old Louis Newman in a more cavalier fashion and chose not to mention how quickly (and with what self-sacrifice) McGaffin was paid off.

By working closely with the Africans, my father was breaking with a powerful Afrikaner tradition. The native was to be considered sub-human, and those who didn't find him subhuman were, accordingly, somewhat lower than subhuman. After my father's production figures made it clear that the inferiority of African miners was a white myth, his real troubles began.

The Africans had no reason to do the job well. They were rich only in insults. The human genius for seeing difference (any difference!) as inferiority made life in the mine brutish and (as my father tirelessly pointed out) inefficient. But he was an American and had no way of knowing how different that made him. Tocqueville says, "When the ranks of a community are nearly equal (as they were then in the United States), as all men think and feel in nearly the same manner, each of them may judge in a moment the sensations of all the others. He casts a rapid glance upon himself and that is enough. There is no wretchedness into which he cannot readily enter, and a secret instinct reveals to him its extent. It signifies not that strangers or foes are the sufferers; imagination puts him in their place. . . ."

This is the Enlightenment speaking, and it was my father's point of view. The South African attitude was, to his mind, a violation of reason. Unfortunately, prejudice was sacred to the Afrikaner. It had less to do with race than tribe. It was sacred because their survival as a European tribe depended upon separation. It is not the same thing as American racism. The Dutch Reformed Church told the Afrikaner he was there to redeem the heathen native. He survived, not because he had European guns, but because God had assigned him South Africa as a spiritual task.

The European Enlightenment had bypassed white South Africa,

leaving the Afrikaner with the world view of a seventeenth-century Calvinist. His little golden age had ended abruptly when the British saw the potential for mineral wealth around the Vaal River. A single decade (1870–80) was time enough to transform South Africa from a legend in Genesis to a lesson in Darwinism. Heavy European technology was trundled in to dig enormous, filthy holes where there had been modest farms with oxen grazing a year before. Sandwiched between the lowly African below and the lordly Britisher above, the Afrikaners were in danger of becoming a lost tribe, an economic nonentity.

My father, raised in the remote and provincial Northwest, was an especially innocent American. He admired Ben Franklin and gave me his own battered volume of the *Autobiography* to read. I looked in it for adventure, but found only practical advice. My father valued Franklin's genius for linking democracy to efficiency through good business practice. This was pretty much what he had in mind for South African mining. Racism obstructed production. The Afrikaner insisted on distance, but it is hard to maintain distance when you lie side by side with black men in a four-by-four tomb, bathed in your own sweat.

Caught between the British above, and the African below, the Afrikaner was frozen in place, afraid that even the expression on his face might betray him, might start him on the short slide to the bottom of the heap. The British had stripped his land, his freedom, and his self-respect. His defense was a kind of violent immobility. Underground, he kicked his men; he demanded they keep their eyes lowered. Aboveground, he was stern, silent, or sardonic.

When my father bypassed the Afrikaners and took his ideas straight to the Zulus, Afrikaner resentment became focused on him. As for the Africans, once they realized he was treating them like men and not some nameless subspecies, they had no trouble turning those machine bolts in the right direction. Soon he was running the most efficient crews in the mine.

Manager Williamson was delighted. I'm not sure that anyone else was. A heavy truck was backed directly over my father's bicycle, reducing it to a work of modern sculpture. White miners, alone in their cars, ignored him as he trudged six miles to work down a long, hot, dusty road. For being too good at his job, he was to suffer far worse. After Williamson was gone, his Ben Franklin efficiency would prove truly self-destructive.

4

Secret War

THE ROLE OF MARRIED WOMEN IN NIGEL WAS DEFINED PRECISELY. Miners who intended to crawl from underground to a manager's position needed a wife who was very good at pouring tea while she chatted brightly about nothing in particular. My mother soon discovered that making small talk and serving tea uses up more than time. In her first letters home she tries to suppress her misgivings by identifying herself entirely with his job. "This is supposed to be easy country for white folks but Gus and I both declare that neither of us has ever worked as hard before in all our lives. He is still on the three A.M. shift and working flat on his back in a narrow stope. We expect about a £5 bonus this month. The bonus is all we can eke out for saving. It just about takes all of the £20 to live on."

She meanwhile looked for some way to employ her intelligence. Her university degree in librarianship was of little use in a society where no one read anything but pulp fiction and mining manuals.

Upwardly mobile society in Nigel resisted any temptation to deepen understanding or improve the mind. The town library was housed in the dingy basement room of the post office and contained a few novels of Dickens and Trollope and the *Encyclopedia Britannica,* with selected missing volumes. She offered to take over and bring the place back to life but was gently persuaded to return to her teapot.

Provincial Nigel curiously resembled her youth transposed into a South African key. An immigrant child from Croatia, she'd been raised in a home with four half-brothers and a stepfather, Petar, who sounds in every story I've heard like Ivan the Terrible. If his boys showed signs of independence, they were taken down in the basement and beaten. His stepdaughter, my mother, was the first child and only girl. She imitated obedience and employed energy, charm, and subterfuge to get her way. Her mother's life was a lesson in what to avoid.

Her stepfather was a Serb. As a child, his parents chained him to a table like a dog, leaving him with bowls of food and water while they tilled the fields on their farm near Sarajevo. Petar was small and handsome, a narrow man with a vicious temper. The wrong word could whip him into a spitting fury. He never could adjust to the American attitude toward children and tried to wallop some old-fashioned respect into his boys. The results were not good. My mother never spoke his name that I recall. His sons all moved out as soon as they had the means. His wife eventually went insane and spent half of her life in a madhouse.

Attracted to art, my mother escaped from home into the library whenever she had free time. Petar was suspicious of anything that got in the way of earning a good income. He had the provincial's suspicion of books and learning and could not fathom what use a woman might have for education. He probably understood it was a kind of tunnel through which the unhappy prisoner planned to escape. My mother persevered, saved her money to buy a piano, and put herself through university, where she started out in the School of Fine Arts. She switched to librarianship when she realized how impractical painting would prove for a penniless young woman from the working class.

Her mother, Mari, was all emotion. Her daughter, having inherited an unknown father's intelligence, combined barbed wit with high spirits. At the University of Washington, she began to enjoy life for the first time. Her friend, Haroldine, wrote me that "Pat got a kick out of accosting half a dozen men in the campus quad and stinging them with her wit." (During the last year of her life, 1949, a university student phoned our house by mistake; my mother gave him such an entertaining runaround that he insisted he must meet her. She had to put me on the phone to convince him she had a fifteen-year-old son in the room.)

There still exist two snapshots of my college-boy father visiting his Slavic in-laws. They stand together in the Martincevic vegetable garden on Seattle's Beacon Hill. Mari exhibits the baggy shape of a woman who no longer cares. Petar stands formally for his portrait. With his wing tip collar and dark suit, he resembles a diplomat from some Balkan principality managed by the Marx Brothers. People from the Old Country seldom smile when their pictures are taken, but the expressions on these grim faces set a new standard for staring down the camera. My father looks like someone beamed down from another planet. He smiles at the ground.

Aside from his good looks, my mother was attracted to my father's calm, his clear intelligence. He had plans. He knew his own mind. He never lost his temper. The year he spent in Alaska he sent back a steady stream of letters. She didn't understand then that marrying a miner is like marrying a seaman or soldier or someone who writes poetry—a bad choice. No fortune-teller informed her that when she married this person she married the deserts of South Africa as well.

Around her twentieth year (1926), my mother fashioned herself after Victorian paintings. This combined the erotic with the funereal, a self-absorbed expression, misty backgrounds. Her photos remind me of Alma-Tadema's paintings. This artist made a career painting pretty women in Greek silks draped along marble terraces high over misty seas. His stage-set world was slavishly imitated by a Hollywood that was already inspiring the young to look like everything they were not.

There is an Alma-Tadema painting titled *Under the Roof of Blue Ionian Weather* where the dark-haired model bears a precise likeness to my mother when she was eighteen. The subject lies on a curving marble seat, head propped on hand, listening to a flute player. Seated beside her is an idealized blonde, a dead ringer for her best college friend, Haroldine. Both models' heads are wreathed in flowers. The painting was executed five years before these particular young women were born, suggesting perhaps that even kitschy art may come in a generation ahead of plodding old nature.

My mother's suitors included a man from California, who was sure he could get her into the pictures, and the son of an undertaker, who rolled around Seattle in a Stutz Bearcat wearing a raccoon skin coat and porkpie hat. Her mother, Mari, was upset by the young man's association with death, but nevertheless went for a ride in the Stutz Bearcat. Mother and daughter came home about midnight and found Petar in a fury. He was overcome by jealousy and (once again) accused his stepdaughter of degrading the morals of his family. He then tried to throw her out of the house into a driving rain. But John, the eldest son, wakened by the uproar, threatened to leave with her.

Determined to put herself through university, my mother visited a series of administrators looking for work. The dean of the School of Librarianship, William Henry, gave her a job in the library office. There she met Haroldine, who describes hearing my mother's voice ringing out as she came through the offices, greeting her friends. ("I wondered who this person was, so sure of herself, behaving as if she were running the place.") Dean Henry became a kind of surrogate father during her university years. On their first meeting, she felt so sure of her ground that she hit him up for a loan. He mentions this in the letter he wrote her when she quit her job four years later. His note on University of Washington stationery is dated December 27, 1927—the year she was awarded her bachelor's. His affection for her makes him slightly incoherent. He sounds to me more like an unrequited lover than an employer:

My Dear Patricia,

Thank you very much for your recent note informing me of your desertion of our ship. I am sorry to have you go, for as you know I like you very much and I am perfectly willing for you to know it, but I am not the only one that likes you, and my opinion upon your departure from our library is not a question of my likes or the likes of anyone else other than yourself, except on the grounds of what is best for you. If that is what you want to do, that is the thing I want you to do, and if you can succeed in getting there better than what you can get here for your taste I am not only willing but anxious for you to do it. My interest in you now is just what it was when I made that great big loan of $9.00 without security. You see it was an awful risk to take, but I believed so completely in you I took a risk that might have frightened a millionaire. I believed in you then and I have believed more firmly in you ever since. Now what I want for the future is for you to have a position where you can devote your whole soul and use your exceeding intellect, and if you see at any time a thing that is better than you have at that time tell me if I am here, and I will do everything I can to help you get the other position. My one fundamental interest is to help as best I can those of my three hundred darlings that are out in the state serving the young people.

Some day when it is convenient for us both, and especially for you perhaps, I would like to talk with you about your new work, and find out what your liking is for it, and if you want to continue in that, let me help you if I can, to secure a place where you can use your entire power and do a great work.

Very truly yours,

W. E. Henry
Dean

This highly regarded young woman now sat staring out of the window at a dusty street where African women passed with enormous loads balanced on their heads. Her new world had a surreal cast. "Some of the Africans keep their private organs in a kind of little red hammock that's kept in place by a cord around the waist. And when there's an urge to water the lawn, they merely pull their skirts aside and lower the hammock. The passerby can't help but notice these little details. And one gentleman I saw evidently got part of a dress suit from somewhere—no shirt, only a vest and the coat with tails and a wing collar. He had two bow ties, so he wore them both—one on each side of his neck."

The English were no less interesting. "Their salt shakers have just one big hole. The English put a big mound of salt on their plates and pick it up with a knife and salt each individual mouthful of food!"

Energetic, well-educated, and free at last, she must have felt cut-off. She had dreamed life would be a remarkable adventure. She was surprised, as the young are, to find that real adventure includes tedium, monstrous discomfort, and the possibility of death. Days in South Africa moved through a viscous medium that bore little relation to time in the nimble United States. Their lovely grand tour had rapidly dwindled into scrabbling for a little expendable income. The cottage they rented early in 1933 sopped up most of the money my father earned. The excess must have gone to McGaffin. What they longed for most was a company house that would come rent free.

"I hear that some of the mine houses were given out yesterday and the women are having a regular cat fight over them, some having got better ones than others. As for me, I'll be thankful for anything. . . ." Making the most of doing very little, my mother decided it was time to have a child. I was born before they acquired their company house, and it still looked "pretty hopeless. There are 120 applications and only 35 new houses and I'm feeling grumpy with my nasal catarrh and the drought and heat."

My father's professional progress was their great obsession. Their chance for a company house, the money to pay off "the national debt" (to old Louis Newman), the means to go home, everything depended on making a better salary, getting into management. Williamson soon designated my father a "contract" miner, that is, a miner who worked at his own pace with his own crew. Supervising his own men, he began to make ten times the bonus money he'd got before.

"We are just dying to see the number of fathoms of rock he breaks this month—and see the check," she wrote home. "I figure if he gets the expected fifty pounds bonus every month, Daddy [Newman]'s thousand will be returned in six months. Yeah, seems like the *Arabian Nights,* all right, but we shall see."

My mother became so involved in his job that she copied out questions from the certificate examinations for Bess to examine— how does one timber a station in a five-compartment vertical shaft?; how does one charge a stope with dynamite?

That September she wrote home, "I'm all agog. Mrs. James is coming for me today in her DeSoto 8 in view of all the neighbors, all sitting on their verandas. Mrs. Will told me yesterday that Mrs. James told the compound manager all about 'that charming young American, Mrs. Pifer.' How tastefully appointed the tea was that I served her. How wonderfully dainty were the tea cakes, etc. And how pleased Jimmy (her husband) was with Mr. Pifer. So we are getting along all right. I only hope all of this helps us to secure a house. It certainly makes me feel pretty good, believe me!"

In October, a month after the wildly successful tea with Mrs. James, she wrote, "My head is going around and around and I don't care. WE HAVE BEEN GIVEN A HOUSE! Mrs. Will told me she heard someone say they couldn't understand why the Pifers got a house after only one year, while others worked here over five and didn't get one."

My father furnished the new cottage with tables and chairs he made from scrap lumber picked up in the mine. But they found the company house powerfully resistant to improvement. In the thirties, South African kitchens were designed (it seemed) to make cooking and cleaning as depressing as possible. Nigel kitchens in 1933 were painted brown or black—colors calculated to demoralize Africans, who detest dark colors. My mother painted her kitchen a pale rose with mauve trim. The wives of managers who peeped in were astonished. "But doesn't it get dirty?" they cried, touching it lightly with their fingertips.

"The idea seems to be that if you can't see it then there's no dirt there," she wrote Bess. "Can you beat that?"

Doing the family wash was torture. A great, galvanized tub was filled with buckets of water drawn from a wood-fired boiler built into the backyard wall. Soap came in big yellow cakes heavy with lye that removed both dirt and skin. After soaping on a corrugated board, the clothes were drubbed, rinsed twice, and stretched on a line across the yard. Shirts were vigorously boiled in a barrel. Rinsing involved drawing fresh water and lugging it across the yard to the tub. There were endless negotiations with washerwomen about how dirty the rinse water should be before it was changed.

Pressing irons were beautifully designed to scorch shirts and create friction between madam and maid. These irons were ugly objects resembling badly designed ships. They were heated by filling with burning coals. When the water supply pipes ran dry, the maid had to fetch water from the public pump two miles up the road. Drinking water was boiled to ward off enteritis, which laid low hundreds of mine workers and their families in 1934, the summer after I was born.

Following the birth, my mother's health became more fragile. Her difficulties were compounded by high altitude and extreme heat. For the first time in her life she suffered nosebleeds and asthma. The air, always thin and dry on the Rand, burned hot in summer and was freezing cold in winter. Air conditioning was, of course, unheard of, and the climate was precisely the opposite of those mild seashore worlds where she had always lived.

She had trouble with her teeth and suffered a series of painful operations on a cyst below the gumline on an eyetooth. The asthma kept her from sleeping, and in the middle of the night I began roaring and had to be fed. She would then catnap and rise at five to light the fires in the freezing house and start breakfast.

South Africa was not organized to accommodate American views. My mother was nervous about hiring a servant, but it was pointless to soldier on without some help. Finding someone looked easy enough. Africans were forever seeking work (though friction between white and black had been built into the system). But it was easier to complain about servants than to take the trouble to train them. My mother would discover that, as a rule, training a cook ensured having no one to cook. The cook would immediately depart for Cape Town, where life was happier and expertise was worth more money.

The South African native population lived then (and lives now) in a sort of perpetual crisis. Thousands, moving from tribal kraals into wretched stick and corrugated metal hovels or into the closed locations set up by the mining companies, lost contact with ancient tribes and existed in a spectral limbo. To achieve the simplest end (a drink of water, a pair of shoes) they had to evolve the most complicated, exhausting techniques. It still requires a Herculean effort to get to work on time without transport, to write a letter without an education, to locate a wife, a son, a daughter who has no fixed address.

The situation was this: the white man demanded from Africans European habits, without providing either European training or European conveniences. Dropped into a ghostly vacuum, the African was asked to perform as if the only inconvenience he suffered was . . . his inability to develop the outlook and abstract drive of a European.

African families were scattered from Cape Town to Bulawayo

without hope of seeing each other for months and even years on end. They existed without hygiene or medical facilities or schools for their children. Babies were no sooner born than they were handed over to ancient grandmothers who lived in huts with mud floors, hovels fashioned from packing crate lumber and sheets of corrugated iron, fastened together with baling wire. They lived with the smell of camp fire smoke, unwashed bodies, food going bad. Cousins, brothers, wives, mothers—someone was always sick or dying in the distant Karoo or Natal or Northern Rhodesia. Whenever a messenger knocked on the back fence, the news was never good. My mother more than once describes this maid or that washerwoman leaning against the gate post with a letter in hand, "crying as if her heart was going to break." Husbands had been arrested, or married someone else, or died in the mines. Children never came near a doctor or dentist, much less an undertaker. The entire African population was in a state of permanent dislocation, and what the white madam dismissed as laziness was more likely the result of divorce, disease, disgust, despair. In 1933 all of this was marvelously invisible to white society. People saw differently then. This would be proved when thousands marched across Europe to kill millions and die for ideas that now seem merely idiotic.

Violet was my mother's first servant. So it was Violet who led her *miesies* into the chasm that exists between white mistress and African maid. Violet had never met an American. Amazing, she said, the way Americans spoke through their noses. My mother describes Violet as "a marvel and very funny. . . . She asked if we had bad people in America. She thinks Gus and I are angels and America must be a kind of heaven. But the other day she saw one of those tobacco ads with a picture of a red Indian fighting a pioneer. She had never seen an Indian before, so I explained how the whites came to America and settled there. She wanted to know if the whites fought the blacks that way in America too. I said no, the blacks were forcibly brought over from Africa by slave traders. She shook her head and said,

'Hhauw! White people fight red man and make black man work!' She thinks the white man very predatory indeed. She sighed and said that it used to be much better in the olden days when the black men lived on their own farms and raised their own vegetables. But now they work hard in the mines for 50 pence a day. Though she thinks it's better under English rule than under the Afrikaners."

After some months Violet fell ill. "She looked quite sick, but she came to make sure I'd hold the job open for her until she recovered. She said maybe another week. Poor thing, I told her yes, of course. I trust her with everything. She is absolutely honest and she adores the baby. She had to see him before she went away this morning."

Violet never returned. My mother's descriptions of servants coming and going provides a picture of this unstable world, of lives lived on the crumbling margins where the old ways had been replaced by perpetual agitation and worry. Now that we drive into suburbs and our feet no longer touch the earth, we admire what seems to us primitive. But these Africans were the most modern people imaginable, living as if some great machine had carelessly tossed them into the air. And no matter how they struggled, they remained in free-fall, dusty and overheated, or cold and wet, abandoned in attitudes of permanent discomfort.

After Violet, my mother hired Nancy, twenty-five, married, the mother of two. Nancy had to leave her four and six year olds with women at the native location in order to come and work for us. My mother had already developed the fatalistic outlook that suits African affairs so well—nothing that works well will work for long. "The secret is, don't count on it. Then you are never disappointed." She describes Nancy as "altogether too good to last."

Returning from their first holiday in Durban, having left Nancy in charge, mistress and master were met by a small African child who delivered a smudged letter written in pencil on a torn shred of pale blue paper. (I have the note in hand so I am able to transcribe it exactly).

"Dear Mrs. Pifer I am in prison so I should have been in my work as I receive a letter from Mrs. my chqe 7 days or I have the honour Nancy Makoba." Translation: I received your letter and check covering the week you were gone, so I planned to be at work, but unfortunately wound up in prison instead.

Nancy had been jailed for fighting with another woman. My father bailed her out and brought her home. Two weeks later she mysteriously disappeared again, leaving every stitch she owned in her room.

Eunice, hired next, could barely understand English. My father, coming home after a quarrel with a shift boss, snapped at her. She assumed he was firing her. She never returned. My mother went looking for her on the location the Sunday following. My parents were, it seems, the only white couple to actually visit the native compound. "One of them came over and then they all flocked around making an incredible fuss! At night it really seems we are in Africa. Then we can hear the chanting and singing and the drums beating about a mile from our place."

She met Eunice's brothers and aunts, but Eunice was in hiding, or had gone to another town, and Africans were never inclined to help Europeans find someone who had vanished. I wonder if my father at that time would have understood the impression it made on a black woman to be shouted at by a white man. But all my mother could do was bawl out my father for his self-indulgence. She wrote Bess, "Ye Gods! If I only had electric appliances I could thumb my nose at all of this!"

Natalie, hired next, is "a little gem. She's only two bricks high, and has a little boy three years old. Speaks perfect English as her father used to be a native schoolteacher for forty years. She is quick and deft, learns rapidly, and is very cheerful and willing to do anything any time."

But soon Natalie fell ill and sent her cousin Lizzie to substitute. "I asked Natalie, who has complications with the mumps, if she'd prefer to give her job up to Lizzie, and she squealed, 'Oh no, Missis! I

couldn't do without you.' " (This provides another theme in this series of failed relationships. Most of these African women found my
mother a congenial employer and tried to hold onto the job by sending substitutes until they could return. But the seldom-expressed
problems in their own lives were too great to overcome, and they
simply disappeared. All across South Africa families were separating,
looking for better pay, traveling hundreds of miles for pennies, then
straining to get back together. They were not likely to tell white
madams that they had taken the job only to earn enough for a train
ticket to Mozambique.)

So Natalie never returned and Lizzie, who was "mission trained,"
appeared, full of half-repressed fury. From the beginning, she regarded her employer as the enemy and every request as a personal
affront. "My new girl has quite an idea of her own importance and
won't let me look at her cross-eyes without getting up on her high
horse. I can't do a thing about it. What an insolent girl!"

The impression Lizzie made was so powerful that I still have a
distinct mental image of her, though I could have been no older than
three. I remember a thin, sallow face, a narrow head tied in a dark
blue kerchief while she slaps a light blue shirt against a washboard. I
remember her weary, halting walk. It would be a familiar walk, for
there are many Africans in South Africa who drag out each step as if
they were weary beyond weary.

My mother decided now to try a male servant and hired Jonas, "a
butler, parlor maid, washerwoman, valet, cook, and nursemaid all in
one. He even does the lawn and heavy garden work. I do hope he
changes his mind about going home to Rhodesia at the end of the
year. He wants to rejoin his family there as he has been in the
Transvaal a year already. Says he came here to work as he gets more
money than in Rhodesia. He wears white duck exclusively and is
in gleaming white all the time. I would never have a girl in the
house again. . . ."

Jonas, who missed his own child up in Rhodesia, made a substitute of me. "He asks to hold Louis and take him for a turn around the garden. He entertains him, knows his meal hours, and sets the milk to boil on the minute. He is the servant *par excellence* all right!

"He commissioned me to buy him a jersey sweater, and gave me exact specifications. But, alas, I picked one with a design in brown and he spurned it. He said it looked like a Shaangaan's—a tribe that is very unpopular. They wear dirty brown blankets, he tells me. He would rather freeze than wear a brown sweater. So I'll just have to get another when I go to Springs to exchange it."

But Jonas, overwhelmed at last by homesickness, could think only about his wife and his baby. I remember him staring out the window in his white coat and trousers, mentally traveling to Rhodesia. And soon he was gone.

Annie, hired to replace Jonas, was an extraordinary thief. Objects disappeared. Underwear, pillowcases, spoons. It gave my mother the impression that either things were mysteriously evaporating, or she was becoming so absentminded that she could never remember where anything was. One morning the silver gravy ladle was gone and my mother called in my father to deal with the situation. "We couldn't find it anywhere. I told Annie to go out to the dustbin to look. She ambled slowly out with Gus after her. No ladle. Then he went to the coal shed and there he found it half buried."

A second Eunice replaces Annie, but she will do nothing unless she is followed about. She sits and stares at the wall. Whether she is exhausted or ill or overcome by some incalculable sorrow, she refuses to say. Given a specific order, she heads in the right direction, then is discovered in the next room collapsed in a chair. Instructions oppress her like lead weights. My mother replaces her with John, a Zulu.

John moves "like greased lightning, knows how to set the table and serve, and even does a little cooking." I remember John because he was so different from the angelic Jonas. John was squat and fidgety, with stumpy, muscular legs, and he had no patience with children. When we were alone he would suddenly leap at me with a threatening yell. Or he would fling up an arm, jump, stamp his feet, strike a wild pose, his face contorted in an evil grin. I was more interested than frightened. His antics were full of rage, but he never batted me about in private (as Lizzie had). Perhaps his stamping was the reflection of some battle dance practiced by Zulu men a century earlier when the bloodthirsty chief, Shaka, had converted the Zulu tribe into a war machine and turned Southern Africa into a killing field.

John took to pouring great mounds of whipping cream into his coffee. Bags of mealie meal vanished and were converted into his own special brand of "kaffir" beer. "The sugar disappears fast and furious and I have to have everything locked up, but that's the least of it," my mother wrote Bess. "He's just lost interest and wants to go home."

No longer greased lightning, John was like a spring-wound toy running down. During his last days with us he barely moved. Setting the stage for an important party that involved "two sets of managers and their wives," my mother needed his help. John, already bored with the whole senseless business, calculated his exit nicely. On the day madam was most desperate, he came to a dead stop. There he sat in the kitchen with an aggrieved expression, as if someone had greatly insulted him. Instead of giving him orders, my mother felt she should apologize for something, though he would not say what it was. Discovering that five pounds of granulated sugar had disappeared, she told him it was perhaps time for them to part. But why, she pondered later, had he stayed on to put her through all of this? Why hadn't he left a week before? Why did he feel obliged to make it all so complicated? In any case, she released him.

John rose on his bandy legs with the expression of a man who has been understood at last and darted out the door like a fish from a trap. I watched him depart through the back gate, his cardboard suitcase balanced jauntily on his head. He wore the same battered old brogues he'd worn the day he arrived. The new shoes my mother had bought him were packed along with the new shirts—also the nice box of sugar cubes he'd quietly removed that morning (much to the consternation of my mother that night).

John's battered shoes I remember more clearly than anything else about him. But I have no doubt confused them with all the other broken-down shoes I would see on the splayed, cracked feet of African men—shoes worn always without socks; shoes plodding through the hot dust, paper-thin soles packed with cardboard or newspaper; shoes laced with baling wire or post-office string or held on with sticky electrical tape; shoes found under bridges, where human excrement dries among the rocks, and bluebottle flies swarm in the choking summer heat; shoes finally abandoned and left on the roadside to split and harden in the pale dust.

As a child, I had the vague impression that those calloused African feet were different from European feet, not suited to European shoes. Shoes on African men were loose. Their feet seemed too broad in the sole, too narrow in the ankle. Shoes would never fit such feet snugly. While pondering the oddness of African feet, it didn't occur to me that these badly fitting shoes were not constructed for their second owners. The same was true of the coats, the pullovers, the trousers that never fit. If you want to make a character ridiculous, dress him in something that doesn't fit. The roads of Africa swarmed with clowns.

After John had ground to a halt and been sent away, my mother tried to make do without servants. She wrote to Bess, "Without John we are saving quite a bit every month. I can keep this up for another couple of months and then I'll have to train another servant. Bah! They are a damned expensive nuisance, but it's got to be done because around October first there will be four of us instead of three. So the secret's out, but don't tell Mama. You know she worries entirely too much."

It took a lot of getting used to, this hiring of people one could not really afford, at prices they couldn't afford to live on—people whose problems were always worse than anything the white madam could possibly imagine. But pregnant by then with her second child and suffering from asthma, my mother felt her own life was going under. They were still deep in debt. They could see no way out of Africa in the near future. She still suffered from the recurring abscess beneath an eyetooth that no dentist in South Africa seemed able to cure. She was daily more anxious about my father, who was losing weight and had broken out in boils that would not go away.

At first light, my father came tramping in off the graveyard shift. Often he was too tired to eat and went straight to bed. Everything that mattered came down to "progress in the profession." My father was perfectly aware that success on the Rand depended entirely on the manager, so he could congratulate himself on working for Williamson. From the first, the men had liked each other. Williamson's death would change everything, of course, but that still lay in the future. My parents were yet to discover that things can always get worse for acrobats who work without a net.

5

Disasters

WHAT COMES THROUGH IN THE LETTERS MY PARENTS WROTE DURING their first years is the euphoria of youth, the irrepressible energy of young people who can't imagine failure. A year after their arrival, and ten days before I made my premature entry into the world, my mother wrote Bess, "Yesterday was the fourth of July [1933], but here it was just another day. Gus and I celebrated by singing the 'Star Spangled Banner.' All we hear about here is England and the Prince of Wales—always something about him." My parents found humor in the hardship: the locusts, the self-defeating habits of the locals that would almost defeat them in the end. They would seldom laugh so hard again. My birth is described to Haroldine as a comic turn.

I first announced myself in this world as a bad case of indigestion. That was my mother's conclusion. She had made up her mind that no child of hers would arrive over a month early. And there was, in any case, no phone, no car, no neighbor. The doctor was miles away, her husband thousands of feet underground. My father came home at midnight and she said she was sure it must be something she'd eaten. He was less sure. After rereading all of their U.S. government pamphlets on fetal development, he hopped on his bike (it had not yet been mangled by the Afrikaners) and peddled off across the veld in search of a car. It was July, the air was ice cold, the fields studded with staring oxen. He was struck by the unpredictability of life. "How could I have dreamed that I would be racing the stork across Africa at three in the morning on a bicycle?"

His friend Zeppenfeld had a car but the rear tire was flat. They repaired the tube but found the tire pump had a missing plunger. My father cut a circlet out of Zep's leather slipper and fashioned a plunger using his pocketknife. Racing home, he found my mother in her best dress, gloves, and hat. The pains were by then so intense she kept slipping to the floor (as I remember her sliding to the floor when she was in the grip of the disease that killed her sixteen years later).

The ride to the hospital was a wild jounce through potholes and ruts that she thought would kill the baby. She imagined it so undeveloped that it would resemble less a human being than a pale rat. I emerged around lunchtime looking more like an undersized pig and in a few days took on the prosperous aspect of a successful businessman, bald as the moon.

I was born the year Hitler seized power in Germany, and as if thoughtfully adjusting itself to reflect the gathering chaos on our planet, the local scene began to breed disasters of its own. "You should have seen the storm on Christmas day," my mother wrote. "The sky turned inky black. We had to turn our lights on . . . and all of a sudden we heard a terrific din and down came the hail, as big as eggs, the shape of cubes in a refrigerator tray. I honestly thought they would come right through the iron roof. They bounced all over the lawn and in a few minutes it looked as if it had snowed. The leaves in all the trees were stripped off. Three of our windows were broken. Cows out on the veld were killed. The Vaal River rose five feet. Down in the village the Indian shops were flooded out entirely. A cloudburst occurred at the same time seven miles away and two people were drowned right in the street. Harry [a friend invited to dinner] arrived looking like a drowned rat. He had to wade through water up to his knees. His motorcycle was ruined. It's still in the backyard. All our peaches are down on the ground."

My first baby-sitter, Evie Wrightson, was permanently maimed on her way to a dance. Her escort, young Gibbs, tried to beat the train to Johannesburg across the tracks behind our house. Young Gibbs was the teenage brother of a shift boss who had demanded my father call him not Gibbs, but Mister Gibbs. "No doubt it's different in your country, Pifer, but here we have manners." In South Africa titles were important. My father referred to Gibbs as "His Lordship." As for the headstrong younger Gibbs, his collision with the train left him barely alive. A young woman in the backseat was killed outright. Evie, in the front seat, was torn apart like a paper doll. Her mother, riding in a second car, saw the collision, the car with her child in it being dragged down the track like a crushed insect. She stumbled through the dark and found her daughter pincered in the wreck, her head a great clot of blood with broken teeth.

Though Evie's forehead had been crushed and creased like a cardboard, she remained as calm and good-natured as ever. Her mother hoped the mining company would come up with insurance money so Evie could travel to America for corrective surgery. But no money was forthcoming. And no gate was erected to keep teenagers from trying to beat the train across the train tracks.

Among the prodigies that greeted me my first year was a locust plague. "For the past three days the sky has been darkened by swarms passing overhead. At first when they began hitting the roof we thought it was hailing. They got tangled in the tennis court fencing, and our trees came alive with them. Others dropped in for a meal off our lettuce and beet tops. . . . These swarms are so dense they obscure the sun. They have stripped Pretoria, fifty miles away, of trees and vegetation."

Naturally, I don't recall these locusts or sweet Evie Wrightson. I remember Nigel as cold, blue shadow and bright, hard light. I remember my mother's voice and her hands. I remember the frustration of being sloppy with urine and feces, and I remember a patch of red brick wall and a washing shed. I remember the texture of the white woolen jumpsuit my mother knitted, the backyard with the brick washhouse, Lizzie slapping clothes on the washboard and scowling at me over a clothesline that hangs suspended in midair. I remember most of all a kind of shimmering happiness that seemed to emanate from the world around me. But I have no recollection of the famous day I almost got myself removed from this life by the same Johannesburg train that maimed Evie Wrightson.

I toddled out of the backyard one day and made my way purposefully down the railway track that ran behind our Nigel house. An old African man spotted me walking between the metal tracks. He led me down the cinder bed to the backyards below and asked the washerwomen who I belonged to. No one knew, and it took him an hour or two to find my mother.

By then the train had long since swept past on its way to Johannesburg. I don't know what state my mother was in or what she said to him. All she could do was give him something to eat in the kitchen.

Nigel remains less a place on earth than a sensation in the mind. I feel those first years embedded in the ground of my memory the way a bass line is embedded in a page of music. There was something glorious about having exploded into existence. And my mother (what incredible luck!) was a being who created order and happiness. So I must be excused for assuming our planet a kingdom of the blessed.

Our second year in Nigel my mother wrote Bess, "Our neighbor's three-year-old daughter just died after being sick for only three days.

Her parents gave her some fish and chips at a restaurant, which they never should have done since the little girl was already in a constipated condition. I went to see her only yesterday and there she was lying in her little cot very quietly. The father had to go three times for the doctor before one finally arrived. . . .

"Today, the distracted father rushed over here to see if we had any brandy as his baby seemed on the verge of dying. Her heart barely worked, and they were taking her to the hospital. Four hours later she was dead, a beautiful little girl who used to come over here to play. One of her toys is still here. . . . The doctor diagnosed ptomaine, but if so, why didn't the parents feel ill? They ate more than she. We have to be careful to keep well because there is very little help forthcoming from these brainless blunderers who call themselves doctors."

A month later, a car driven by one of my father's Afrikaner miners hit and killed a small girl. "She ran across the road to meet the bus on which her mother was traveling, and died instantly with her mother watching. This morning I heard that our neighbor Mrs. Winter's brother died in an auto accident Sunday. Safer being without a car here, so many drunken drivers, and horribly narrow, winding roads."

The mining executives in Johannesburg were enjoying a boom in gold prices, so the pressure to raise production levels was unrelenting. The accident rate underground rose. Jan Viljoin, the Afrikaner who instructed my father in the use of dynamite, was one of the first to go. My mother describes the accident. "Saturday one of the development contractors was blasted as he was charging up. His assistant was killed outright when he received the full discharge. Viljoin had one arm blown off, one eye clean gone, the other blind. A stone has buried itself in his forehead . . . his face is unrecognizable. He's a young man of thirty-five with a family, his youngest is one year old. He lived right across the street. . . . Things like this make me wish Gus was an office worker." Viljoin died the day after.

Nick, my mother's eighteen-year-old brother, arrived in the winter of 1934, July. The most handsome of her four brothers, he would live with us for two years. I remember him a few years later, on holiday in Cape Town, wearing light, floppy trousers and two-toned shoes with perforated toe caps. He bounced when he walked, as if he were about to fly away, and his glistening black hair was combed back suavely like a 1920s film star. He was always upbeat, optimistic, smiling, and I found his breezy American manner unfailingly attractive. Life was easy, life was good, as long as you didn't ask a lot of complicated questions and stuck to the surface of things.

My mother was often frustrated by Nick's dedication to lightness of being, but they had laughter in common. They both loved laughing. In fact her whole family was addicted to laughter, an antidote to their father who looked on life itself as a kind of whipping. This may have been partially my mother's influence. She brought into her mother's family a more aspiring spirit. The father she never knew had been Viennese and there was something irrepressibly Viennese in her nature. As for Nick, he craved action and avoided reflection. He longed for perfect transparency, to be a man with no past, a man who had somehow escaped his own history the way Monte Cristo escaped from the stone cell in Château d'If.

My uncle, who ran away from home at fifteen, could set his hand to anything. The garage he built as a teenager behind the family house on Beacon Hill still looks today as though the last nail had been hammered home only last week. In Africa he would work as a miner, a surveyor, a prospector hired by newly created African nations, an entrepreneur. He was quick-witted, hardheaded, the son his father never beat into submission. Nick absorbed terrible whippings as a child. Petar strapped him down and beat the soles of his feet in the Moslem manner. Instead of becoming obedient, Nick grew more obstinate. He shipped out as a cabin boy the moment he found a captain who would take him on board.

Nick worked at forgetting. He kept moving, he kept smiling, he

kept himself very busy. When he did lose his temper, then the furious face of his father would emerge. I never saw him angry, because
he never lost his temper in the company of my mother. I knew only
the generous, affectionate Nick who read to me, carried me piggy-
back and sang horribly off-key. My mother wrote Bess that aged two
I would run from the room covering my ears, crying, "Leave off,
Nick! Leave off!"

Nick soon began breaking records underground. His movie-star
style belied a steel will, and he enjoyed working longer and harder
than most men. But if the whippings he suffered in that Seattle basement made him tough, they also left him with a fury he could never
completely discharge. The anger was not always explosive. It was an
insidious poison that froze his heart and affected everyone who came
under his domination—miners, women, his children. I would guess
it may account for the disasters that dogged him through his life.

Aged fifteen, Nick had shipped out on freighters that went to the
Orient and around Cape Horn. He was arrested in South Carolina
(and released after my grandmother telegramed the judge, an old
friend of her family). He survived a wreck off the mouth of the Co-
lumbia River. His ship, the *Laurel,* carrying lumber to the Orient,
ran aground on a wild night in 1929. The lumber broke free and slid
overboard into the surf, making a swim through the heaving logs
suicidal. A coast guard vessel strung lines seaward to remove the
crew, but the cable kept going slack, dumping men into the waves
among the pulverizing logs. By timing the give and take of the sea,
Nick rode high over the gnashing lumber. Next morning the Seattle
Times wrote him up as "a cabin boy hero."

My parents brought him out to Africa on their own money. My
mother had expended much of her youth trying to rescue her brothers
from their father. She urged them to study. She insisted they take
music lessons, go to college, enlarge their notions of who they could
be. As a university student, she had appeared on board a freighter
bound for China from Oregon, demanded to see the cabin boy, and

talked Nick into giving up the trip to Shanghai. She insisted he must finish high school. He went back to Seattle and completed two years in one.

A few months after going underground, my uncle saved another miner from being battered to death by his own work crew. The Afrikaner had struck one of his men with a carbide lamp. My father describes the beating of Africans by white miners as routine. Usually, the Africans took out their resentment on each other. But this time the entire crew laid into their white overseer. My mother writes: "Nick, who was forty feet above him on another level, heard shouting and ran to investigate. He brought with him an iron bar and started to lay about him right and left. Two natives got the bar away from him. Nick wrestled with them and kicked them down somehow. When Nick gets good and mad he is a human tornado, and the gang beat it. The miner was unconscious. He was black-and-blue from the beating as they attacked him with shovels, lamps, and rocks. Nick thought he was dead, but he's OK now, though only thanks to Nick. He has a wife and children, the youngest two months old. He might think twice before he hits people with his lamp again."

Two years later, my father and Nick saved the mine from a major disaster and total closedown. We were living then in a mine house across the street from the main gate. One Sunday morning, my mother was awakened by "two terrific explosions. I thought they were blasting at the Number Three Shaft," she wrote. "But then all the mine whistles started to blow. I woke Gus to ask him why all of this noise on Sunday? He leapt into his clothes, called Nick, and they raced down to Betty Shaft where they found the compressor house on fire and flames thirty feet up in the beams."

An electrician had pulled a switch and short-circuited 550 volts through his own body. (Fleisher, who replaced Williamson as manager, would be held responsible for not maintaining the equipment.) My father, first on the scene, carried out the injured electrician whose body was charred black. He died before noon that same day.

"Nick climbed up thirty feet to the ceiling and succeeded in putting out that part of the fire. So by the time Zeppenfeld and Fleisher arrived the fire was out," my mother continues.

Nick and my father had saved the company thousands of pounds sterling. "Gus and Nick were highly commended," she concludes. "No checks in the mail, however."

My father, with his blue eyes and awkward diffidence, had little in common with Nick, whose personality was charged with Mediterranean spontaneity and careless charm. My father considered the mines a career. Nick had gone underground because the work was available. He was up for anything as long as it paid, and years later would own a chain of liquor stores in Rhodesia. When my father spoke about mining, he made it sound like banking or corporate law. He thought of himself as a practical man, one who expects a reasonable return on his educational investment. But I realize now that, like Nick, he secretly thrived on impossible odds—adventure, chance, brute danger. When my parents sold their wedding presents and said they were off to Africa, no one understood. The mines of Africa? It seemed reasonable enough to my father. Later, like a good husband and father, he paid stiff premiums on a wide variety of insurance policies. But in 1933, the whole world was headed for disaster. It was a time when the adventurous survived while the prudent stay-at-homes were bombed, herded into camps, murdered, starved to death.

In my parents' letters, death returns with the mechanical regularity of a skeleton marking midnight in a medieval clock. When they set out for Africa, death was no consideration. They were too young; death was un-American, the child of carelessness, inattention, bad luck. But death had one virtue. His regular appearances reminded them that there was worse than boredom and exile. Death frightened my mother into a heightened awareness of the joy in being alive.

"Our happiness really frightens me sometimes, as I'm so apprehensive of a jealous fate that might at any moment snatch it from us.

But Gus who is always practical, says there's no anticipating. Live in the present."

My mother wrote this some time after Williamson died on the night of April 22, 1935. It was then the odds went against my father. The death of the man who had brought him out to Africa would prove nearly fatal for him as well.

6

The Austrian Officer

"Mr. Williamson died last night. It's a big blow, believe me, especially as it was Mr. Williamson who sponsored Gus and thought such a lot of his ability. But just imagine allowing a man to die because of incompetent medical attention. It makes me furious. These blacks are wise. They won't allow themselves to be dragged off to the hospital. They call it 'the dying place.' And that's just what it is. If you're so badly off that you must go to hospital, it's all up with you, because the doctors are absolutely no good. I feel so awfully sorry for Mrs. Williamson. They were married only a year or so. We've had a terrific gale, biting wind. Winter has definitely set in."

Advancement on the Rand was a game of favorites, and my father was an American. He lacked both the tribal instincts of the Afrikaner and the colonial assumptions of the English. He expected to make up the difference by breaking more rock then anyone else. He had learned Afrikaans, he conformed to the British manner. But the necessary moral arrogance was beyond him. He had not grown up in a tribal world, so his American attitude seemed to him the only morally defensible one. Some tribes were vicious, some benign. The Afrikaners were the tribe with the white skins and guns. But it was the British who owned South Africa, and they might well be compared to the ancient Chinese, who believed their universe rested on the back of a tortoise. The tortoise is slow, ungainly, sad, and unthreatening—a good place to park a universe. And the African nations, upon which the colonial world was balanced, may be described in the same way.

Fleisher was made manager the day after Williamson's death. But he was demoted a few weeks later, after the compressor fire. A new manager was sent out from Johannesburg, the skeletal and inscrutable Mr. Coe. Fleisher, grumbling and fuming, found himself once again an assistant to the man in charge.

Mr. Coe possessed a long, bony frame and a face as pale and expressionless as the belly of a bottom fish. His eyes protruded oddly, as if nature were preparing to shoot them out on stalks. His surefire technique for making money was never to spend it. Spending any money, even company money, made him acutely unhappy. He canceled Williamson's bonus system, which rewarded high achievers with cash. Coe instead rewarded them with time off. My father did once try gently to explain that by rewarding the men with a few hundred shillings the company made thousands of pounds. Surely it was not efficient to reward the best men by sending them home to sit on their bottoms.

"Coe has cut all the men's overtime, including Nick's," my father wrote home. "He thought Nick was making too much. So what he is actually doing is holding up production. Everybody from the Assistant Manager Fleisher down to the lowliest apprentice is against him. He buys the very cheapest machinery so hoists and other equipment are always breaking down. The mine has gone way down in production."

With production plunging, Mr. Coe tried to make up the difference by saving on water and electricity. He ordered the power line to the mine-village switched off at ten o'clock, and he spent a lot of his time checking up on the light bulbs in company buildings. "Nothing over forty watts," was his motto. "Bright light anywhere gets him hopping mad," my father wrote. "When he sees a sixty-watt bulb he lights up himself."

Water in company houses was available only for an hour in the morning and an hour in the evening. Muttered complaints about Mr. Coe were gradually upgraded to expletives describing his relations with his mother and then his dog. All through 1935, dull minds in the Johannesburg office pondered the situation in Nigel. The accident rate climbed. Fist fights broke out underground. Rats appeared in the water supply system. White miners booted black miners in lift lines, and rocks from sources unknown struck white miners in the back. Nick joined in the fun and kicked a black miner who happened to be holding a pick. The pick went through Nick's shin. A day later his leg swelled to twice its normal size. My mother worried he would lose the leg, because he went back to work before the wound healed. "This mine water is full of infections," she wrote. "Even his groin is swollen, the ankle is huge."

My father had been put in charge of drilling efficiency by Coe and liked the idea. He wrote his mother, "There are a hundred and fifty stopes (narrow tunnels drilled along gold seams), so you can see I've a big territory and job, if I am to bring up the drilling efficiency of so many workers. It includes forty-five to fifty whites, each with three machine drill black miners."

The idea of efficiency seemed to elude Mr. Coe. "He even frowns on the expense of keeping an efficiency department—to my mind one of the most important in any mine." My mother adds, "The man just worked his way up from a learner and got his ticket (certification) years before when technical knowledge was rudimentary."

By then my father had passed every examination the South African system required, and he was more than ready to manage any mine on the Rand. Instead, he was idled. No matter how efficient, personable, and responsible he made himself, he would get nowhere until another Williamson came along. His own abilities were irrelevant. His own efficiency, if anything, began to work against him.

The elevation of Mr. Coe had created a kind of running joke that everyone from the lowliest African shovel hand to the assistant manager could share. The new manager was so clearly incompetent that those who followed his orders could only marvel at their irrelevance. For a few months the miners were united in shared detestation. Fleisher hawked stories against his boss to anyone who would listen and judged men by their willingness to find his contempt amusing.

The last months that Nick lived in our little house were a time of rapidly declining optimism. My mother had not adjusted to the violent climate, the dull society, my father's bad fortune. She suffered from asthma, eye trouble, and the cyst on her tooth, which a series of operations seemed only to make worse. The high altitude and dry air brought on nosebleeds. She spent much of 1936 pregnant with my sister, born September 26. Yet her letters repeatedly mention how much they all find to laugh at. Her brother Nick was eighteen, young, and energetic. He paid rent for his room, planted a vegetable garden, bought a motorcycle. Compared to my father's bleak Anglo-Scottish relatives, my mother's family were an irrepressibly cheerful bunch. They played musical instruments, they sang. They were more inclined to laugh than reflect. True, their father was a monster, but they had grown up free from the dark, inward restraints of a Puritan heritage.

"We laughed until we had to sit down and couldn't get back up," my mother writes Bess. Or, describing the locust plague and Nick's attempt to save his vegetable garden, "He looked ridiculous [wearing a miner's helmet and his underwear], swatting them with a tennis racket. We fell down laughing and couldn't do a thing to help him. And of course the locusts ate everything anyway, including all the leaves off the trees across the street, and then flew off to eat all the trees in Pretoria as well."

The best laugh of 1935 was provided by Mrs. Bertram, a writer of romantic novels. Mrs. Bertram and an American, Mrs. Latham, were the only two literary figures in Nigel, and they owned the only two typewriters in town. Mrs. Latham was married to a poor pipe fitter who brought her back from Paris, having mistaken her for a well-spoken American heiress. The plumber had made a modest sum on gold stock and passed himself off in Paris as a rich mining executive. It was only when he brought her back home to Nigel that he admitted the awful truth, suggesting she purchase a house for them. That she was broke came as the worst shock of all.

As for the novelist, Mrs. Bertram was married to a carpenter. One midnight, returning from the neighboring town of Springs, they almost ran down a line of Africans stretched across the road, holding hands. Bertram managed to brake in time, skidding to a stop in a shower of sand and dust. Figures swarmed around the car; faces pressed against the glass. An enormous hand reached through the driver's window. Mrs. Bertram (suddenly cast as the heroine in one of her own gushing tales) seized her husband's handgun, stashed in the glove compartment. Jerking the trigger hysterically, she fired a bullet into her thigh. Bertram took the gun from his screaming wife and jammed the barrel into the face of a man leaning through his window. He had the presence of mind not to pull the trigger. The African, observing the gun up his nostril, extracted himself from the car. The rest of the mob melted away in the dark.

Visiting Mrs. Bertram in the hospital, my mother found her in a euphoric mood. The doctor had sliced the bullet out of her thigh and prescribed aspirin and brandy to kill the pain. The plump novelist was wallowing happily in bed, eating chocolates, and drinking all the brandy she could. "The dear lady had drunk about a dozen quarts of brandy in the last week and was stewed to the eyebrows. She weighs about three hundred pounds, but in her condition she imagines herself a slim, fairylike creature and kept gurgling on about 'little me' until I was ready to split. The insurance agent was there and she made him hold her hand, and called him 'sweetheart,' and told him she idolized him. I made my escape PDQ!"

In the spring of 1935 Mari and Petar were visiting Yugoslavia, taking with them their twelve-year-old son, Marion (later called Emil). My mother decided to leave South Africa for a few weeks. Sarajevo, in Serbia, would provide a convenient midpoint between Johannesburg and Seattle. Because someone had to foot the bill for her expensive excursion, my father and Nick remained underground.

Thus I came to travel first class with my mother up the west coast of Africa, passing Gibraltar, and disembarking in Genoa. Our ship was the *Julio Cesare*, a lovely liner, bombed and sunk six years later by South African beaufighters. We took the train to Venice, my mother's favorite city. After Venice, it was straight to Kreševo, a village near Sarajevo, where Petar was born. There my second birthday was celebrated among squabbling relatives.

My mother sticks to local color in her first letters to Bess, describing "old village women who wear big baggy trousers and black kerchiefs, and white embroidered blouses. The men wear trousers with baggy seats and tight legs, red sashes at the waist, red embroidered jackets, and a high cossack cap or red fez. Their shoes are red with pointed toes and the stockings scarlet. Nearly all of the habitués here are Turkish with very few Christian, and the place teems with little tinplate generals and overfed soldiers, same as Italy." My mother also remarks that Petar visited the house where he was born and was "quite overcome as he walked through all the familiar rooms."

Everything in Yugoslavia was taxed three and four times over with nothing to show for it—"no sidewalks, poor roads, no public hospitals, government schools to the fourth grade only, no playgrounds, no libraries, only three parks in all of Sarajevo. . . . The butter is half sour and always soggy. There is no hurry, no bustle. The sidewalk cafes are always full up with every available chair occupied on every sidewalk where we sit and drink Turkish coffee from tiny cups. There's dancing from eight to three in the morning and we come home at four."

It was only in a letter composed a year later (when she was able finally to write about it) that my mother detailed for Bess what was really going on in Sarajevo, describing the emotional explosions that made her break forever with Petar. It is the only existing letter in which she allows herself to write openly about her stepfather.

"I'm just letting the dishes go till I get this off to you. Every time I think of Nick's father, I simply choke. I think I've shed just about enough tears over him and the dreadful way he acted up in Europe. I wake up in the middle of the night many a time thinking about it, and it's like having a nightmare. It's not so bad now as when I first came back. . . . You can't imagine how horribly disillusioned I was when Mr. M[artincevic] unmasked himself and showed the hatred for me that he has been treasuring up ever since he married my mother. It all sounds like some fantastic melodrama. He has it firmly fixed in his mind that I have alienated the affections of all his sons—that he could do nothing with them because of my influence over them. He called me a she-devil and an ungrateful wretch and a liar, and said what he'd do with me if I managed to get Marion away from him. Such ravings can only be attributed to a madman!"

As for poor Mari, she associated happiness with Crikvenica, the Croatian town south of Trieste and Fiume. She had grown up on the Adriatic coast where her family owned a hotel. As a child, growing up surrounded by people from every nation in Europe, she had loved music and dancing. In 1905, when she was twenty, she fell in love with a young Austrian, a customs officer for the Hapsburg monarchy who came down from Fiume to walk on the beach with her. Until she lost her mind, Mari would preserve a photograph of this officer in a secret album, and the first time my mother took her college friend Haroldine home, an album was brought out and the picture displayed. The officer's surname was Lucian, and my mother confided to Haroldine that she always wished it were her name, too.

A studio photo of Mari, taken in Fiume the year she met him, shows her wearing a high-necked, tight-fitting dress with a narrow waist. Her expression is inward and dreamy. Her dark hair, cropped short, marks her as a woman with independent ideas, or perhaps as someone who works too hard to be bothered with long hair. In 1905, flowing tresses were required once a woman had squeezed herself into half a dozen layers of underwear and cinched her fashionably tortured waist into a corset ribbed with whalebone.

Mari was volatile, sensual, and combative. In photographs she tends to raise her chin and stare down the camera. Emil recalls his mother swimming in Seattle's ice cold Eliot Bay years after she had immigrated to America, paddling out a good half mile. Her squabbles with Petar were constant, a kind of irritable obligato playing all through my mother's childhood. Mari was also clairvoyant. More than once she woke in the middle of the night to announce, through tears, the death of a sister or cousin. And soon a letter would arrive confirming her bad dream. My mother inherited the same uncanny gift, but downplayed it. She did not like looking into the future.

Still in college, shortly after her marriage, she awoke from a nightmare and told my father she had seen Nick in danger of drowning in icy seas. The dream upset her so much that she could not sleep the rest of the night. In the morning, the Seattle *Times* headlined the story of Nick's rescue from the *Laurel*, which ran aground off the Oregon coast.

In Sarajevo, Marion deserted his father for his sister, and she put him to work baby-sitting me. He remembers herding me through the streets of the town, past the naked white heads of slaughtered animals and long strings of black sausage in butcher shops. He also recalls my mother flirting outrageously with a pharmacist. Her freedom of spirit made a lasting impression on him. When they came on a man masturbating by the river, she burst into laughter.

The close affection between my mother and her half-brother sent Petar into a jealous rage. Taking Marion aside, his father warned him to stay away from us. My mother writes Bess, "He told Marion that I was a dreadful person, that I would corrupt him, and that there were terrible things he would tell him about me as soon as they got back to the U.S. He threatened the boy with dire punishment if he repeated any of this to me. Marion stole away and came with me anyway and said his father must be crazy."

The old family pattern was repeating. Petar saw himself undermined, cheated, ignored. His stepdaughter had always made him feel like a man chasing a butterfly with a sledgehammer. Now she was older and it was worse.

Bolstered by female cousins, he set out to even the score. He opened up the subject of his wife's immoral youth. As a young woman she had had an affair with an Austrian officer. The officer had disappeared when she told him she was pregnant with his child. Petar, a poor, hardworking Serb, had saved her reputation and given the child his name when he married her. He had taken mother and child to America and supported them for years. His reward was to see the girl grow up and steal what he valued most in all the world, his sons.

Mari had no idea that Petar was telling tales behind her back. She had waited twenty years for this trip. She could hardly wait for the short journey to Crikvenica. But Petar was not one to give up an advantage. My mother, embroiled in his melodrama, felt that her presence in Sarajevo was ruining everything for Mari. No matter how pleasant she made herself, she was still Mari's illegitimate daughter, and Petar took every advantage of the fact.

Petar told his cousins once again how the women of Crikvenica had stoned Mari after hearing she was having a child. My mother was furious. Petar was furious. The female cousins were furious. There were furious squabbles whenever Mari was not present. My mother grew so incensed that she refused to speak with Petar. This stratagem shamed him in front of the men. He took my mother aside and insisted she preserve a facade of amiability. She said she could find no reason to treat him any better than he was treating her mother. She describes how he "flared up and said all manner of filth, insults, and lies. He must have a very diseased mind. I can't credit a sane person with his thoughts."

Meanwhile I turned two, was stuffed full of cake, and remained blissfully oblivious of the fury raging around me. Petar continued to find excuses for not taking Mari to Crikvenica. These soul-destroying squabbles reminded my mother, once again, that her childhood had been the worst period of her life. "It's only since I've been married that I know what peace and happiness is."

She saw that she must leave her mother and go alone to Crikvenica, or Petar would never take Mari to see her family. In his small way, he had won the battle, and my mother and I went by train to the Adriatic coast where we had time to kill. The waves came slipping in to shore without haste. The small white hotels stared at the blue horizon, as they had looked out during that guilty summer of 1905 when Mari strolled on this same beach with her officer. Nothing had changed but the women's hair and hemlines.

My father would later say that the Austrian officer had died young. We were led to believe, we were told outright, that Mari had been a widow. Long after my mother's death, when I guessed she was not legitimate and asked the question, my father refused to admit the truth. She had charged him to keep her secret, and he kept it until he died.

As a child, I imagined the Austrian officer, in a red uniform on a black horse, cut down by Serbian bullets. The truth was less romantic. Told in late summer that Mari was carrying his child, he vanished. Why, then, did Mari keep a photo of his handsome face in her album? I can only guess.

My mother could identify her father only by comparing her face to those of her brothers. She bore no resemblance to her mother.

Perhaps she recognized him, too, in the quality of her intelligence, her talent for languages, her power to charm, her ambition. Because Petar was not really her father, she could fashion herself as his opposite. She may well have longed for her missing father. She must have thought about him on the beach facing the Adriatic. But she never mentioned him to me. She didn't want to raise questions that would lead us back to those streets where her mother had nearly been stoned to death by the Christian women of Crikvenica.

Petar did allow Mari her moment in Crikvenica—five days in all. Then he dragged her back to Sarajevo. My mother walked me up and down the beach, until it was time for us to depart for Genoa. Of this sad trip into my mother's past, I retain only the vaguest smudge of memory, a glimmer that lights dim images—a white beach with waves curling in; unshaved men in soggy, dark suitcoats; a pale figure emitting a bright stream of urine under an arch.

On the return voyage, an Italian count became infatuated with my mother. I imagine him slim, black hair slicked down with brilliantine, a pair of crisply creased trousers, prominent bones in his wrists, and a nose like a scimitar. Her letter to Bess reports that she enjoyed the attention, but refused his gifts. Whereupon the count loaded me down with toys instead. I arrived in Cape Town with a suitcase full of stuffed animals and a red metal truck. Nick and my father were at the dock to meet us.

Back in Nigel, my mother went to bed for a week. She had, she told Bess, always laughed at the idea of a nervous breakdown. But no longer. "You choke on your own fury. You don't know whether you are spitting bile or blood." She knew that one day Petar would drive her mother mad. She knew she was helpless to do anything about it.

7

Fleisher

DURING COE'S YEAR ON THE JOB, PRODUCTION FELL BY HALF. THE brilliant minds in the Johannesburg head office decided at long last to remove Mr. Coe, who never went underground and spent his days checking light bulbs and water meters. Coe was replaced by Fleisher whom Coe had replaced to begin with. And after Coe had departed for whatever dusty oblivion is reserved for failed mine managers, Fleisher threw a party in Johannesburg. The triumphant new manager and his plump wife used the April fancy dress ball to celebrate their success. My mother describes Fleisher as a "tied-in-a-knot, sputtering, inarticulate little man." With his purple cheeks, veined nose, and wet lips, I imagine him as a kind of South African deity carved in heavy stinkwood—harbinger of destruction, breeder of discord, disaster, and sorrow.

My father, having determined that mining efficiency meant changing the way the races worked together, was bound to run headlong into Fleisher. But this was not apparent to him at the beginning. Fleisher had always put on a friendly face while Coe was in charge, and my parents were invited to sit at his table with half a dozen other couples at the new manager's big bash.

"We got all dressed up as a Dutch boy and girl," my mother wrote. "We put our makeup on at Zep's, then went to the Fleishers' where we were introduced to the Carleton-Joneses and other bigwigs from Jo'burg. We had two tables reserved for us at the dance, which was cabaret style—free whiskey and soda supplied by the Fleishers."

My mother, four months pregnant with my sister, was dead beat by ten. My father, who didn't trust hotel food, had already consumed a full meal at home. He now tucked into "avocado, pear, and grape with sharp sauce, soup, sole with asparagus in butter, grilled lamb chops and new peas, roast turkey and fixings, two kinds of wine, and champagne, cherry trifle, mint, nuts, and coffee." The dancing continued past midnight, and he was still going strong at one-thirty when my mother finally pushed him out of the door.

Quite aside from his color-blindness, there was something about my father's genial kindness and slightly tentative social persona that didn't sit well with the new boss. Given an order, his leap to obey did not demonstrate the right degree of deferential agility. What Fleisher craved, he regarded as garden-variety bootlicking. Despite his six-foot frame, there was about my father a curious vulnerability, a kind of private distance that might well pique the interest of a sadist. The narrow shoulders, the articulate hands, the light touch, all of this excited in Fleisher a powerful desire to knock my father about, teach him a good lesson.

Fleisher had a bully's solid bulk—plump shoulders, a happy paunch extending over a broad belt, blunt fingers with nails well chewed down. The man was full of good-natured abuse and noisy good-fellowship. He could be heard coming from miles away. He pounded backs, he grabbed arms, he berated cronies. Filthy language exhilarated him. The words *bloody bastard* often eased whatever inward pressure caused his bloodshot eyes to bulge. When he ran into my father, he would squeeze his hand hard, harder, harder and ask, "How's America getting on?"

After my father and Nick had put out the compressor house blaze, Fleisher was effusive in his congratulations. But secretly he was not pleased. The head office blamed the fire on him. A couple of underlings had made themselves look good at his expense. That his benefactors were American only made the pill he must swallow more bitter.

After Coe departed in disgrace, Fleisher invited my father to his office and made a big show of handing him a plum assignment. Since my father was so all-fired interested in efficiency, Fleisher wanted to give him a chance to make a name for himself. Fleisher had heard that Carleton-Jones and the rest of the head office lot were bringing in the best efficiency experts in the world. The idea was to make over the way mining was done in South Africa. These experts were engineers from the Bedeaux Group. The Bedeaux Group was the brainchild of a Frenchman. Now based in London, Bedeaux engineers traveled over the world using techniques developed by the genius, Monsieur Bedeaux. The group modestly promised to revolutionize South Africa (as they had revolutionized factory production in Britain). Fleisher gave my father the job of dogging the Bedeaux experts and answering their questions while they studied the miners' work habits.

My father began to express serious reservations after only a few days. Monsieur Bedeaux had come up with the bright idea of analyzing men at work as if they were machines. After reducing human work to motion in time, he then reassembled it along more "rational" lines. Turned loose in a dairy farm, for example, Bedeaux might suggest that milch cows be marched up inclined planes into platforms. This would make it easier for milkers to pull their teats because the teat pullers would no longer have to squat on stools with their cheeks pressed against the cows' udders. Moreover, they could move easily from cow to cow without bending their knees. If the cows were made nervous by standing on high platforms and refused to drop their milk, then Bedeaux might suggest some soothing music (Glenn Miller, Mozart) to get them in the proper mood.

Underground, it was a case of Laurel and Hardy meet Frankenstein. The Bedeaux engineers stumbled about bumping their heads, measuring, clocking, coming up with mechanical solutions to human problems and generally irritating everyone who had work to do. It was clear to the shift bosses that the Bedeaux Group knew little about mining and nothing about conditions in South Africa. What irritated my father most was the way these good folk remained blind to the problem he saw as primary—friction between black and white miners. Unfortunately, the word *interface* did not yet exist and cybernetics had yet to be invented.

Months passed. My father became associated with the Bedeaux Group in the minds of the miners who blamed him for undermining their production. He had no idea then that the company directors (and Fleisher—and some friends of Fleisher) owned stock in the Bedeaux Group. This stock would rise if the company hired Bedeaux to reorganize all the gold mines in South Africa. When Fleisher handed my father the job of checking out Bedeaux methods, he was playing both ends against the middle. He may have guessed that the notion of turning miners into automatons was foolish. But he knew the company directors wanted to hear that time and motion study was the wave of the future. The head office people longed for a quick fix, science to the rescue. Unfortunately, someone would eventually have to give them the bad news—tell them their science was a fiction. It was my father Fleisher saddled up for the job. And while he was working on his final report, Fleisher sold his shares of Bedeaux stock.

By August (the month before my sister was born), it was clear to my parents that Fleisher was our enemy, operating behind a screen of lies and bluster. My mother wrote Bess, "Three men have been made mine captain since Gus got his ticket—all Fleisher's men, much younger and with less experience and no college training—and Gus is still on the shelf. It makes us mad, but all we can do is sit tight and do the job assigned and say nothing."

My father finished his Bedeaux report a few days before my sister was born. He concluded by rashly making some suggestions of his own, suggesting that his ideas might well raise mine efficiency by half. European and African workers needed to see each other in a new light. They needed special schooling. This idea he would vainly push all his years in Africa. No matter how disparate their traditions, black and white must eventually find some common ground. He produced figures to show how thousands of pounds could be saved (and made) by changing the way people above handed down responsibility to those below. As an antidote to the Bedeaux formula, he suggested a more human alternative. Simply, put every man in charge of his own accomplishment and he won't begrudge you interest and effort.

Fleisher accepted the report with a broad grin. Weeks passed. My father stopped by the office and asked if there had been any response from Johannesburg. "There are more important things on their minds than your report, my friend," said Fleisher.

The Bedeaux Group was still busy underground. My father suggested Fleisher press for a response. "Telling me how to do my job, are we?" said Fleisher. "Maybe you should take over from me!"

Every few days, my father dropped by to ask about the report. Fleisher was losing patience, and one hot December day he dropped his mask and snapped, "I must tell you your report is no good, my friend."

"No good in what sense?"

"It is not responsible."

"How do you mean, 'not responsible?' "

"That is not for me to say."

"I'm sure you can tell me what the objections were."

"If it was your business to know what the objections are, then you would know that," said Fleisher.

Conversations with Fleisher were always loaded with the oblique, grinning insinuation that comes naturally to the Afrikaner who knows he must steer a cunning course between the British above and the African below. Generally, he prefers the African. But there is nothing more perplexing than an American, especially a west coast American, who has no instinct for class distinctions. In the Afrikaner's world it is never wise to speak directly, and humor often slides into sly ridicule. Most ridiculous of all is the man who believes that reality is accessible to reason. Nothing in the Afrikaner's history would lead him to so ludicrous a conclusion. But the American is just such a man.

"It would be very helpful if you could tell me what is wrong with my report," my father said. "Unless you are saying they intend to keep you in the dark, too."

"Whatever they said to me," Fleisher shouted, "it is not my job to report it to you. But I will say, my friend, that I had to write a report to cover your report. You made a lot of work for me, Mr. Pifer."

"Well then, is it possible for me to see what you wrote in your report?"

"Are you actually going to question what I wrote!"

"I am interested in learning from you. After all, I spent months doing a report you now say is irresponsible."

"Are you calling me a liar, sir?"

"I really must insist that you let me see the report you sent to Johannesburg. Otherwise I don't see how I can do a good job for you."

"Didn't I say it was confidential? Do you know the meaning of confidential? It seems you Americans have even more difficulty with English than we Afrikaners!"

"Can you at least tell me, Mr. Fleisher, what you personally thought of my report?"

"I think you have a lot to learn," said Fleisher. "But don't worry. We will teach you. You know I am on your side, my friend."

Unfortunately for Fleisher, my father's report was so detailed that he could not send it to Johannesburg without discrediting himself. So he had dashed off his own report, using bits from my father's. (My father got the story two years later from his friend Lute Parkinson, who knew someone in the head office.)

The Bedeaux people meanwhile were tried out on other Rand mines. But they ran into resistance everywhere and in the end were sent back to England. It cost someone a lot of money. It made someone a lot of money. And my father saw that he had no hope of going anywhere under Fleisher.

He faced a bitter decision. To look for another job meant losing the seniority time he had spent three years accumulating. He would have to start at the beginning and hope for a new manager with some intelligence. Moving to another Rand property meant earning less than half the little he was earning. It meant departing with no reference from Fleisher, who would cry that he was being deserted, stabbed in the back after all he had done for this useless American. Starting again meant his time in Africa would be extended indefinitely.

So for the time being he held on, hoping Fleisher might be assigned to another job. Nick, with less to lose, had already moved on to another mine. Finally, there was something in my father that refused to toss it up. Fleisher sensed an adversary and went out of his way to make sure my father got no raises, no advances, no bonuses. He assigned his American friend the jobs others had failed to perform, difficult or dangerous jobs. My father found himself working double shifts in filthy water up to his armpits, or crawling in dusty, badly ventilated stopes where the timbering had been botched and overheads threatened to collapse. He was handed rebellious, demoralized crews, who didn't seem to care if they blew themselves to bits. Years later, whenever I asked him about the Rand an absent look would come over him and he would change the subject.

My mother wrote Bess, "Gus hates this job like poison. And the hours! Yesterday, he went at 6:30 A.M. and got home at 6:00 P.M." Some jobs kept him underground from midnight till four o'clock the following afternoon. "He gets only one decent meal and then is too tired to eat it. I can see where he is absolutely up a blind alley here with this manager who favors all his own friends and former associates first. . . . Fleisher promised Gus a raise when he got back from leave. Instead, they put him on another job which he has to learn from scratch. One miner and three natives were killed by a fall of rock this week. Hired a new girl, Agnes. Quite grand after being without for three months."

My unborn sister was approaching full term. Her fetal life had been a time of increasing anxiety and tension. My mother just then was hiring a series of servants who seemed overcome by agonies and failures of their own. Africa was a vortex whirling people about meaninglessly. "I don't understand why they take the job, and I really don't think they know themselves. They walk in and then they walk out in a state of distraction."

My father had been in South Africa a little over four years. The bone-breaking work he took for granted. But he had counted on his education and his intelligence to make a difference. Now he found himself sliding back down the career ladder. "I've never seen such a place for not saving money," he complained to Bess. "With this salary at home I'd have a house in the Richmond Highlands and a couple of cars with money to spare. I keep careful accounts to see where the money all goes and see that none is wasted, and I know where to cut down when things get a little out of hand, and still no bank balance!" His letters home become more occasional, more evasive.

"This way of working here will kill a man off before he's forty and I'm not talking through my hat. You should see how quickly some of the men age under the pressure of conditions underground, the heat and high humidity. Standish Will [his friend and neighbor] has grown a deuce of a lot older in the past two years. He overworks, is underground more than he should be, puts in two twelve-hour shifts a week underground. . . ."

He was describing himself. When he arrived on the Rand he thought he looked too young and grew a mustache. Now his hair had gone white and he shaved off the mustache for good. He was often sick and developed infections in his arms and legs. My mother wrote that she was "boiling inside most of the time." Fleisher was quietly, gleefully doing him in.

The January after my sister's birth, my father was down to his lowest weight ever. "Gus has been laid up with a large boil on his left elbow [from propelling himself up and down the stopes]. The biggest core I have ever seen came out this morning. The doctor removed it. I knew Gus would come down with something the way they've been working him. He's lost fifteen pounds and the doctor told him he's anemic. This damned mine isn't worth the sacrifice in health. Fleisher made another fellow mine captain, who got his ticket only two weeks ago. You can just imagine how this eats our hearts out. . . ."

Nothing could shake his faith that excellent work must eventually make a difference. The idea had been to make his mark and go home in three years. Four had passed. My parents began to comprehend that they were economic exiles. There was no way back home.

That my father spent his best years underground strikes me as astonishing. That Nick came all the way to Africa to do the same thing seems an additional madness. I worked in a mine just one summer and thought it the next thing to being buried alive.

8

Park

THAT SAME APRIL THAT FLEISHER WAS GIVING HIS BIG BASH, AN-other American couple appeared on the Rand. Lute Parkinson was a professional clarinetist turned mine manager; his wife, Margaret, had been trained as a concert pianist. They came to our house for the first time exactly one week after Fleisher's blow-out. Park was to be our good angel in Africa. That was always my mother's view. As for me, from the moment I was able to focus my attention, I regarded Park as a kind of demiurge. I have never met a man since who matched the impression he made, or the shadow he cast. His power-ful blend of self-assurance, sophistication, musical talent, wild hu-mor, engineering experience, and skeptical irony put him in a class apart.

It is possible to view Park as a kind of Mephistopheles. While he remained in Africa, my father appeared to have a future. The mo-ment he vanished, my father's future went with him, as if someone had turned off the lights and dropped the curtain. Had the Parkinsons never appeared, we would all have sailed to America in 1937. My mother may well have lived years longer. My father would have become the Dean of Mineral Engineering at the University of Alaska, in Fairbanks. We would have lived happily in a frozen wasteland instead of a burning desert.

Park changed all that. Hired by De Beers, elected to the company board in the middle thirties, he found himself playing Mercury to Jove—messenger and consultant to Sir Ernest Oppenheimer who was the true successor to the legendary Cecil Rhodes. Sir Ernest, enormously wealthy already, used American capital to assume control of De Beers and the world diamond industry. In 1919 he negotiated a merger of the six German diamond mining companies in South-West Africa and gradually gained control of diamond output throughout the world. Over the years he changed from a neatly put together young man who resembled the psychologist, Carl Jung, to a powerfully built centaur with a strong nose and great head that thrust forward like a charging stallion's. He became chairman of the board in 1929.

It was Sir Ernest who clipped off my father's career at the eleventh hour. Success, like so much in Africa is a *fata morgana* that turns into heat and dust when the traveler staggers close enough to make out the fine detail.

Margaret, Park's wife, was beautiful. An accomplished pianist, with a soft, round face framed by luxuriant, dark hair, she took you in with a direct, self-assured gaze. These Parkinsons had me convinced that America produced godlike people. Margaret looked as I imagined Athena must look. Park was nothing if not magnetic, a tall, well-built man, with amused, observant eyes and a Roman nose that wandered a bit on its long descent to his grin. His casual American dignity always seemed wonderfully right. His conversation was leavened by a kind of sly irony that seemed to me similar to the humor Africans employ.

Just out of college, Park had come to Africa in 1923 to work for Forminière, the same company that hired Joseph Conrad thirty-three years earlier. Like Conrad, Park boated up the Congo and walked into the heart of Africa. He was among the first Europeans to explore the rivers that flow north toward the Congo—the Chiumbe, the Luana, and the Luembe. Forminière had hired him to slop in the river pits for diamonds.

On his first leave home, he played a series of public concerts with Margaret, talked her into marrying him, and took her back with him to Africa. Her first house had mud walls, a grass roof, and mud floors. The windows were covered with muslin cloth to keep out the bugs. He described her as "a rather discouraged bride," lacking every amenity including a mirror. He hammered together their first kitchen stove himself from scrap metal. She had to have a piano, so he bought one from the British consul in Kinshasa (then Léopoldville) and had it shipped into the interior. The music they played attracted every European within a hundred miles, including the Portuguese governor of the district, who used to drive up from Saurimo on a road constructed of sticky anthill material. Park said the governor was an "amateur violinist who dearly loved to play classical numbers somewhat above his ability."

Their daughter, Peggy, was the first white child born in that part of Africa. People from outlying districts made journeys of two or three days to take a look at the white-skinned infant and to give her presents of eggs and live chickens. The house servants named her "Sankisha"—bearer of happiness. But after they were better acquainted with her, Park reports, she was renamed "Mai Munene" meaning much water. As for the chickens, they thrived in a shed until one day they were attacked by some ambitious ants. Despite a lot of hysterical squawking and desperate dashing to and fro, the fowl were done for. Park found he could do nothing to stop the ants, and what had been chickens minutes before were quickly reduced to little mounds of feather and bone, stripped clean in an hour.

Before the diamond market collapsed in the early thirties, Park had managed mines up and down Angola and Namibia. He switched to gold extraction and was hired to manage a mine on the Rand. Hearing rumors that another American was in the vicinity, Park looked him up. He found the poor man in bad health, pale and underweight, with boils all over his body.

By the time he looked up my father, Park had already developed his lifelong aversion to "Rand management." Fleisher was a typical Rand product. "Jobs for pals" was the watchword. Park's ironic detachment marked an essential difference between him and my father. When I knew him later in life, I realized that Park was saved from the disappointment my father suffered by his interest in music. He trusted music, not mankind. The mindless favoritism that made other men grind their teeth in fury, he dismissed with a quip. Like many skeptics, Park lived in a fallen world, where trust and love counted as bits of amazing good luck.

Park was elusive. His manner was casual, but his arrivals always had the character of something unannounced and his departures seemed sudden. His wit made him impossible to fix. A day in his company was like a visit to the zoo, or a glimpse into an alternative life. A born actor and mime, Park's imitation of Fleisher always left my mother limp with laughter. Tensing his shoulders, going red in the face, and spasmodically sputtering, he would clump across the room with his feet turned out, his hands opening and closing helplessly. He would then imitate himself looking at Fleisher, shooting his eyebrows high, raising an upper lip and crossing his eyes in utter disbelief. My mother later made my father film this famous "looking at Fleisher" look.

I remember Park dancing with my mother in Oranjemund to "Boompsadaisy," a wildly popular song during the war. The words went something like "One, two, boompsadaisy / I'm in love with you," and involved partners striking bottoms together on the "boompsadaisy." Park would perform the "boomp" with an expression so serious that my mother could never get through the dance and would collapse on the couch laughing helplessly.

My mother's enthusiasm for everything about the Parkinsons included their two kids. We heard so much about Peggy and Jimmy that they gradually assumed the pure vitality of mythic creatures, more magically alive than ordinary children. The Parkinson kids still sparkle extravagantly in memory though I wonder now if we spent more than half a dozen afternoons with them in our brief time together.

Jimmy was impressively eight. Peggy had achieved the incredible age of nine. She was lovely and tall, with chestnut hair cut straight across her forehead. As fidgety and temperamental as her brother was dreamy and good-natured, Peggy would joggle impatiently against her father's knee and lift and drop the gold chain that trickled down across her delicate clavicle. I was of less interest to her than the white daisy she slowly tore into pieces with her long fingers.

Peggy was famous for her temper. Whenever she visited I hoped she would display it. We'd heard she'd worked up such a fury once that she tried to brain her brother with an ax. That she might soon murder Jimmy made her especially valuable and attractive. I examined the youngest Parkinson for facial scars but found none. (My sister did a better job on me a few years later, bashing my nose with a plank after I threw sand in her hair.) I wanted to ask Jimmy what he'd done to get Peggy so worked up, but my mother firmly put the subject of Peggy's temper off limits.

Park's kids had inherited their parents' magic. The scope of their lives was staggering to contemplate. Growing up on the banks of the Luembe River, they had gorged themselves on the flying ants that appeared after the rainy season. Park describes how a rolled mat was poked into the underground ant nest and the ants were eaten as they emerged. His children, he said, "loved to join in on this treat and apparently found the taste a delightful change." The Parkinson kids would always have the jump on us. The years that separated us later caused me to ponder the mystery of time. My beautiful Peggy would forever ignore me from the throne of her inflexible maturity. Four years had put her on the far side of a chasm I could never jump. The logic of time allowed them to cross seas infested by U-Boats and pick up interesting American educations and profound American accents while we remained fixed in our twittering British insularity.

Our exposure to these demigods was confined to a few precious summer afternoons in 1937. That was the year my parents would have returned to the states had Park never appeared. The week that Park got my father signed on at De Beers, a letter arrived from the School of Mines in Seattle. Dean Milnor Roberts at the University of Washington was offering him the job in Fairbanks. But my father saw no contest between lecturing in a classroom and managing a mine. He had, in any case, given his word to Park.

The Alaska misconnection is part of a pattern. After leaving the Navy, I found myself in Alaska, bush piloting for an oil company. One day in Icy Bay a geologist mentioned a friend of his, Jimmy Parkinson by name. It was the same Jimmy, Park's son, now working as a geologist for the government near Anchorage. There were no phones in Icy Bay, and I never could find an excuse convincing enough to get myself off the job and up the coast to Anchorage. I kept asking about Jimmy, and the geologists I was flying around the mountains all said he was the best man up there. But I never did catch up with him.

Thirteen years earlier, we had managed to see Peggy just once. It was the summer of 1949, during the last months of my mother's life. My father had a new Packard. My mother was apparently recovering from her cancer operation, and our trip was a kind of celebration. Pausing in New York, we met Peggy for lunch. She was quite grown-up, sophisticated in a restless, twitchy sort of way, at the height of her beauty. She greeted us as if we were her oldest and dearest friends which, in a way, we were. She had attended exotic private schools thousands of miles from her African home and flowered into a stunning independence.

My sister and I were confused teenagers, still tied to our mother and an adolescent narcissism. Peggy, years ahead as usual, was so much at home in New York, so well adapted to its erratic pulse, I felt the place had been designed with her in mind. She talked to my mother. It all felt very familiar. I was a sixteen-year-old American male in a sloppy suit. I had adapted myself to the monosyllabic world of football, baseball, and furtive desire. I had had more to say when I was four. Peggy clinked her bracelets, drank a glass of water, wriggled about in her attractive manner, then had to dash to an important appointment. "Absolutely have to be on time. It's *dire*," she said. I glimpsed her through the window, slimly flashing across the street, negotiating traffic, chasing after whatever it is New York pretends to offer. And we never saw her again.

Park said that Fleisher was only one symptom of the general incompetence that emanated from the Anglo American office in those days. When the gold markets had revived in 1935, conditions grew worse. Good men were dying, losing hands and eyes. My father wrote Bess: "Dozens of mines are starting. One new proposition about three miles from here was floated in Jo'burg the other day—capital stock of two million pounds was oversubscribed by ten million, just minutes after they opened the books. So somebody sure has the money. But we don't see it."

In 1936, the international diamond market began to revive and Park was hired by De Beers in Kimberley. At the end of the year he posted us a letter, a letter my mother was convinced saved my father's life. She mailed it on to Bess, so I am able to quote from it directly. It must be born in mind that this letter arrived a week before the one offering him the job in Fairbanks. "It occurred to me today," Park writes with characteristic understatement, "that you possibly may want a change of location badly enough to take on a job here as shift boss. Well, I've had a little word with the General Manager who likes the idea . . . I told him that since we have you in mind as a likely candidate for a better job in the immediate future, I did not like to take the responsibility of bringing you into the company's employ without his first having a look at you. I suggested that you could probably come down any weekend. He was very much in accord with the idea and said, 'Bring him on!' . . . I do think you would like the work here. No shouting and cursing and 'bloody bastarding' is necessary to function efficiently in any of the local jobs—at least as far as I have observed."

Park continues: "A Namaqualand job will be going in July. You might get it, and yet I can tell you nothing definite about it. But your prospects would certainly be much better if you were already a company official at the time." He warns: "There are no company houses and the whole of Kimberley offers nothing decent to rent. So be careful before you leap, brother."

My father leaped on board the train to Kimberley that same weekend. The De Beers officials met him and he was hired on the spot. He gave Fleisher notice the first day he was back. And the following Sunday we left Nigel for good—driving 340 miles through the dust and narcotic heat to the promised land.

9

Sudden Ascent

WE GOT ROYAL TREATMENT FROM PARK AND MARGARET WHO IN-
stalled us in their house for the time being. My mother writes, "The
hotels are full up, and so are the boardinghouses, and there aren't
any empty houses to let for love or money. Kimberley is booming."

Somehow Park finagled an empty manager's property that stood
outside of town near the Dutoitspan mine. My father's lowly status
(shift boss) was magically ignored and we moved into a mansion.
Suddenly we found ourselves in the colonial Africa that movie stars
inhabit in Hollywood films.

"As big as the Fleishers' place," my mother chortled. "Twelve
rooms, three screened in verandas, fireplace in every room, pergolas,
summerhouses, flower gardens, a bowling green, tennis court, and
swimming pool!" She goes on: "It's no exaggeration to say that Parkinson saved Gus's life, or at least added ten years to it. Gus is a
different man now—self-confident, buoyant, and very self-assured.

That man, Fleisher!—I'd like to crush like a beetle, as he tried to crush Gus—that so called big executive. . . ."

Our gardens were fenced away from the red dust and white heat by hedges set between brick posts with white wood crossbars. I had turned four the previous July. At that age the memory retains only fragments that stick to consciousness like shards of eggshell to the fluff of a newly hatched chick. My picture of this paradise (compared to what had been and what would soon come) was reinforced by later visits when the Parkinsons lived in the same house. There were pine trees and a long shaded road softened by pine needles. Beyond the main gate the line of pines gave way to eucalyptus. The eucalyptus marched past our tiny swimming pool into a distance that vanished into total obscurity. I pushed my sister's pram through gardens that had no boundaries.

I retain a vivid image of sickle-shaped leaves floating on the light green water surface. I basked on the damp edge where the concrete had begun to crack. I sniffed the camphorous odor of the leaves that sank gradually to the pool floor like tiny drowned figures, and I will always associate the sight of leaves floating in a swimming pool with a sensation of joy and hope.

Joy was palpable in our lives that year. My father, instead of being sent into collapsing, waterlogged stopes to clean up the messes other men had made, was being considered for a shot at mine management. It seemed that hard work and expertise might count for something after all.

My mother wasted no time enrolling me in dancing school. I remember only my black dancing shoes with their metal taps, and the music, which I found intolerable—the tinny sound of the thirties was thin and sickly after the vital roar of African drums and passionate singing of the miners in the Nigel compound.

In Nigel there had been distant drumming almost every night. This is how my mother describes the dances that took place on certain Saturdays. "Yesterday more than a dozen teams of dancers from all over the reef were competing. The SubNigel group was the best as far as we could judge. The whites sat on the porch of the compound on benches forming a circle about five or six deep around dancers dressed in their Sunday best. They came whooping it up with cerise feathers in their hair. One of them made a tail for himself out of garish colored plumes of some kind, loincloths or sarongs like the Maoris wear. Small mirrors set in ostrich feathers decorated their hair. The orchestra was made of a dozen natives who are the 'women.' At home it is always the women who do the singing and hand clapping for the men dancers. The rhythm is sustained by this chorus who hold pieces of wood. They sound rather like Spanish castanets. Some of the musicians bound their heads in silk kerchiefs, and wore blouses and skirts. Several had stuffed their chests and hips, à la Mae West. One had silk stockings with his skirt above the knees so we couldn't miss the stockings. He improved on these by tying different colored handkerchiefs around his ankles and below his knees. When the dancers work themselves up they stamp the ground till it shakes, roll their eyes, throw back their hands and generally appear raving mad. When it's over, they fall down and pant like marathon runners. And oh boy did baby enjoy it! He sat on the front bench and the solo dancers danced for him mostly. Now he tries to imitate them, and it's too funny to watch him."

My mother describes me, aged nine months, dancing "up and down whenever he hears music—whistling or singing in perfect tune. Everybody thinks it's marvelous and so do we." This is doubtless mother's pride going over the top, but sound has always affected me more than language or visible design. I can still re-create in my mind's ear Park's Colorado accent rolling out across the garden in Kimberley. The American voice was immense—grand and broad like the movement of the ocean waves, a sound that evoked great prairies, quite unlike the twittering English I used, precise and sharp as the chirping of birds. Once in the desert we would hear very little music, unless I count the Nazis in Oranjemund bellowing their patriotic marches. But there was still the wind, the roar of the surf, the leaves rustling, the cicadas chirring, and the B-flat seventh of the mine whistle. It was African music and the singing of the desert that taught me to listen to landscapes and cities as if they too produced music.

During the half year we luxuriated in Kimberley, half a dozen servants came and went. We lived too far out in the country and had no car. The bus stopped running early in the evening. My mother tried hiring Afrikaners. Her letters mention an old Afrikaner woman whose husband had been killed in the mines, and a young Afrikaner girl who never changed her underwear. My mother struggled with the girl over her "linen," but it was no use. In the end, overwhelmed by the woman's body odor and the constant embarrassment of having to raise the subject, my mother asked her to go. An American nose in Africa often proves a problem.

The only servants I remember in Kimberley were Mabel and Gertrude, eighteen and twenty. They were sisters hired as a pair because they refused to separate. "Mabel is the cook and Gertie is the nurse-maid and general assistant," my mother wrote Bess. "Both can wait on table to perfection and they are neat, efficient, and very willing to do anything and everything. Gertie looks like a white girl except for her light brown hair done in neat curls at the back and held by a net. Mabel has the flat nose and thick lips of a Zulu but has a very light color. A strange mixture they are but they certainly know how to work and are very civil."

I have a clear memory of Gertie's cool, haughty face with the light blue eyes, white lashes, the saddle of reddish freckles across her nose. She had neat little nostrils that flared when she was annoyed. I was dimly aware that I annoyed her. Her sister was as warm and bashful as Gertie was cold and imperious. Only now, a lifetime later, am I able to imagine the excruciating difficulty of their relationship.

It was Gertie's apricot skin and European features that lent her

status. They were like a pair in some Nathaniel Hawthorne story—
dark goodness yoked to luminous sin. The darker sister with her Zulu
features compromised Gertie's pale superiority. Wherever Gertie went
people had only to glance at her sister to see that Gertie, too, must
have African blood. White people, black people, Indian people, everyone stared. And Gertie had to endure the insipid comprehension,
always the same surfacing in all those eyes. "If that one is Zulu then
the other one is Zulu too, even though she looks white. Isn't that
interesting, that a black can look so white!"

Gertie's back was as stiff as a sergeant major's. She never smiled
and she dominated Mabel with a stern look, a toss of her head, a
curt gesture. Obedience was the price she demanded for this humiliation by association, the constant outrage of having to acknowledge
that nothing was what it seemed.

I inflicted myself also on the gardener's son, a spindly little boy
about my age, but half my size. His diet had consisted mostly of
mealie meal, the universal gruel poor Africans consume in South Africa. (Up north, in the jungles, they had *chombi* a sour-smelling mush
made from pounded manioc.) My mother used to seat the gardener's
child with me in the kitchen and urge a soft-boiled egg on him with
buttered toast and milk. I remember his large, abashed eyes and
loamy smell, and the way he drank his milk with a strange little
sucking sound. My well-fed energy fatigued him, and my mother
would warn me to stop terrorizing the child.

When he was gone, when my infant sister was asleep and the
afternoon stretched out as endless as the world outside the gate, I
would go in search of Gertie. She would glare at me with her strange,
lynxlike eyes, then turn her face away, refusing to dignify my prattle
with a reply. It was my impression that I had done something wrong.
Those cold, green eyes with the yellow flecks and her willful silence
inspired a sense of guilt. More than her beauty, it is my guilt that
fixes her so firmly in memory.

10

Hottentot

OUR TRAIN PULLED OUT OF CAPE TOWN EARLY SUNDAY EVENING. WE
were heading north into the desert. Table Mountain, with its blue
flanks and flat top, faded with the light and was replaced by our own
faces peering into the window of the dining car where we could now
see only the South African Railway logo (SAR), delicately inscribed
in the glass. We slept in our bunks with the windows open, the desert wind tickling through our hair. In the morning, there was only
the desert and a double telegraph line that swooped down, then
swooped up, only to drop again after being slapped in the face by
another unforgiving pole.

Because the price of diamonds was rising briskly in 1937, Sir Ernest Oppenheimer reopened the alluvial pits at Kleinzee on the
southwest coast. The Kleinzee digging required a manager who could
work in one of the most inhospitable deserts on earth with a camp
full of illiterate Afrikaners. Park had insisted my father could do the

job and Sir Ernest had finally nodded his heavy head. So here we were, advancing into Hottentot Land, though there were almost no Hottentots left. The diamond territories were off limits to everyone but the police.

The locomotive clanked to a stop at rail's end in the wretched town of Klawer. It was six in the morning. Waiting for us was round-faced, round-eyed Jannie Oddie, the company chauffeur. The vehicle that would get us across the desert was a sand-pitted company Chevrolet equipped with balloon tires for "floating" over soft sand. Our bags were tossed into a flatbed truck driven by an Afrikaner with a face burned bright red. He followed behind us to Kleinzee, much too close behind us. But no matter how often my father suggested that he would do better to drop back behind the dust we kicked up, the obstinate fellow insisted on driving a few feet behind our bumper, skillfully keeping himself in the thick of it. The Afrikaner was apparently operating by a logic inaccessible to my father. Why place yourself in the center of an eternal sandstorm?

Before we motored out of Klawer my mother suggested we all stretch our legs, shake the cinders from our hair, and search for some fresh fruit. Wherever we traveled, she was always on the lookout for fruit. But Klawer at half past six in the morning has never offered fresh fruit. I doubt you'd find much fresh fruit in Klawer even today, no matter the hour. However, there we were searching for a greengrocers, though it seemed clear every door was locked up tight. Discovering a gate in a fence, she pushed through. No thriving market lay beyond. We found ourselves in a tiny, dust-dry courtyard occupied by a family of very small people.

They were housed—an old man and woman, a young man and some watchful children—in a couple of packing crates. The old woman was boiling coffee in a smoke-blackened tin rigged with baling wire over a fire of dried cow dung. They were tiny and wizened, the color of pale yellow clay. Just as nature has supplied camels with humps, she has given the Hottentot large rumps to help them survive the forced abstinence of the desert. And when they age, their eyes seem to recede into a pair of cracks just as lizards hide in fractured rock during the hot time of day.

The wind-wracked faces of the old people were startling, but no less startling were their clothes. They were all got up, the lot of them, in Victorian dress, ladies and gentlemen in cast-off evening wear—long skirts, underskirts, and button boots. The old lady wore a hat with a torn veil. The young man squatted in a cutaway coat, spats, top hat, and shredding khaki shorts. They looked like children with prehistoric faces playing in clothes that Cecil Rhodes might have worn to pose for his statue. As surprising as their layers of formal wear was their indifference to the heat. The sun was up early, as it always is on the desert, and the moment it popped free of the horizon it burned like a stove; but they kept on their coats and waistcoats, their hats and spats, the tattered ascots.

The Hottentot long ago were cattle herders. They believed that everything in the world has a soul—stones, stars, bushes, caves. So they passed through the world with great diffidence, and that diffidence is still in them. They begged forgiveness from whatever springbok or wild rabbit they killed. Amused by their diminutive size and irritated by their quiet refusal to labor, Europeans made a sport of hunting down the Hottentot and their companion tribe, the Bushmen, on horseback. By 1937, these tribes had been reduced to begging or thieving or washing clothes in littered backyards. The males were regarded as a public nuisance and, according to stories my mother heard, were still being casually murdered. The concept of private property lay outside their view of the world. They never could grasp the unholy European wisdom that said when a man owns nothing he belongs nowhere.

Having wiped out most of these people, some Europeans today feel nostalgia. Is there a word for the regret that follows a mass murder? Some kindly anthropologists have tried to show a belated respect for these decimated tribes by calling them the Khoikhoi, which is their own name for themselves. But Hottentot was the only name we heard when I was growing up, unredeemed by the euphemisms and science of the present age. If I persist in using Hottentot here, it's because "Khoikhoi" sounds to me like an affectation—too correct. Can a word redeem history?

While eighteenth-century Europeans cut down the Hottentot the way American plainsmen shot down buffalo a century later, news of their quaint customs circulated among philosophers back home. The Enlightenment critic Gotthold Lessing wrote, "The filthiness of the Hottentot is well known, and what they regard as beautiful and holy excites our disgust and aversion." He draws a scholarly example from a humor magazine, the *Connoisseur*, where Lord Chesterfield amused his readers by satirizing a Hottentot marriage ceremony:

"Knonmquaiha made a varnish of the fat of goats mixed with fire ash, with which she annointed her whole body as she stood beneath the rays of the sun. Her hair was clotted with melted grease, and powdered with the yellow dust of Buchu. Her face, which shone like polished ebony, was beautifully varied with spots of red earth, and appeared like the curtain of the night spangled with stars. She sprinkled her limbs with wood-ash and perfumed them with the dung of Stinkbingsem. Her arms and legs were entwined in the shining entrails of a heifer. From her neck there hung a pouch composed of the stomach of a kid. The wings of an ostrich overshadowed her fleshy promontories behind. Before, she wore an apron formed of the shaggy ears of a lion."

The Hottentot were surviving in the most inhospitable desert on earth, but Chesterfield neglects to mention this, so one is obliged to imagine the ceremony taking place in a little chapel in Surrey. The Lord goes on, "The Surri, or Priest, approached Tquassouw and Knonmquaiha, and in a deep voice chanted the nuptial rites to the melodious grumbling of the Gom-Gom and, at the same time, bedewed them plentifully with the urinary benediction. The bride and bridegroom rubbed in the precious stream while the briny drops trickled from their bodies like the oozy surge from the rocks of Chiri-griqua."

The Namaqualand Desert does not enjoy a benign climate and a considerate rainfall. By ignoring the whole point, the European can chortle over a couple of aborigines getting high on urine. Had Lessing and Chesterfield slogged alongside Tquassouw and Knonmquaiha for a week or two in the Namaqualand—their lips dry and flaking, the water blisters on their feet swelling and breaking—they might have learned to love urine too. I have certainly felt its attraction. To spill liquid into the sand, any liquid, feels worse than wasteful. It feels sacrilegious. Urine is a pretty good disinfectant, too. And if your most useful possessions are a slack bow and a few flint arrows, then the slick entrails of the beast you ask forgiveness for killing are more meaningful, I'm sure, than the diamonds on a dowager.

The Hottentot were a scattered remnant when we drove into their desert, but it was still their desert and whatever formed their world would touch my unformed mind as well. How human history gets into a landscape when its only mark is a few graffiti in stone, I don't know. Perhaps it is written into the horizon and the hot sand. What formed the Hottentot was to alter me as well.

We dashed out of Klawer at very high speeds on gravel roads that quickly degenerated into a hard dirt rut cut by deep transverse corrugations. Oddie slowed down only when the car threatened to capsize. Driving at a reasonable speed was not practical, because the corrugations set up a vibration so violent that it rattled teeth, cracked shock absorbers and broke axles. On the horizon lay black rock mountains set like reptile fossils in a sea of sand.

The farther north we drove, the more often the road vanished under drifting dunes. Approaching heaps of sand that rose higher than houses, Oddie would slow slightly, then floor the accelerator, gauging his forward momentum to carry us over the crest. A fine, choking dust churned up through the floorboards. Behind us came the young Boer in the flatbed truck, gamely eating our dust. The temperature calmly passed one hundred degrees.

Soon everyone was sick except for the driver and my baby sister. Patsy was red as a boiled lobster, but was otherwise just fine. Every hour or so my mother begged Oddie to stop so she could stagger out and vomit. "I was never so sick in all my life," she wrote, "and heaven knows I've done some touring—all the way to Victoria Falls and back, but I never saw anything like this."

While she retched, we stood and waited in the heat, peering at the horizon weaving like a snake under its cap of liquid air. An obligatory vulture circled. The sand burned through our shoes like a stove top. The rocks were too hot to touch or sit on. There was no breeze. White as a sheet with red blotches on her cheeks, my mother staggered back to the car and we roared off again.

As we jounced northward toward Kleinzee, sand and stone gave way to giant lakes of hard salt. The temperature rocketed up through 110. Approaching these giant dry pans you are blinded by their dazzling whiteness; but beyond them rise blue hills, and then orchards and cool villages with white houses set on blue lakes. Soon this *fata morgana* world, with its false promise of lilting fountains and orange groves, dissolves. As you rush forward, the hot air swallows everything, as if some demon were rolling up the world like a rug, removing the vineyards and the châteaus moments before you arrive. Only the salt crystals are real—flinging the light into your eyes like a spear point. And ahead lies yet another range of bony, sterile hills, each with its back arched like the black fin on a half-buried brontosaurus.

We passed through sand blasted *dorps* (small towns): Nuwerus, Garies, Kamieskroon. Feeling good and sick after drinking too much tepid water in Springbok, we at last veered westward toward the coast.

We passed over a low range and suddenly everything changed. My mother wrote Bess, "When all I wanted to do was get out and lie face down on the hot sand, we arrived. And when I was able to look around me, the hills and valleys were completely covered with a riot of flowers—orange, pale blue, white, yellow, and crimson." Chance had been kind. We had arrived during the best week in a "wet" year, when the desert flowers bloom.

Kleinzee was set in a slightly rolling flatland of broken rock and shifting sand that tilted down into a cold sea. The desert, with its high dunes, is narrow—only fifty to one hundred miles across as it follows the coast north, paralleling a cold Antarctic current. Behind it stretch badlands, drylands, a tumbled landscape that strikes travel guides as magnificent, and prospectors as an interminable hell.

The unpaved, gravelly street that ran past the wire fence in front of our house continued on directly into the sea. Across from us were the diggings—open trenches dug by Afrikaners with picks and shovels. There was a wire fence, a tiny porch, a few cactus plants, stones white as bleached skulls.

We stumbled into the tiny gray stucco house. The front door faced the Atlantic. The backyard consisted of a single clothesline. But we were the manager's family and our neighbors had felt obliged to pack in a few supplies. The kitchen was stocked: sweet condensed milk, tins of Alaska salmon, bottles of Boveril. The beds were all neatly made. My mother lay down and slept like one of the dead. The high waves half a mile away sighed and thumped. A sea breeze fingered the blind. I don't remember that night at all—but the night wind is part of me, and the ponderous roll of the surf that obliterates time and suggests eternity. Naturally I had no word for eternity that year, but I had arrived from that region so recently myself that I knew it better then.

11

The Wind

OUR HOUSE OCCUPIED THE FIRST PLACE IN A LINE OF FOUR, BUT IT was identical in every detail to the others. Set at an oblique angle a few yards down the road were the tiny, single-room huts of the diggers—three hundred Afrikaners. The only Africans in the Kleinzee camp were housed servants and most of them were of mixed blood, "Cape Coloured," as they were designated. They spoke Afrikaans and were brought in from godforsaken little inland settlements (Kommaggas, for example), which simmer in the same heat as their white neighbors but appear on no map. Only the senior staff were allowed to bring wives and children into the camp, and only two other children in Kleinzee spoke English.

My mother could never accustom herself to the afternoon winds— ninety-mile-per-hour gales that ripped shirts off the line and sent them straight up out of sight while the sun shone brightly. Mornings were heavenly calm. By noon, the light sea breeze would start to dress itself out as a real desert wind. Around two in the afternoon, dust devils carried scraps of cotton wadding from the power plant high into the sky. These whirling funnels of wind descended on our row of houses, lambasting the neighbors—the mine accountant, the pit superintendent, the head engineer—tearing at our rock gardens. Dust and sand began to obscure the horizon and soon the dust devils were scattered by a headlong gale off the sea. Restlessly hauling at the roof, violently rattling the windows, blowing a fine dust through every keyhole and crevice, the wind stripped paint off cars, pitted windshields, and howled in electric lines overhead. It knocked us off our feet and it sent old Mr. Orpen flying into our fence. We grew used to the sand in our hair, our eyes, our milk; we expected grit in our butter and porridge.

A still day was a gift, a piece of incredible luck. On one of these miracle days, a Sunday morning, my father took me for a walk in the wasteland beyond the pulsator plant. The sun was hot. I was sweating and no breeze came to cool me. But oddest of all—I suddenly realized my presence *here*. A sense of my own identity flashed over me. I woke out of my infant dream and stared at the sandy shoulder of the road that ran back into town, past the rickety pulsator plant to the sea beyond. Like an alien from another star, I landed on earth with an almost audible thud.

The wind had many voices, and I imagined a face for every voice. I would catch their intonation in the lightest breeze and when the wind was strong it was as if a crowd assaulted the house, tapping at the window, crooning at the door. Sometimes one of these voices would pronounce my name quite clearly. In the electric wires, I heard women singing. Some trick of auditory perception set up by that desert wind has supplied me with these whispering associates throughout my life. But out there their presence was so palpable I would often whirl around expecting to see a face. When my mother said, "The gods have been good to us," I thought I had some notion of what she was talking about, and it seemed to me a palpable consciousness looked back into my own or beckoned me somehow from somewhere in the hills.

When it rained, my sister and I were filled with such wild excitement that we dashed out into the road and danced in the puddles, stamping and singing in a frenzy. I brought with me to Kleinzee my own version of the Zulu dances at Nigel, where the African men had invited me to join in.

Next door to us lived Mr. Wilson, the mine accountant, a plump man with a bristly mustache, famous for his snore. A grand honking sound would wake us up in the middle of the night. Everyone wondered how his poor wife could stand it. My mother said that Mrs. Wilson must, like Ulysses sailing past the sirens, put wax in her ears to get any sleep at all. However no one in town would have dreamed of mentioning Mr. Wilson's snore to Mrs. Wilson. The Wilsons were very proper people and dinners at their house were heroic affairs entailing many courses, linen serviettes, and a lot of heavy silverware. Considering the howling wilderness outside, my mother found the Wilsons' elaborate dinners somewhat overdone. But as the manager's wife it was her duty to give as well as she got. She was aware how the formalities of Europe could lead to a kind of inner grace, providing you didn't topple over into pomposity. Informality had a dangerous way of degenerating into a lack of self-regard. She achieved grace with a touch of American informality.

The Wilsons' daughter, Paddy, was eight. We were all drafted by Peter Carstens, the youngest son of Jack and Minx Carstens. Peter installed us in his private army, and we marched up and down the street with popguns over our shoulders. It was Peter (aged nine) who suggested that since Paddy was a girl and different, she might like to take off her clothes for us. She had no objection, so we all hopped into a ditch. I was profoundly impressed by the economy and smooth perfection of her nakedness, which Peter thought we should kiss. Again Paddy was amenable, so we did that too.

Peter didn't stop at sex. He was the first to inform me that one day I would die. When I objected, he said that I was not alone. My mother and sister would die too. This seemed a bit farfetched, and I went to complain about him to my mother. She said it was true, but hardly worth worrying about until it happened. And then it was all over with and other people had to worry about it.

She might make light of it, but it was still a nasty shock—the idea of not existing at all. I insisted she tell me exactly what death was, how we were buried, and what would happen to us after that. She said it was a bit like going to sleep, only more so. Or perhaps less so. No one knew for sure.

Faced now with death, I comforted myself with the thought that all of us were still so young that our lives extended virtually forever. However, Peter's revelation marked the moment when I first glimpsed the perverse nature of birthday parties, which are really little funerals. Later, when I turned ten, I was profoundly unsettled by the absolute knowledge that my age would henceforth contain two digits; I had been banished from single-digit status forever.

That a boy of ten will never again be nine was one of the few bits of absolute knowledge I was ever to pick up. And like most bits of absolute knowledge, it was perfectly useless. Pushing on with the inexorable logic of the very young, I reflected that if I ever achieved triple-digit status it would be in the year 2033. But by then I would have changed into something even more decrepit than Mr. Orpen, who was only seventy. Besides, the year 2000 looked even more distant than the moon, so I tried not to worry about it.

Peter's mother, Minx Carstens, had once been a schoolteacher and she opened a class at her home for Peter, Paddy, and me. She would read to me from the Old Testament, pointing out the words as she went. The story that made the greatest impression was Jonah and the whale. All through childhood I dreamed of whales, perhaps because my mother, in Durban, had once led me into the mouth of a dead whale. The giant jaws were propped wide with timbers and the stench of death was overwhelming. I couldn't leave my mother alone in the whale's mouth, so I tried to hold my breath and just about fainted before she led me back out into the breathing world again.

Peter Carstens's father, Jack, was the man who first discovered diamonds in that remote desert south of the Orange River. But instead of becoming rich and important, a fortune had somehow slipped through his hands and into the pockets of the wily Sir Ernest Oppenheimer. The De Beers Company had generously made Jack pit superintendent on the site. He was the pit super when Park started up Kleinzee a few years before we got there, and he was pit super when my father arrived. When we left, my father insisted on making him a chief prospector, which apparently upped his salary. But in the end, all he really got for making a find that netted De Beers millions was a job on a wind-wracked coastline redeemed only by its surf fishing.

Kleinzee marked my father's arrival in the Africa of his dreams. Responsible for everyone and everything in sight, he enjoyed the freedom of total control. It was his genius to make people under him feel free as well. On weekends he joined Jack Carstens carrying a long bamboo rod and hardwood reel, its fittings green with corrosion. Jack wore an old tweed jacket. My father sported floppy khaki shorts, and both men had ancient, battered hats. They fished for stumpnose and hottentot (so-called). They also netted herring fish called harder. Scrabbling among the rocks, they came up with enormous lobsters— crayfish to the English, *krief* in Afrikaans.

Jack looked like a sea captain. He had a lantern jaw and a wonderful pair of gray-green eyes. He soon taught my father how to cast into a strong wind, and the two men would stand in the breaking water, leaning into the storm, the cold spray soaking them through as they flung their lead weights against the gale. The high arc the weights describe as they rise and fall has always seemed to me the best moment in fishing, more satisfying than reeling in the frantic, doomed creature with a hook in its gill.

Every Sunday we would see Jack loading his gear to go fishing. My father would trudge off to join him, happy as a kid out of school, in floppy British shorts and shredding tennis shoes. My mother would sometimes join them with a picnic lunch bringing Minx along.

My mother was very fond of Minx Carstens. She was one of those hardy, uncomplaining Englishwomen scattered around the globe by the Empire and still found occasionally, exiled in Pretoria, Patagonia, or some Arabian desert. Her reddish brown hair was cut no-nonsense straight across her broad forehead. A magisterial wen graced her right cheek. Her life would have been much the same had she lived in Chile or Chichester. During the wild afternoons my mother would sit with her in the Carstens's small glassed-in porch, chatting while the wind howled and flung sang against the glass.

Our family, we knew, would move restlessly on. The Carstens would remain. Jack would fish in the cold waves while his wife read Penguin paperbacks, put on the teapot, and knitted away the years. How could the Carstens live year after year in a howling sandstorm with empty, windscrubbed beaches stretching from one salt-hazed horizon to the other? It perplexed my mother. "Is this really all they want? I should go mad," she wrote Bess.

Kleinzee was, of course, my father's big chance. But there had to be more to life than this! Time was passing. Youth had already mysteriously slipped away. Is it possible to find the meaning of life in a perpetual sandstorm?

My mother would wonder aloud how she had wound up in such a desolate setting, surrounded by barbed wire fences. There was something wonderful about the absurdity of it, and something frightening. When the wind faded at twilight, she could hear the waves falling and retreating on the long beach. At night the surrounding sand was swept by restless searchlights.

She should be grateful; she was grateful. As the manager's wife, she was expected to set the social tone and she did so without strain. Her asthma had cleared up in the bracing air. Except for the wind and dust, the climate might be compared to Southern California.

When the wind picked up each afternoon, the house would shake and rattle like a live thing. A fine dust would neatly line the window-sills, and the midday light would darken to a yellowish brown. Men would pass in the street wearing goggles and kerchiefs over their faces, leaning steeply into the blast.

My mother would haul in the wash from the line. She would visit Mrs. Wilson, or Mrs. Agenbag, or knit with Minx. She would go home and write another letter to America: "The day is filthy today—sand seeping in through every crevice though the windows are all closed. The wind continues without respite. We can't see across the valley, the sand has obscured all vision. The wind blew one of the big sheds over. You can't imagine how queer it is to have the sun shining brightly with the wind blowing a ninety mile gale at the same time. . . . I really can't neglect my teeth any longer or I shall soon be a toothless hag. Have to have that cyst cut off my gum again too. . . . Park writes that his wife, Margaret, is still in poor health as a result of a tick bite which she got on their holiday almost a year ago. She had tick fever badly and it has left her in such a weak condition that she's prey to anything that comes along. She has been in bed for a long time. Park is taking her to a specialist in Jo'burg. Up to this time, Margaret hasn't been sick a day in her life. . . . Five years of idleness have rotted the machinery here and it is constantly breaking down. Put in one new assembly and another breaks down. Everything rusts in no time in this salt air. . . ."

12

Acts of Patriotism

THE KLEINZEE ALLUVIAL MINE HAD BEEN SHUT DOWN AROUND 1931. That was the year Sir Ernest had taken advantage of a falling diamond market to acquire a string of mining companies that included the Cape Coast Exploration Ltd., owners of the Kleinzee diggings. Park had managed Kleinzee briefly before every diamond mine in Africa closed down in 1932. My father started up the Kleinzee mine again on October 2, 1937. On that day the ditches once again were full of Afrikaners with shovels. Little dump cars rolled on narrow-gauge track to the processing plant, pushed by white men with the healthy faces of farmers. My father was set on breaking every record his first day out. The logbooks showed that Park had got twenty-three carloads of diamond-bearing rock to the plant on his opening day. My father set out to process one thousand.

At eleven that morning a line of cars ran off the track, and my mother heard shouting on the hill. Peering through her front window, she saw my father leading his entire office staff out to lift the ore cars back on track. Every spare hand was on the line in shirts and ties, while he dashed up and down the line like a mad thing, determined to show the Kimberley office they had hired the right boy.

By quitting time that day, he'd trundled 622 cars through the plant and no one in town seemed to hold his monomania against him. Everyone on the executive staff at Kleinzee was older than him. Wilson, the accountant, was about forty, Jack Carstens, his pit super, was near fifty. The head of company security, Mr. Orpen, was seventy-four. Mr. Orpen was a philosopher, a sort of Diogenes of the desert, an Afrikaner who carried himself like an Englishman. He distrusted electricity. He regarded mechanical efficiency as a snare and illusion. He argued that machines were fundamentally unproductive. "Where are we all rushing off to?" he would murmur. Mr. Orpen had seen the metallic fungus of technology blight South Africa; he had observed the multiplication of drive belts, gears, and gadgets. He had seen gaping holes hundreds of feet deep dug in the earth, and endless tunneling far below the earth's crust, where the heat was intolerable and men lived their whole lives breathing gray dust in artificial light. This knowledge had perfected his skepticism. Machinery, he confided to my father, was man's overwhelming ambition given free rein. Old Orpen recalled a time when there were no machines and he believed people then were much happier.

He liked to describe the golden years before British power had descended on South Africa and laid waste Afrikaner society. Back then, with the Battle of Blood River and the Zulu wars behind them, Afrikaners and Africans had lived together in harmony. It was a biblical vision, the lamb and the lion lying down. Orpen regarded Cecil Rhodes as the worst of the European moneyman. But Barney Barnato, the prizefighter and circus clown who sold his share of De Beers to Rhodes for over five million pounds and a seat in the prestigious Kimberley Club, was hardly better. Barnato had later killed himself by leaping off a ship in the mid-Atlantic. In Orpen's view such men were all men damned—bullies, braggarts, pirates like J. B. Robinson, who enjoyed beating up on men smaller than himself, and wound up a millionaire. These were the kinds that dragged South Africa into modern times. Such creatures exhibited a boundless lust for scratching giant holes in the innocent South African soul. An unholy alliance of greed and technology had swept the Afrikaner off the map. Kimberley and Johannesburg were unnatural cities, symptoms of an English disease, grotesque camps that sprang up overnight.

Orpen could recall Johannesburg back when it was a filthy tent city, spawned by prospectors from Natal who camped on a *spruit* east of the original strike, setting up tin shacks in places they called Natal Camp or Ferreira's Camp—now degenerated into the Ferreirastown slum. Orpen, himself, hated the hegemony of money. After forty years with De Beers, the old man hadn't saved a penny. He was aware the company made no provision for retiring old hands. Employees were expected to handle their own retirement and not beg Sir Ernest to do it for them. But Mr. Orpen, having come this far, and disapproving of company policy, had placed his faith in God. De Beers could go to the devil. The De Beers directors, not wanting to see him starve, sent him out to the southwest desert where they thought he would do the least harm. And that was how my father inherited him.

Mr. Orpen had lived so long in the desert that he knew every Afrikaner family in Namaqualand. He was a fine translator and go-between. My father depended on him because the Afrikaner Boers (farmers) who showed up to work couldn't drive a tractor, much less repair one. When a carpenter or bricklayer was needed, my father had to train the man himself, picking among the three hundred Afrikaners digging in the sand for the most talented. They were a contentious and unambitious lot and finding the right man was not easy. But Orpen knew every one of them by name.

Among the supervisors, the sorters, the technicians, and the clerks

there were slackers, thieves, drunkards, and exceptionally able men.
The nineteen-year-old electrician, Gottseif, could fix anything, but
he was from Cape Town. Carey Lee, my father's private secretary,
became a lifelong friend of my parents. But his father was English.
When I asked Carey in 1993 about Kleinzee in 1937, he went into
the next room and came back with a small diagram of the single
men's housing in Kleinzee. Fifty years had passed, but he could still
assign a name to each house—Duncan, Darling, Giles, Smiley, and
the two Germans, Dunkel and Steeger. He recalled that Duncan was
the postmaster and had only one arm, which didn't stop him from
playing an excellent game of tennis. And suddenly Duncan was before me exactly as he was then, as if he still lived; and I saw again
his thinning red hair, his long jaw, and freckled face and forearm.

Carey Lee had seen Namaqualand first from on board ship returning from England where he went for the coronation of King
George VI. Observing the wild coast and wasteland beyond, he'd
remarked that he'd rather live in hell than Namaqualand. Three
weeks later, he was assigned to Kleinzee by the Kimberley office. But
he describes my father as "the best manager I ever worked for."

The staff, like Carey Lee, were British South African or German
mostly. The diggers were all Boers, aged sixteen to sixty, wind-
burned, their cheeks and jaws almost black from the sun, their fore-
heads pale under broadbrim hats banded by sand goggles, Afrikaners
hired in from sunbaked, windswept towns like Springbok, Okiep, Nababiep, or nearby Grootmist. Their fathers and grandfathers had
come out into the desert to escape the domination of the English. In
one of our old photographs they look like college athletes—strong,
handsome, honed by hard exercise. Their working clothes were
loose-fitting trousers and shirts worn by dust, sweat, and repeated
laundering to a light tan with the texture of fine suede. They often
sang while they shoveled, and they loved a good laugh.

The company provided no machinery for excavation, no sand-
moving equipment. Everything was done by lines of men digging all

day like convicts doing hard labor. The small dump trolleys, hauled by mule or pushed by hand, were fastened to a cable and winch to drag them up the pulsator plant incline where the rock was crushed, washed, and refined for sorting. My father considered putting in for a company steam shovel. But upon reflection, he decided it would never work out. The coastal atmosphere rotted the steel teeth that held conveyor belts together and popped gears like dislocated joints. These Afrikaners had been raised with horses, cows, and goats, and they had developed a mysterious resistance to technology. Perhaps heavy machinery reminded them too much of Britain.

So from morning to night the diggers shoveled their way down to bedrock, heaved stones into the tiny railcars, and pushed them by hand to the winch line that drew them uphill to the plant. Boulder by boulder, the ancient riverbed was hauled to the pulsator, crushed, washed, sieved, and inspected by sorters under a layer of water. In the old days children, with their sharp eyes, had proved best at spotting diamonds in the bed of tiny green-and-black pebbles that collected at the center of the round sieve. In Kleinzee the sorters were selected for their honesty. The company's greatest anxiety was diamond thieves.

My father had barely got the mine started when thirteen diggers appeared in a body and demanded their pay be doubled. Otherwise, they would quit. Park had warned about this sort of thing. "Our American manner works against us. If I were you, I'd put on some weight, grow a big beard, stick out your belly, and speak at the top of your voice. Smile too much, you'll probably get a mouthful of sand."

My father asked the diggers to come back on a Saturday, and he asked old Orpen to act as translator. But the day before the negotiation, a telegram from Johannesburg notified Mr. Orpen that his daughter had shot her husband. This delighted Mr. Orpen, who loathed his abusive son-in-law. Old Orpen skipped around camp telling everyone the good news. Another telegram soon followed. The police were charging his daughter with attempted murder. So as the striking diggers were assembling in my father's office, old Orpen drove out the main gate headed for Johannesburg to bail his daughter out of prison. Whether he succeeded, my mother never said.

My father's Afrikaans was almost as bad as the diggers' English, so he asked the young electrician, Gottseif, to translate. "I am sure this is all a joke," he began. "Because you know very well I have over three hundred applications for the jobs you are giving up. I hope you won't blame me if I give the people who applied for work here jobs before you when I need diggers again."

"You need us more than we need you," said their spokesman. "And if we quit, don't be surprised if everyone on this mine quits. No one in the camp is going to go on working like slaves unless De Beers makes it worth our while."

"Well, I hope you will at least tell all of those who are going to quit that they will make a lot of people who are eager to work very happy."

He was bluffing. He was short of workers and could ill afford to lose anyone. The next day the thirteen walked out of the camp. He held his breath, but no one else joined them.

My mother's letter to Bess contradicts itself. "The men he does have work like mad, but he needs many more and can't seem to get replies to the application forms he has on hand. It seems these Namaqualand farmers are just lazy. So many quit after just a few days. The hard work is too much for the loafers. Though they're half-starving at home, they'd rather go back and do nothing."

My father, who had no power to raise the workers' pay, pondered this little rebellion. Why did men who needed cash to keep their farms going and their families fed make demands they must know he could not meet? While he was pondering, Company Protection Officer Ter Blanche appeared in his office to set him straight.

"It's quite simple, sir," said Ter Blanche. "They are diamond thieves."

"Perhaps I don't understand you, Officer Ter Blanche."

"You must understand, sir, that these diggers come here only to steal."

"That's a little extreme, isn't it! All of them?"

"Not every one of them, possibly. But why do you think thirteen diggers resigned the very same month you arrived? Either they had diamonds they were trying to smuggle out and wanted to do so before you caught on to their game, or they decided you were not going to make it easy for them to steal, so they gave it up."

"Officer Ter Blanche, are you actually telling me that I have three hundred thieves working for me?"

Ter Blanche was a patient man. "Of course you are quite right, sir. You would never catch me saying there are no honest men among them. But who exactly are these honest men? Only God can tell an honest man as I am sure you must agree."

"But really! I cannot assume that my entire work force consists of thieves!"

"Of course not, and no one is saying that, sir," said Ter Blanche. "But you must learn to think in a way that allows you to see what is happening here. A manager can only see the situation clearly when he views every man as a thief. Except, of course, for those who are paid by us."

"Paid by who?"

"Those employed by security, sir."

"You mean spies?"

"Observers, sir."

"Spies, in other words."

"We would be in great trouble without observers, Mr. Pifer."

"I would guess the great majority of these men are honest, and I'm not sure I like having hired spies among them. Doesn't that make us dishonest?"

"I never said that one or two of the men may not be honest," said Ter Blanche. "They may all be honest. That is for God to know. But you are new at this, if I may say so, and perhaps I know these men better than you. I have learned that they are honest only if they are very simple or very religious. I am religious myself. But I am afraid you cannot run a mine by hiring only very simple and very religious men."

"I am perhaps less suspicious by nature than you," said my father.

"In America I am sure it is different," said Ter Blanche. "Here we must be realistic."

It gradually became clear what Ter Blanche was telling him. Afrikaners felt no overwhelming reason to play by English rules. The English were, in their eyes, an occupying power. Thus stealing was moral, a political act. It was a patriotic duty to steal. The De Beers Company was, after all, not very different from the invading British army that only thirty-four years before had killed the fathers and grandfathers of these very same diggers. The Boer War was well within living memory. The diggers had only to glance at the barbed wire perimeter fencing to see how their place of work resembled a concentration camp. The British had used concentration camps to control the Boers. (They had taken the camp concept from the Americans who used it to control Indians along the Mississippi. And the German government at that moment was employing it to apply Nazi science to an imaginary social predicament.)

Given this history of conflict, Ter Blanche treated the diggers with extreme suspicion. He was forever marching around the barbed wire perimeter, improving on the system. There were X rays, there were three concentric perimeter barbed wire fences, there were guards and dogs and police spies. When the Alexander Bay golf team drove down from the Orange River mouth to play their annual golf tournament against Kleinzee, Ter Blanche insisted the players kindly check their clubs at the gate. Wives and children were parked in the police station, while the team played with borrowed equipment.

My mother (the manager's wife was not x-rayed) brought the wives and children tea and milk. The golf game was lent additional interest by the wild wind that sent balls curving away on eccentric trajectories into the dunes. The Alexander Bay team was badly beaten by the

Kleinzee gang, who were more familiar with their unusual golf course and winds aloft. On his way out, each visitor was x-rayed. Full of tea and roentgens, the defeated group drove the hundred miles back to the Orange River mouth through a howling sandstorm.

My father was forced to take the situation seriously when stolen diamonds began to pop up everywhere. He himself discovered a little box of gems secreted in the pulsator plant. "Oh, I find them all the time," said Jack Carstens. "They tie them to rocks and try to heave them over the perimeter fences. Accomplices come in after midnight and pick them up. We've found diamonds in their boots and their teeth, not to mention even more popular orifices. You've got to expect a few diamonds will walk out of here. And just as well the company has no idea how many."

One morning Ter Blanche found signs that someone had tried to dig under the barbed wire, got stuck, struggled, bled, and then returned to camp. As a matter of course, police checked the sand for footprints each morning before the afternoon wind blew the spoor away. Small sacks of stones were found lying about in the no-man's-land between perimeter fences.

That February Ter Blanche asked my father to meet him outside the community building. His eyes were sparkling. His smile was joyous. "I have received some quite depressing information," he said.

"Your observers have observed something?"

"I am afraid so. If you will kindly accompany me, sir, there are two interesting young men I want you to meet."

They went out to the diggings, my father tagging along after Ter Blanche, who had the alert demeanor of a bird dog. He paused by a ditch and called out to two diggers who were diligently shoveling sand as hard as they could. "Hey, Piet. You, Simon. Be kind enough to join us in the community building. Mr. Pifer would appreciate your company very much."

He led the men to the locker they had in common. "Would you boys object to me looking in your personal belongings?"

"Not at all, sir!" Piet and Simon were eager to cooperate. They threw open their locker gladly. They laid all their belongings out in a neat row on the floor and jumped back to give Ter Blanche plenty of room. Nor did they object when Ter Blanche poked about in their armpits, ran his fingers under their genitals, and began to empty out aspirin jars and palpate the dried apricots they kept in a tin. The officer soon became absorbed in a jar of cold cream. After sniffing the sticky white stuff, he ran a finger into the jar. The diggers leaned against the wall and joked. "You don't need cold cream, Ter Blanche. You've got lovely skin for a policeman."

Ter Blanche removed his finger from the jar. There was a diamond on the tip. He fished out seven diamonds in all. He spread his handkerchief on a bench and laid out the rocks in a row, polishing each one carefully. This was accomplished in solemn silence. The diggers shook their heads in astonished disbelief. Ter Blanche sat looking sadly at the diamonds and said nothing. The diggers slammed their fists and heads into the wall. They began to howl and cry. They insisted they had been set up. They were so upset that my father was half-inclined to believe them. Ter Blanche continued to look at the diamonds as if he too could not believe what he had found. "What am I going to tell your mothers, eh? I'm afraid it's off to the magistrate in Springbok with you."

"Can you be sure?" my father asked. "They seem genuinely upset."

"Their friends told them that hiding rocks in cold cream is a sure thing. Their friends convinced them that we are very stupid. They believed what their friends said. So they feel betrayed. That is why they are emotional."

That same evening thirty diggers angrily announced that they were quitting in protest. Ter Blanche was amused and annoyed. "You can see how it is, Mr. Pifer. Now they think we have put a spy in their midst."

"But we do have a spy in their midst, don't we?"

"Yes, but what difference is that? The point is that every man who hooked a diamond this month now believes we've got his name on our list. I can tell you only one thing for sure. Every one of these thirty boys is a thief, and he's trying to smuggle diamonds out of here. You must look sharp, sir."

"But surely they know we'll search them!" said my father.

"We may catch one or two," said Ter Blanche. "The rest have either got their stones out, or they'll come back for them later. Or they've figured out a method we still don't know about."

A search force was assembled—the medical orderly, ancient Mr. Orpen, two secretaries, and three policemen with shiny pink faces. This select group worked all day rooting through the diggers' trousers, shirts, Sunday suits, and private parts. Cheerful insults were bandied about as the officials probed orifices. "Come now, Mr. Orpen, any woman knows better than to look for the family jewels up there!"

One digger was arrested when diamonds were found sewn into the seams of his trousers. Another had seven stones wrapped in tissue and inserted up his rectum. When he was shown the X ray, he broke into tears. "Rage and mortification," my mother wrote Bess. It was embarrassing, a grown man sitting in a chair, crying like a baby.

Ter Blanche told my father, "These Boers refuse to believe a machine can look through solid flesh. They think it's just a lot of De Beers propaganda. They're good fellows, but the one with the stones is a real *domkop* (meathead). A few weeks in prison will teach them a little wisdom. Jail time is a good thing within moderation. It's the only place really that a man will find time to contemplate."

X-ray plates turned up four more stones in the gullet of another digger. Pictures were made each day, tracing the diamonds as they made their way through his stomach and intestine. On the morning of their expected emergence, Ter Blanche accompanied the digger into the toilet in order to confiscate the rocks. The man objected strongly to a police officer peering up his bum. My father agreed that this was really going too far. "We have to leave these men some dignity! The X ray showed us how many stones he has to hand over."

Ter Blanche wore the expression of a sad bird dog. "The X ray is often wrong because two stones may show up as one on the plate. And if I am not there when the stones come out they often pop one or two back in their mouths. And what if he throws one out the window or hides it and says he washed one down the sink? Then we have to tear out the plumbing to see if he's telling the truth. You have to understand, sir, these Boers feel the company owes them a stone or two for all the inconvenience. And they may be right. I won't dispute it. But we have our duty to do." And Ter Blanche went with the digger to the toilet and did his duty.

Each month the Kleinzee mine produced diamonds worth $250,000 to $300,000 (multiply by 30 or 40 to approximate their worth in today's dollars). Four or five times a year, Park and a gaggle of officials flew in from Kimberley to check out the digging. Park then packed up the diamonds in a flat metal box that slipped into his battered old attaché case.

For Officer Ter Blanche the high point of 1937 was news that professional criminals had turned up in Springbok and were planning to hold up my father and Park. Ter Blanche's spies reported that the thieves, up from Cape Town, had been spotted with a schoolteacher and garage proprietor from Grootmist, the tiny farming community two miles from Kleinzee. The four had been observed at dinner and they were probably planning to hold up the De Beers officials between Kleinzee and the airport.

This delightful news put new spring in Ter Blanche's step. At last he had an adversery he could respect. He made the rounds of the barbed wire perimeter and inspected the no-man's-land between the sections, whistling under his breath (a habit which always annoyed my mother). If he bagged four robbers, two of them professionals, his reputation would spread from Klawer to Lüderitz. He would take his wife to Cape Town and buy her a new wardrobe. Ter Blanche was very proud of his wife, a tall, slow-moving, slow-speaking very beautiful woman whose fingernail polish matched her russet hair.

On the day designated for the holdup, Park and my father drove to the airport through the midafternoon wind and stinging sand. They were led by a car full of goggled policemen and followed by another. Guns bristled. No robbers showed up.

After the plane had taken off safely (sand blowing into the engines was the real worry), Ter Blanche sent his men into the desert. They stumbled around in the blasting sand, peering through their goggles, until they came on the garage proprietor huddling behind a dune. He was sitting on a revolver but insisted he was out hunting springbok.

"In a seventy-mile wind?" cried Ter Blanche.

"That is my way," said the mechanic.

"Then you are the only Boer I ever met who hunts springbok with a revolver," shouted Ter Blanche.

"That is my way," said the mechanic. And to every question put to him the reply was, "That is my way." He refused the policeman's offer of a ride to Grootmist. Ter Blanche drove away in a foul temper.

The schoolteacher was found at home in bed. "Taking a nap," he said. "In your shoes?" asked the police. As for the two professionals, they had lost their way driving across the open desert. Their Willys car had bogged down in the shifting dunes. Abandoning the car, they headed due west into the pelting sand. Five hours later, their hair and their eyes full of sand, they spotted the dim outline of a car and ran toward it, crying gladly and waving their arms. But it was their own vehicle buried to the windshield. They would have died, but they were discovered by a family of Hottentot traveling on foot from Nababiep to Springbok.

In October, a sorter and an electrician from Kleinzee were arrested on holiday in Cape Town. The police found them with $25,000 worth of stones in their possession. They swore they had acted alone, but Ter Blanche's spies whispered they were in contact with the Parvys, a medical orderly and his wife in camp. Parvy, a pale man whose sad face resembled an internal organ, was in charge of searching diggers on their way out of camp. Ter Blanche believed Parvy's wife was the problem. Mrs. Parvy was a dour Brunhilde, with plump, dimpled arms and astonished blue eyes. My mother had invited Mrs. Parvy over for tea two or three times, once with Mrs. Ter Blanche. Mrs. Ter Blanche kept a close check on her slim figure and ate almost nothing. Mrs. Parvy spoke only when asked a direct question, but quietly consumed everything on her plate and put away two pots of tea. "Twice her husband's size," my mother described her for Bess. "She never looks you in the eye. She's a menace."

The tireless Ter Blanche had meanwhile arrested two other workers—Dunkel, a sorter, and Steeger, an electrician. Ten thousand dollars worth of diamonds (1937 value) turned up in Dunkel and Steeger's possession. Dunkel and Steeger got three months and five months, respectively, in the Springbok court.

After all the trouble they had caused, this seemed a very light sentence to my mother, who was inclined to strong vengeance when her husband's reputation was threatened. But Ter Blanche explained that a "real sentence only complicates the manager's job. You'll find all the diggers in camp walking off the job if you start handing out real sentences. It destroys their morale." This implied that all the diggers expected to go to jail sooner or later.

Ter Blanche soon got word from his spies that Mrs. Parvy was certainly the brains behind the Dunkel-Steeger caper. So one morning around breakfast time, the officer knocked on the Parvys' door and asked them to kindly stand aside while he searched the premises. He had brought with him a small work force armed with crowbars and a sledgehammer. While Mrs. Parvy sat glumly spooning some kind of oatmeal sludge into her baby, the floor around her was pried up, the furniture dismantled, the stove disassembled, the plaster smashed. The unfortunate couple were extensively x-rayed. So was their baby. Mrs. Parvy complained to my father and he went to Ter Blanche.

"Officer, excuse me, but Mrs. Parvy is complaining you're treating her baby like a handbag. This really is going too far! People do have certain rights, even out here."

"This would not be the first time a baby was stuffed with diamonds," said Ter Blanche. "I have seen babies with four or five stones in them. And there's no harm in a snapshot."

Because Ter Blanche had recovered so many diamonds it was hard to argue with him. At year's end, he took a few days off from the Parvy investigation to take his beautiful wife to the hospital in Springbok. She had been complaining of pain in her abdomen. In Springbok, the doctor decided the best thing to do was remove her appendix. He said it was a simple operation, though it might have been a good thing to bring her in a week earlier. The job was hopelessly bungled. A week or two earlier, Mrs. Ter Blanche, in excellent health, had appeared in pale chiffon at the regional ball in Port Nolloth with my parents. She died in Springbok the day after the operation.

Ter Blanche came back to Kleinzee, followed by a truck carrying her coffin. At night he could be heard sobbing in his house. During the day he walked along the new third-perimeter fence, kicking the posts. One morning he told the electrician Gottseif to order a large reflector globe from Cape Town and install it over the police gate, to dispel the darkness. As for the Parvys, they were never caught with the goods, so no one could dispute their innocence. My father had the company rebuild their gutted house.

13

Gottseif

I WAS ALMOST FIVE; HE WAS IN HIS EARLY TWENTIES, MY FIRST ADULT friend, Gottseif the electrician. My mother describes him as "an extremely handsome young man, Gus's height and weight, with curly brown hair and blue eyes and fine teeth—the only son. He has a mother and two sisters in Cape Town. His father is a bridge builder in India."

I met Gottseif after the axle of my wagon broke in two. The wagon, manufactured in America, was all metal, painted a bright scarlet red. The mysterious word *Radiogram* appeared on its side panel. The significance of the word was beyond me and eludes me to this day. My father took me and the broken wagon down to the electricians' shop near the pulsator plant. Gottseif was there, bent over his workbench, and he advanced through a shadow to shake my hand. "Take care of each other," my father said and left.

Gottseif loaned me welder's mask and showed me how to adjust it so I could watch him repair the axle. The arc light, he said, was brighter than the sun. Look directly at it and I would go blind. I called him Mr. Gottseif, and though I have pondered long and hard, I cannot remember his first name. The shadows of syllables flit through my memory (*ri, ric, eric, heinrich, riemann, niemann?*), but their secret combination evades me and appears nowhere in my mother's letters.

I used to slip over to his shop whenever I could dodge Emma, our nursemaid. Gottseif, I knew, was usually there in the morning. Afternoons he scaled the tall poles that looked over the perimeter fences or crawled through the spaces where high-tension lines snaked through the pulsator plant. Occasionally, I would spot his tiny figure moving high under the roof like a human spider. He would give a shout and wave with his free hand while dangling by the other.

I recall his shop better than I do our house in Kleinzee. There was something profoundly satisfying about the thick stench of tar and creosote, the pretty electrical boxes, the smooth black cable wound on drums and resembling fat rolls of licorice. Festive lighting fixtures hung along the corrugated iron walls. More than any toy, I valued a certain type of light bulb that Gottseif saved for me. This lighting fixture was used by the police to throw a brilliant glare on the surrounding desert at night. Gottseif showed me how to smash the spent bulbs to extract the glass core without cutting myself. The core, with its copper filament arms and lead boots, resembled a tiny robot. The head was clear crystal. These light-bulb men resembled astronauts hatched a generation early from their glass eggs.

Gottseif taught me how to make a tiny tractor toy by assembling in cunning combination an expended cotton spool, a rubber band, a candle end, a paper clip, and a lollipop stick. Powered by the twisted rubber band, the toy would creep across the floor, and it was the first in a series of devices I would make for myself after the world began to employ its toys for the serious business of killing on a planetwide scale. Engineers by default, we children constructed planes of aloe wood, sailboats with lead counterweights that kept them from capsizing no matter how murderous the wind, submarines powered by carbide and water.

Gottseif went out of his way to save these bulbs I valued so much. But already this fine, solid bulb (manufactured only in Germany), was being perniciously replaced by a flimsy British update that sported a single contact plate. The new technology caused me anxiety and distress. I placed great value on the outdated version and later, in Oranjemund, whenever I found one of these extinct light bulbs, I would remember with a stab of pleasure and regret my great friendship with Gottseif.

Whether we spoke English or Afrikaans, I forget. My playmate, Theo Agenbag (Aschenbach is the German form) could speak no English; nor did Emma, the nursemaid. Thus in Kleinzee I probably spoke more Afrikaans than English. My sister, just learning to use words, was confused. Together we prattled in a double tongue that only we could understand. My mother wrote Bess that she would stand in the next room and try not to laugh aloud once we got going.

What I recall most clearly of all is the way Gottseif and I would laugh when we ran into each other. Exactly why we laughed is impossible to describe exactly. I wonder if I have ever experienced anything so pleasant since, the feeling of being overwhelmed by the sensation of meeting a friend whose sensibility somehow matched my own and expressed itself as laughter. When I showed interest in his work, he would stand me directly on his workbench so I could have a perfect view. A thick strand of his hair would drop over one eye and tickle his nostrils, until he jerked his head sideways to clear it. Then he would pummel the end of his nose with the back of his hand to keep from sneezing.

We wasted a fair deal of company time constructing a toy British battleship from sheet metal, copper, and wood. It had turrets that turned, guns that trained up and down, and tiny metal railings. Gottseif drew in the fine detail with blue and black ink. Whenever I popped in for a visit, he would eventually take down our model and add another porthole or big gun. The battleship was soon on its way to becoming the most extravagant toy I could ever hope to own. And still Gottseif kept improving on the detail, putting in piping, rivets, anchor chains, cable drums.

On the morning that he went to fulfill Ter Blanche's demand of a new high intensity light over the main gate out of town, Gottseif passed our house and called out cheerfully to my mother, who was planting succulents in our rock garden. With him was his teenage assistant, Van Syl. At the police gate they set up a high ladder and Gottseif climbed up forty feet, hauling a big reflector globe behind him.

The day was still with a slight breeze and high silvery clouds. All of these details are recorded in my mother's letter home or preserved in my own memory. She writes that Mr. Orpen, passing directly below Gottseif, was struck by a small piece of wire falling from above. He pretended to scold the electrician, saying, "Now don't be throwing things at me, young man." When Gottseif made no reply, the old man shaded his eyes and saw Gottseif, a dark figure in the sun, bent over the high tension line that fed the X-ray unit. A greasy gray smoke was streaming up from his body.

Mr. Orpen began to tremble and cry, but pulled himself together enough to totter across to the police station where he phoned the central power station. Too upset to give details, he could only stutter, "Shut off! Shut off!" The power station operator, having no idea who was speaking or what the words meant, did nothing.

Young Van Syl meanwhile scrambled up the ladder to pull Gottseif off the wire. A farm boy who knew nothing about electricity, he had no idea of the force concentrated in Gottseif's body. When he seized Gottseif from below, twenty-one hundred volts threw off a flash of light and Van Syl was flung from the ladder and snagged, unconscious, by the tangle of lines below. He hung by one leg, twenty feet in the air. Above him Gottseif burst into flames.

One of the policemen had by then jumped into Mr. Orpen's car and careened over to the power station, where he shouted at the operator to turn everything off. Orpen phoned my father, but made no sense whatever. He did manage to say "Police station," and clearly something terrible was happening. Bringing with him a medical orderly, my father ran from the office as fast as his legs would carry him.

Ter Blanche showed up about the same time. He and another policeman lifted Gottseif and Van Syl free of the lines and worked them down the ladder. The orderly tried to give Gottseif first aid. Van Syl's leg and an arm were burned to the bone. Writhing in pain, he wanted only for someone to tell him that Gottseif was alive. My father splinted up Van Syl's charred limbs to keep him from damaging himself further.

Gottseif had phoned the power station that day and asked the operator to switch off the current. The power had been switched back on three minutes before the electrician reached across the lines to wire up Ter Blanche's new lighting fixture. It was a holiday and half a dozen diggers wanted to leave the camp and visit their families in the river bottom. It was necessary to x-ray them, so the operator had flipped the power switch without thinking.

The telegraph service closed down on holidays, so there was no way to tell Gottseif's mother that her son was dead. There was no doctor in Kleinzee, and no formaldehyde to embalm the body. It was necessary to bury Gottseif immediately in the graveyard at Grootmist, "a desolate little spot in the riverbed consisting of a store, post office, school, church and a few farmhouses." So my mother describes the place.

Gottseif's shroud was sewn from hospital sheets by Mrs. Agenbag. The company carpenter spent his holiday fitting together a coffin. The women went into their gardens and picked every flower in town. Assembling at our house, they wove eight wreaths of geraniums, mauve statice, daisies, and a few carnations and then fashioned a cross. By picking every flower growing in Kleinzee that day, they had just enough blossoms to cover the grave.

Oddie, the chauffeur, had left at once to find a minister in Alexander Bay. He arrived back the following day with a Dutch Reformed churchman. The afternoon of the funeral the wind died down and a light breeze blew in from the sea. The air down in the Grootmist river bottom was almost still.

The pale yellow pine coffin was lashed to the company's flatbed truck to keep it from bouncing off on the broken track that led to the cemetery. I stood in the window of our house and saw the truck pass with Gottseif's body in its box. The image of that coffin merges oddly in my memory with the later image of a jet fighter sinking into the sea. A friend of mine is seated in the open cockpit of the plane as our carrier heaves past. Hearing the racket of a plane tearing up the landing deck, I dashed up from the ready room and arrived on the catwalk just in time to see a helmeted head nodding in the cockpit fifty feet aft. Twenty years separate Gottseif's coffin moving past on the empty Kleinzee road and the jet slipping astern with its unconscious pilot, but the sky was identically overcast and streaked with thin silver clouds. And the hour of day was the same.

My mother wrote Bess: "To follow that poor, unstained, newly made coffin strapped on a huge green truck over the rough, sandy roads through that lonely waste of desert just as the sun was setting, is a journey I won't forget. The cemetery was a most desolate forgotten sort of place with only rough stones marking the graves, and engraved with an initial or two—but more often no name at all. The one tombstone suitably inscribed was put up by the company to the memory of Captain Crowder, the former diamond detective who died here five years ago.

"Gottseif was placed by his side. Children from the Grootmist school, about twenty little girls aged ten in khaki gabardine dresses and barefoot, sang 'Nearer my God to Thee' from slips of paper, as they didn't know much English.

"I kept thinking and thinking of the poor boy's mother and wondered how she would have felt to see her only son being buried by strangers in a lonely waste place in the desert. I do hope we never have to go through any more harrowing experiences like this on this mine.

"This morning Gus went out to the grave, rearranged the flowers, took photographs of the grave, and also brought back one of each kind of flower still fresh and heavy with dew to send the boy's mother with all the cards. I put the flowers in the fridge since the mail doesn't go out till this evening. Gus has the painful duty of writing her a letter telling her all about how it happened. I do hope we're doing the right thing. We certainly never know when we're going to be cut off suddenly. Makes one feel so weak and puny and ineffectual. If only we could remain as a family intact until Gus and I are really old, that's all I ask. But it's such a lot to ask for."

The battleship Gottseif built for me sailed straight out of my memory the day he died, so I never went to collect it. In fact, it was blanked so perfectly from my mind that only now, as I write this, does it come steaming back out of his shadowy shop, with the drums of black cable and arc light that he said was brighter than the sun, and Gottseif himself, who has no first name, turning from his workbench to laugh at me.

14

Emma and Maria

DE BEERS HAD SENT US INTO ONE OF THE GREAT DESERTS OF THE
world. The Namib is long and narrow, fifty to one hundred miles
across, eight hundred miles from south to north. The ocean carries
the icy Benguela Current that swings up from the Antarctic, denying
the atmosphere moisture, drying the burned land to a faded rust red.
In Namibia are found the highest sand dunes on the planet. Getting
there had not been easy; it would prove even more difficult to leave.
But my mother waxed enthusiastic. "This chance here is one in a
lifetime," she wrote Bess. "Everybody has such regard and respect for
Gus already. He is the youngest of all the senior staff, and the manager. I wish you could see him. He's the picture of health and I
wouldn't mind staying another year here. Park certainly saved his life
as a couple of years more on the Rand at the pace he was going
would have done him in."

As the months unrolled, she had to remind herself often that everything was for the best. If this was purgatory, she recalled that Nigel was hell. There Fleisher had tried to finish off her husband. Here, the constant wind and dust infected her eyes, but at least my father was in charge. Her teeth still bothered her. Several times she had to make the long, insane trip to Cape Town to see the dental surgeon. She lost weight. To defend herself from the sun, wind, and sand, she used olive oil and unguentine (a substance she made up herself and which we children regarded as a fabulous panacea).

She wrote Bess, "I've been giving the servants hell. It seems I wake up livid Monday mornings and it's the servants who get it in the neck. I go around finding all the silt that blows in everywhere on everything, and the careless cleaning, and what a jerking up they get. The nursemaid, Emma, listens respectfully until I'm finished, then she takes up her humming where she left off and continues on blithely with her work as though I had merely passed the time of day."

Emma was indifferent to everything but her daydreams. One Sunday she almost swallowed a seven carat diamond, mistaking it for an aspirin. Carey Lee had brought the week's diamond haul to the house, but my father was off fishing with Jack Carstens. My mother signed for the stones and, picking out the biggest one, showed it to Emma, who dreamily popped it into her mouth. My mother managed to extract it before she swallowed. "She had never seen a diamond and she thought it was a huge joke, trying to eat a $1,200 pill."

Like most servants, Emma had a secret life hidden from those she served. And like most children, I knew the servants' secrets better than my parents did. I saw her make faces behind their backs and let her gobble up my breakfast, as well as her own. She would cut two slits in an orange and, fastening one slit to her nose, wedged the other over mine and pretended we were stuck together until we both fell down, laughing hysterically. She was often temperamental and sulky, and would slap at me to drive me away, then pull me against her, then shove me away again. One evening after my parents had gone out somewhere, Emma began splashing water in my face while I was taking my bath. I retaliated by taking a healthy shit in the tub. (I remember a vague feeling that I was taking revenge on my mother for having gone away without me.)

Emma cleaned up the mess without complaining, which should have struck me as ominous. She then took me into my bedroom and pulled the blinds. Taking off all her clothes, she lay down on the floor and told me to crawl over her. Even more vivid in my memory than Emma's light brown skin is the calm, deliberate nature of her disrobing, and the sad, brilliant light of the setting sun forcing itself through the yellow blind into the darkening room. I felt some vague pleasure in this sport, unfocused as mist. Emma had made me the doubtful gift of my own secret life.

Kleinzee, the smallest town we would ever live in, was always always full of scandal. From my point of view, Mr. Wilson's snore was fascinating—the idea of a man lying dead asleep and emitting that much noise was beyond belief. There was also Mrs. Parvy, the suspected diamond thief, stuffing herself on cake and glaring at my mother as if the cat had her tongue. And there was the uproar over Jack Carstens's cousin from London who said he wanted to marry an Afrikaner woman from Grootmist. Nothing like this had ever happened in the region within living memory.

Just out of university, Jack's cousin had been sent to Kleinzee to pick up valuable engineering experience. Jack had assured the young man's parents that there would be no temptations in a camp full of dusty men. But the young fool had found his way to the Buffels River bottom and fallen in love with a farmer's daughter. My mother wrote Bess, "They were supposed to look after him and make sure he stayed out of trouble. They have no idea how they will explain this marriage to the groom's parents back home."

The Afrikaner bride, Maria (Marr-eye-yah), was born in the Buffels River bottom, a kind of Siberia without snow. My mother appeased the Carstens by pointing out that the girl had descended from the Earl of Warwick. (She doesn't say where she got this information.) In any case, she was soon friends with Maria's mother and took care to point out the young woman's "genuine English complexion and English features." With the manager's wife taking their side, Maria and Jack's cousin had no more difficulties.

Maria was my first love, though I was too young to identify the obscure pain I felt when I saw her. She resembled one of those rural maidens painted on tins of English cookies but miraculously transformed into warm, living flesh. She was easily the most lovely creature I had ever seen. Her light hazel eyes were often hidden under dark lashes. Her skin had a translucent, golden clarity, and she wore a cap to shield her face from the sun. Like all the Afrikaner girls from Grootmist, she was shy as a springbok and spoke in a low voice, usually quite inaudible. She was even shy around me, though I was not yet five. It was my overwhelming impression that the closer I got to her the more she withdrew, and when I reached out to touch her she dissolved. It was as if her real self had been sent away beyond the hills and the girl in our living room was an apparition whose tentative smile aroused only acute frustration.

Although her family didn't speak a word of English and Jack's cousin knew no Afrikaans, the couple seemed to understand each other very well. In company they did little more than exchange an occasional look. Even I could see that their joy baffled them and words were hardly necessary.

My mother invited Maria over to our house a number of times just to make sure all the English in town knew how much the manager's wife approved of the Afrikaner bride, and I was usually trotted out to translate. I would stare at Maria, and she would laugh quietly at my staring and look away.

Maria's Afrikaner parents were much more upset about her marriage than the Carstens. The idea of their only daughter sailing off to a remote, rainy island in the North Sea with some bloodless Englishman was hateful. Her father would not allow it. There were angry confrontations in their Grootmist house. Maria had been raised to do her father's bidding, but her passion for the Englishman was too great. She had been taught to lower her eyes, to never raise her voice, and this she did very well. But in the end she proved tougher and more pigheaded than her father. Like a champion arm wrestler half his size, she bent his will to her own and got her Englishman.

My mother traveled back and forth between Kleinzee and Grootmist, trying to soothe the ruffled feelings in both camps. There were still men alive in Grootmist whose brothers and fathers had been killed by the English in the Boer War. Englishmen were seldom if ever invited into an Afrikaner home, but Maria's wedding was an exception. Maria's father, having bowed to his inflexible daughter, now found himself nodding to the mine manager's wife. He could assert what was left of his dignity only by laying on a terrific feast. My mother, for her part, made it her business to see that every Englishman on the staff showed up with his spouse.

So the lot of us drove into the river bottom where the Grootmist farmers had their little orchards and vegetable gardens, past low houses laid in a straggle between the dry banks (as if the Buffels River would never flood again and the land would remain dust dry till the end of time). Packed into two of the cars in the little caravan were the Wilsons, the Carstens, and the Pifers—churning through the stones and sand dunes to the gray little *dorp*.

In the house where Maria had grown up, we ranged ourselves around the edge of a bare, unvarnished floor on straight-backed chairs. The awkward talk was nudged along by my mother, but even her gift for greasing the conversational skids was sorely tried that evening. The triple divide of language, history, and social class was almost impossible to negotiate.

The bride, her face pink with embarrassment, sat next to her pale, kindly Englishman who kept reaching over to touch her arm, as if to assure himself she was not a painting on a cookie tin. I was stricken with passion for her and tried to overcome the ache by stuffing myself with Afrikaner lard cake. It was awful stuff. Those Afrikaner farmers could ill afford butter, and the white flour was gritty with sand from the grinding stone.

As she often did when people were tongue-tied or isolated by a foreign language, or simply unable to find anything to talk about, my mother called on art to inject life into what looked like a very dismal evening. She ordered the children to entertain the grumpy company with a few songs. Always ready to show off, I advanced stomach foremost and sang the old Afrikaner standby, "Sarie Marais," and "Good night, my love, the big yellow moon descending," though the last word (my mother reports) came out "desembering." This broke the ice, and Maria's brother and father brought out their guitars. Things warmed up with some spontaneous dancing, which I was only too glad to lead. Before we drove for home, I insisted on a kiss from Maria and for a few hours the Boer War was forgotten.

I saw Maria only once again. Five years later, in Kimberley, she came to stay with us for a week. Walking into the bathroom without knocking, I discovered her sitting in her bath. She quickly turned away. Her small ears curled neatly on each side of her delicate head from which the hair had been pulled up and back. Her back and damp shoulders gleamed like the interior of a seashell. I beat an embarrassed retreat, and she vanishes from memory the way a white pebble dropped in dark water is erased from sight.

15

Nazis

It was 1938. Everywhere there was talk of war. The market for diamonds was falling. Sir Ernest Oppenheimer was once again closing down Kleinzee. Salaries would be cut in half, the diggers sent back to their farms, the staff reduced to a skeleton few. We would return to Kimberley, and my mother could hardly wait. But the longed for trip back seemed never quite to materialize. Every time Hitler danced another one of his spastic jigs around the conference table, the nervous businessmen of Europe adjusted to his tune, and Sir Ernest found himself dancing with the rest. Prices were bouncing erratically. Bits of countries cracked along ancient seams and fell into Germany. The Germans in South-West Africa wanted their desert to end up there too.

My father wrote home, "Another five years here is the limit. I'm just glad we paid dad [Louis Newman] off during this short period of affluence. We'd like to make the trip home but there isn't time to save the fares. If there was a job at home, I'd come." My father was being tugged in two directions. He was committed to going home for the sake of his family. But he wanted to make a difference in the world, and his world was now South Africa. He felt Sir Ernest would have to take note once he proved so good that no other manager could possibly match him.

Across the Orange River to the north lay the town of Oranje-mund, which Park described as "quite a lively place." He was allud-ing not to its social life, but its politics. Oranjemund lay at the south-west tip of the territory that comprised the old German South-West Africa. After Germany lost the war in 1918, this desert was man-dated by the League of Nations to the Union of South Africa. It comprised a hostile landscape of 322,400 square miles inhabited by some 20,000 Europeans, mostly German. Seventeen thousand were settled in the capital, Windhoek. The remainder huddled in Oran-jemund. The 237,323 Africans (faithfully recorded in my ancient *Bartholomew Atlas*, circa 1928) were still biding their time.

In 1939, Oranjemund was a German town. Its inhabitants (engi-neers, clerks, restless adventurers, wives, and children) had been swept up in the excitement Hitler was creating at home. The works were owned by Sir Ernest under yet another title (Consolidated Dia-mond Company), and he was becoming increasingly worried about the Oranjemund management and staff who had put up pictures of Hitler on every available wall.

Park suggested that Sir Ernest must take advantage of the old man-ager's retirement. The staff were agitating for a politically proper replacement. They longed for a satisfying reunification with the fa-therland. Hitler himself sent down agitators to excite the political conscience of the population and prepare them for a glorious future where Germany would play with the planet the way Charlie Chaplin (playing der Führer) had palpated a globe of the world. The Führer dragged in the South-West Africa question at every international conference. The democratic leaders were in their usual disarray. Like nervous trainers who throw steaks at a pitbull to pacify him, the statesmen of Europe were feeding chunks of land to Hitler. Sir Ernest was afraid his diamond mine in Oranjemund would be next.

In Oranjemund, a plump little Mephisto called Dr. Rudi Mehl had appeared. Politically impeccable, the ever smiling, magically unctuous Dr. Mehl was a surveyor with Nazi sympathies. Mehl had been sent into the desert to write a detailed report on mining conditions in Oranjemund. He took his time, and every evening organized serious little talks in the living rooms of the more serious-minded engineers about the future of the German people. Sir Ernest wanted to see him back in Kimberley, but Mehl insisted on German thoroughness and refused to return before the report was perfect.

The men in Kimberley were afraid that sacking Mehl would create a political incident that the Germans might blow up into some kind of international uproar. This would give Hitler an argument to pry loose the southwest desert and gain Germany a toehold in Sir Ernest's fiefdom.

Park suggested to Sir Ernest that my father might provide a solution. He was good with staff and workers; he had raised production levels at Kleinzee to their highest level in the mine's history. Best of all, he was an American. The Germans would loathe a British boss and despise an Afrikaner, but what could they say about someone from the blandly neutral United States?

Oppenheimer hesitated. Sir Ernest always hesitated. He was among the most powerful men on the planet. Every day, in every newspaper in the world, his name appeared on the page where stock quotations were published. But powerful men often resemble muddy-eyed old crocodiles who know how to stay out of sight until the moment for the kill. To maximize surprise, Sir Ernest created worry and confusion. He generated what Park described as "the Oppenheimer atmosphere"—the corporate equivalent of smog, a highly toxic compendium of rumor, cocktail gossip, judicious silence, and subtle smiles that might or might not mean something. The result among his subordinates was nervous apprehension, high anxiety, and poor health.

Sir Ernest did not trust newcomers. But, in the end, he went for my father. The Germans had worked themselves into a state of high political excitement. They were lighting bonfires at night and singing patriotic songs. So the word came down. We were off to Oranje-mund, and my mother was obliged to set aside her dream of Kimber-ley and adjust to more time in the desert. More wind, sand, and sun.

Between her stepfather's domination at home and the dust-choked mining camps in Africa, my mother had enjoyed her best moment of freedom at the University of Washington. There, for the only time in her life, she was free to be as witty and outrageous as she pleased. As the wife of an American manager in a Nazi town, she was aware that every word must be monitored. Her letters home are guarded. But she assumed war was inevitable. She used the word *holocaust* to describe what she sees coming twenty or thirty years before the term was put into general circulation.

"Those poor damn fools," she writes Bess, "dead these twenty years, who are rotting away in France and thought they were fighting the war to end all wars! It makes me incoherent with rage when I think of all the waste and misery then, and ever since then. . . . So Europe is going to turn into another holocaust. What a tremen-dous waste of life and money. This time I hope they scotch Hitler properly."

Dr. Mehl tried to remain elusive. But time was running out on him, and Hitler was more occupied with Czechoslovakia than South-West Africa. De Beers, meanwhile, sent Park in to flush him out. My mother wrote Bess, "They are keeping us under cover until Mehl produces his survey report. Then they will cut him adrift with three months pay. The company hasn't liked him for a long time and has been trying to get rid of him. He's a very strong Nazi."

Kleinzee was shut down and, with three months of leave coming, my parents decided to tour Europe. My mother wrote Bess, "I couldn't bear to stay up here for much longer—I get so terribly homesick for people, streets, shops, shows, civilization!" My father thought he might pick up some German and observe what the Nazis were doing at home before dealing with them in the desert.

They were in Prague a few days before Hitler marched into the city and got out more or less as he marched in, just before the trains were stopped. In Berlin, my mother complained, there was no way to greet people in a civilized manner because every desk clerk, hotel manager, and waiter used "Heil Hitler, including the children and dogs."

The Carstens agreed to take care of my sister (two) and me (five) during the months our parents were in Europe. That final Christmas in Kleinzee (1938), just before our parents left us with Minx, was the first Christmas I can remember, and I remember it as the most opulent festival of my childhood. My sister and I goggled that morning at an incredible array of gifts arranged under a real fir tree shipped in from Cape Town. Stockings were stuffed with candies and fruits, crayons and watercolors. A stack of books had been shipped by Grandma Bess. My sister had a new wicker doll buggy and a high society doll with painted china cheeks and blue eyes that popped open when she sat upright. We were loaded down with several kinds of building blocks—alphabet squares, miniature timbers that snapped together to make log cabins, construction blocks in odd shapes that produced grand English houses with fluted columns and dormer windows. My only disappointment was a tiny toy piano with notes that clunked like a dropped dinner fork.

There was joy in Germany, too. Hitler's society resounded with goose-stepping soldiers and pirouetting panzer divisions. The attack on Poland was nine months and five days in the future. The statesmen of Europe assured nervous nellies that bits of paper (bearing Adolf's self-assured signature) guaranteed peace in our time.

The people who manufactured children's toys knew better. Under our fir tree that Christmas, World War II was laid out in voodoo miniature. Like tiny sorcerer's apprentices, we European children held in our little hands all the delightful technology of death — spring-fired cannons with tiny shells; attack planes with heavy, military wings; locomotives that hauled troop trains, and flatbed cars fitted with ack-ack guns; sentry boxes; gun emplacements fastened together with smoothly functioning little nuts and bolts. We had warships and troop carriers and tanks with solid rubber treads that knocked down block houses.

Above all, I loved my platoons of lead soldiers, a Scottish Highland regiment clad in green-and-red plaid kilts, some carrying rifles, some hoisting bagpipes. A smaller box contained Tommies in khaki, led by an officer in a flat British helmet. His arm raised, he was half turned, leading his men into a hail of machine-gun fire.

I felt a profound pleasure opening those cardboard boxes of solid soldiers, each with his black dot eyes, eyebrows, and tiny red mouth. They were cast in deliciously heavy lead. Each man was fitted securely into the cardboard box through a slot. I gave them all a name and a personality — stolid McGregor; Bartlett, the born survivor; McDavitt, whose machine gun broke off; and the lieutenant with the revolver, who was me in miniature.

Forty years later in London, I spotted an identical Scottish regiment lined up in an identical flat box and selling for a small fortune in a shop outside Kensington Station. It was the same box, the same Highlanders, my lost platoon still marching in bright plaid, still hoisting their bagpipes. They had probably been gathering dust in a London attic for a generation. For a moment I was five years old again, back in Namaqualand, the wind rattling the windows, my tiny sister in her terrycloth jumpsuit, pushing the new wicker pram, my magical parents still alive and worried about Germans.

16

Oranjemund

WE ARRIVED IN ORANJEMUND NEAR TWILIGHT. THE DESCENDING SUN threw a hard, horizontal light across the desert. Identical white houses threw identical blue shadows on the stony ground. There were no streets. A single unpaved road led out of town. The black Atlantic lay invisible across the western horizon. The river, too, was out of sight. The only tall building in town was the power plant, resembling a black church stripped by barbarians. It housed a bank of green dynamos, each machine linked to an enormous green flywheel by a whirling black drive belt and tended by a genial and perpetually drunk Englishman named Jones. Close by the power plant rose a squat wooden water tower bound with metal bands. And over the water tower a spindly crane lurched into space at an improbable angle.

The town appeared deserted. No one showed up to greet the new manager, and I had the impression that everyone had gone away a very long time ago. The spaces between the buildings swept clean by the wind, Oranjemund had the polished, Euclidian look of a grave-yard. From horizon to horizon the sand stretched out, strewn with small black stones. There were no gardens.

I have no recollection of our arrival in Kleinzee and have con-structed the event from my mother's letters. But I remember Oran-jemund with surreal clarity. In Oranjemund, the cloudy fragments of my world began to assemble as I emerged from dreamy infancy. So if I write more elaborately here, the reason is that I hesitate to fix in words too simple an item as shadowy, contradictory, and mysterious as waking consciousness. If there is anything entirely my own, any compound that composes my identity, it must be these refractory im-ages and sounds. And if I were to lose the memory of my sister's frowning smile; the feel of my mother's hand, warm on my forearm; or the awkward heave and slash of my father's attack on a tennis ball, then I would vanish without a trace, leaving only an organic hulk for doctors to ponder. These images are the capillaries of my spirit, and a false phrase, it seems to me, may cause the past to crumble and go dark, like the fiery netting in the Coleman lantern that lighted our house those first months in Oranjemund; so fragile it might be destroyed by a breath.

Geometry dominated Oranjemund. Oranjemund was geometry. But I hardly noticed then what would seem deadly to me now. The houses were divided into three-room, prefab family units and single-room, prefab huts for single men. The huts, like the houses, had been laid out with a tape measure and set well apart at dead-even intervals. Each hut was furnished with a single door, a single win-dow, a single table, a single chair, a single bed, and it contained one single man. It was German order lacking the saving sugar of *gemüt-lichkeit*.

The family houses, including ours, were constructed of three single prefabs bolted together. The former manager had not bothered to cut doors through the walls. To move from the bedroom to the living room, or from the living room to the kitchen, he and his wife and his children and his servants had simply gone outside and tramped through the sand. Our back door opened directly on the western horizon. To the north, tennis courts cut off a clear view of the power plant. The courts presented themselves as a disheveled sheet metal fence, hammered together haphazardly to keep out the afternoon sandstorms.

Our backyard was a dune. Containing several tons of sand, this agile dune often danced from the west side of the house to the east overnight, depending on how the wind blew. Aside from a vine draped around the front door, there was no greenery. No screens warded off the swarms of black flies. No electricity had been drawn from the power plant to light our house or any other house in town. There was no indoor plumbing. I don't recall my parents complaining. They never complained. "We have plans for this place," my mother wrote home. They found the Germans' lack of initiative as appalling as their politics. They intended to make the town over, add rooms to the house, electrify everything, run pipes everywhere.

On that first evening, my mother fired up the heavy iron stove with wood and warmed water from the single faucet in a large black kettle. The setting sun painted the kitchen wall a brilliant chrome yellow. The big cast-iron stove threw a black shadow. My sister and I took our bath together, as we often did. The sun was replaced by the Southern Cross, and candlelight lent mystery to the evening. Our shadows skittered after us to bed, slithering up and down the walls, creeping across the sand when we went outside to go around to the bedroom.

My Oranjemund was composed of wind, flying sand, the horizon with its great watery puddles of superheated air, and the garden my father began to assemble. Private life in Oranjemund was watered by politics. We arrived the month before Hitler invaded Poland, and every carpenter and mechanic had turned himself into a political theorist. German blood and Hitler's economic plan and the expansion of the fatherland were all mixed-up together in their heads like a great Caesar salad. The Führer's tight lips and staring eyes were proudly displayed in every living room, framed above a pair of swastika flags. In the spring of that same year, getting out of Prague just as Hitler was marching in, my mother had written Bess, "Really, that man is only a big time gangster. What all of the 38,000 poor Jews in Prague are going to do I don't know. They've already issued orders for all Jewish doctors and lawyers to give up their practices to Aryans. It looks like the colonies will be his next move. And if England has to hand over anything more to that brigand it will be South-West Africa since that is the most settled by Nazis. They have their own schools, organizations, and agitators. I can't understand the South African government allowing them to keep up so much propaganda in a British mandated territory. We saw shops in Germany with show windows giving the people an idea of what Germany means to have in the very near future and it included *all* of their former colonies in Africa. But the worst of it is that the Afrikaners are all for the Germans."

The summer before hell broke loose with the Polish invasion, our local Nazis sat in their geometric houses in their geometric town with their ears glued to shortwave radio sets, waiting for the great event. On the first day of September it came, and our neighbors went mad with joy. They sang and threw their arms around each other. They wept like children. They worked themselves into such a state of political orgasm I may as well have been a child wandering about a Hamburg whorehouse. I got my first whiff of history and found it rich and strange and satisfying. I, too, felt glorious though I had no idea about what.

Oranjemund, so rigidly laid out on the stony sand, imitated in its own way those great assemblies of the party-faithful lined up in straight rows—stretching from the Führer's polished boots to the marching children on the margin, with flowers in their hair. I experienced my own version of this German euphoria, though the Nazi honeymoon with Hitler was confused in my six-year-old mind with dreams about flying, and Mowgli in the jungle, and Hermann Goering turning into a white balloon, and a naked arm rising from a lake grasping a sword.

Quite aside from the Nazi business, Oranjemund was suffused for me with a mysterious significance. Because my imagination could run free, I provided the town's geometric outlines with obscure meanings. The straight lines, the dozens of small dunes raised by the tireless wind behind each house; all of this was peopled with images and sounds that filled me with a nameless pleasure. The flat world ended at a blue sky swallowed at night by countless stars. The days were full of light, and every evening our mother read us stories at bedtime. King Arthur and Theseus and the Minotaur inhabited the twilight stretch of desert that ran out to the sea behind our house. And after the light was out, I heard blind Pew banging with his stick in the wind at the front gate.

The desert, the wind, the sandstorms that obscured everything never made me feel isolated or cutoff. The clouds piling up like castles in late evening, the voices I heard in the breeze, these assured me there existed some source shifting for itself at the heart of things. I felt myself securely situated at the heart of the world.

One morning we left before sunrise for a trip to Pomona, where the X-ray station was situated. Michael McIntosh, a boy my age, lived there. As I lay half dreaming in the backseat, I watched the sun rise over the flat horizon, and then rise a second time and then come up again, and again. I knew this was impossible. But it was happening nevertheless. And each time it rose a kind of wild joy grew in my body until I felt I would dissolve with pleasure at the impossible beauty of the thing.

After that, whenever we drove anywhere before sunrise, I waited for the sun to repeat its performance. I even got up early myself and stared at the eastern hills, daring the sun to rise more than once. But apparently the star had given up on me and did only as my father assured me it was bound to do. So I had to look somewhere else for my ecstasy.

Oranjemund had been founded around the turn of the century when the Germans first discovered diamonds in the ancient riverbed. The river had brought the stones down from volcanic rocks to the east and dropped them in layers of sedimentary rock just below the dunes. After Germany lost the southwest desert following the First World War, Sir Ernest Oppenheimer secured title to the diamond territory but left manager Horlein and his staff in charge. The Germans had no reason to improve the town, which was controlled now by Consolidated. The French and the British had created an elegant colonial style—screened verandas, gardens, stone buildings with cool interiors. Colonialism meant trying to get as comfortable as possible in ridiculous climates. The Germans in Namaqualand lived in prefabricated squalor. They imported a few tinned foods (sausages, sauerkraut, beer, spinach, sweet condensed milk, whose cloying taste all children loved) and left it at that. They had no illusion of permanence. The history was German; the money was not. Their wretched huts, raised in a day, turned into furnaces when the wind burned in from the east. They ignored the aggressive flies that collected in the eyes of their children and didn't put up window screens. They washed in cold water and suffered snakes and fleas gladly. They pulled down their trousers in outhouses and wished they were back in Berlin.

I was sitting peacefully in one of their outhouses with the door open one night when I saw my first shooting star. Afraid that something was going wrong with the world, I ran inside to wake up my father, who assured me the sky was not falling in. I learned that stars do not fall. The sun, moreover, rises only once every day. My father never doubted that science has given us the one true picture of the world. A few days later, he brought home bits of black meteorite to show me what my shooting star was made of. I felt considerably let down by his science.

Because the manager before us had not bothered to punch doors through the walls in his house, much less plant a garden, no one else in town had done so either. Good Germans all, they would never dream of appearing better off than their manager. But as soon as our corrugated iron fence went up and my father put in a lawn and a fishpond and flowers and flagstone walks, gardens began to sprout all over town, each carefully calibrated to appear less grand than the American manager's.

A few yards north of our pale red fence, a windmill had been raised on spindly legs by the former manager. He had used the wind to charge a battery for his shortwave radio. This windmill marked the center of the world I measured out for myself in Oranjemund. My private domain extended east into town, then cut straight across to the power plant and water tower. It included the new recreation center my father was building in the center of town and it was bounded by the power station and the airfield behind our house. The landing strip was marked by an enormous blue, yellow, and red target painted on the sand. This series of circles within circles gave the company pilot something to aim for. Captain Halse, whom I recall only as a leather cap, took me on my first flight. The aircraft was a biplane with two open cockpits. I sat on my mother's lap and goggled at the earth below, which appeared neither far nor near. I remember my perplexity. The world had become a freezing blanket of blue wind that wrapped around us.

On the enormous red bull's-eye at the center of the airfield target, I placed the entrails of slaughtered chickens—a sacrifice to whatever spirits I had heard hissing my name in the wind. Whenever I went out alone in the desert, I was followed by invisibles who, to judge from their voices, meant me no harm. The sacrificial bits I carried into the desert were always gone when I checked the next day, and I knew perfectly well that some jackal or hyena had made off with them. I didn't imagine Zeus or Aphrodite would zip out to Namaqualand to pick up a heap of chicken guts. But the vanished offering made me feel I was magically connected to whatever was out there in the desert—the creatures with gleaming eyes who owned the night the way I owned the day.

The southern boundary of my private Oranjemund was marked by two big water wells, dug before pumps were installed to bring water directly from the river. My sister and I would lie flat on the gray, rotting boards and peer into the dark below. Pencil-thin shafts of sunlight lit the gruesome sides, and once I thought I saw a pale woman with an eager expression clinging to the dank wall and peering up at me. We ran away, shrieking with fear, and my sister accused me of inventing witches to scare her. True enough, but not on that particular occasion.

The eastern boundary of my Oranjemund was marked by the blacksmith shop and slaughterhouse. The disorder in the smithy was oddly satisfying. There were tangled, rusting scraps of metal in every corner, but I knew the chaos was an illusion. All of these tangled bits of iron would melt into a white slag; the smith would then bang them into tie bolts, horseshoes, hammerheads. The smith wore a leather apron and pumped a mechanical bellows with a foot treadle. His anvil resembled a small black hog. The white-hot metal he plunged in a barrel of water emitted a reptilian hiss before emerging, iridescent and cold. Thus the hardest and most stable things were easily transformed. All it took was a small fire and a stream of cold air.

The slaughterhouse was right next to the blacksmith. The killing yard extended from under a low shed into an open court, smoothly paved. A groove ran from the shed to a drain, and a line of darkening blood oozed along the groove, like a red worm gradually turning black before wriggling underground. I went there for the first time with Theo Fourie, an older boy. Advancing boldly into the dark under the shed, I saw a man in a blood-spattered apron pick up a sledgehammer. Outside in the bright light, cattle in a chute stared distractedly at us, showing the whites of their eyes. The butcher approached the ox and casually brained it with a single blow. He then slit the throat, and a stream of hot blood seethed around our bare feet, crimson and sticky. The black hide was slipped off the cadaver as neatly as a fur coat lifted from the back of a plump lady. It was chastening to see a living creature reduced so quickly into greasy piles of meat.

The sight, however, didn't put any of us off our evening meal. In Oranjemund I accepted without question whatever I observed. A living creature was brained before me, I saw the bright blood leap from its throat, I saw the broad knife hack through its shivering limbs. I went home for dinner and asked for a second helping. The world lived by eating itself. I ate the living world, while time nibbled on me.

In Oranjemund, I saw a thing even more mysterious than fire and blood. One day I ran into Phillip Broughton and Theo Fourie, who were hurrying across town. They wouldn't say where they were going, but allowed me to join them. We stopped at the door of a brand-new house and Theo knocked. It was opened by an Englishman—the new engineer in town. "Oh, you've come to see our baby," he said and led us into the house.

All the blinds were drawn. I noticed something odd about the father's movements, as if he were freezing cold in spite of the warm afternoon. He led us down a short hall into a small bedroom where there were toys and a child's crib. An infant lay in the crib. I had seen sleeping babies before. This one looked like all the others except for the coins covering its eyes. I realized with a horrible qualm that I was seeing my first dead person. Its father removed the coins. The eyes remained closed, slightly flattened under their delicate, bluish lids. Everything about the baby was bluish and perfect, as if it had been cut and polished in pale blue marble.

When its father suddenly began to laugh, I felt as if I had been thrust off a cliff. For a moment there was nothing beneath me. I glanced at the engineer and understood that this was how grown-ups cry (a thing I had never imagined). The sight of the man weeping alarmed me even more than the dead baby with the wrinkled eyes and blue hands. The sound of his sobbing made me think of the Spartan boy who steals a fox and hides it under his coat. When he is confronted and accused, he denies his guilt while the fox gnaws its way into his entrails. Before he fell, the boy must have made a desperate sound like this.

I quickly turned away from the baby's father and left the room, taking great care not to run, which would have been (it seemed to me) terribly rude. The baby's father followed right behind me. He opened the door and thanked me for coming. Perhaps the sight of living children gave him some kind of solace. The only thing I could think to say was, "You're very welcome."

I didn't mention the dead child to my mother. I thought she might be upset with the engineer for displaying his dead baby to children in town. Three years later, when I persisted in questioning my father about the death of his good friend, Ziervogel, killed during the invasion of Italy, he would lose his temper. My questions about dying, corpses, coffins, and embalming were too much for him. When he began to shout at me, my mother objected, saying that my terrible curiosity was "only natural." Of course he backed down at once, as he always did when she intervened in her sure and certain way.

I was often in danger of unsettling my father. His nature was sweeter, more troubled, more reasonable than mine. Drawn to look without blinking at whatever rejects looking at, when I stared down at the engineer's dead child, my alarm was mixed with cold equanimity. The child's terrible blue forehead, the engineer's desperate sorrow, this was profoundly interesting because it was so disturbing. Some level-eyed and coldly detached monster in me looked at the world without judgment or fear. I had left the dead infant with a jagged fragment of reality fixed in my memory like a sliver of broken glass. In that fragment I could see reflected all the dead and, even one day, myself.

Yet, years later, when my father died I could not bring myself to see whatever the embalmer had done to him. (I had gone through all of that with my mother, and once was quite enough.) I preferred to remember him alive. My sister was brave enough to visit his corpse, and when she returned said, "He was simply very dead." My slight advantage is that I remember him alive, only alive.

17

Myths

THESE WOULD BE OUR FAMILY'S HAPPIEST FEW YEARS, BUT HOW COULD
we know that? Each day passing seemed timeless and absolute. Taken
together, my parents combined American reason and European art, a
potent mix. My mother still had trouble with her eyes, her teeth, an
occasional asthma attack. But my father's success created a sensation
of rapid forward motion. The future appeared to lift like the curtain
on a play in which they were writing the script. "We are going to
make big changes here," she wrote Bess. And within weeks she had
set up a dairy and a modest chicken farm, hired a schoolteacher from
Holland, and brought in weekly Hollywood films from a Cape Town
distributor.

Few of the women in town had more than a grade-school education, and many of the Afrikaners were simply illiterate. Only one or
two of the Afrikaner children could read. Distressed by their ignorance, my mother pressed books on whatever children came to our

house. Our bookshelves served as the first library in town, until she came back from Cape Town with over three thousand volumes and put the local teenagers who could read to work labeling and organizing the titles.

Time in Oranjemund bore no relationship to whatever time has since become. A day then lasted a year, or a lifetime. A day easily contained a hundred pages of Mark Twain, hours in the jungle with Mowgli, a snake hunt behind our house, and a gallop to the sea. But reading was the experience that cut deepest, because it furnished the imagination with everything in the world, and there was little to compete with Shakespeare, Dickens, and Herman Melville in Oranjemund.

By the time we drove out of town, many of the younger children in Oranjemund were better read than the American high schoolers I graduated with ten years later in Seattle. With no radio, few films, and television still years in the future, books were all we had, and we were insatiable. After *Grimm's Tales* and the Greek myths in various versions, I made my way through the Norse legends.

I relished the dark, rainy world of the Norsemen and their obsessed and demented heroes. These myths became a journey no less real than our trips through the desert to Cape Town. The wet forests where they lived were the antithesis of our glaring desert. The Greek myths seemed to me pallid and blighted by comparison. But the Greek stories had been raked over by editors who wanted to preserve my generation from images of rape, murder, and incest. We knew perfectly well, however, what Leda was doing with her swan, and why Psyche spent those nights with Eros. We had already been seduced, had observed death and dementia. I had crawled over a nude woman in a dark room, and my sister had had her teeth knocked out by a flying bottle. I had made sacrifices in the desert, seen the faces of the dead, walked in warm sticky blood on the slaughterhouse floor.

I wish that I could read now as we read then. I was taken over so completely by the troubles of Oliver Twist and traveled so far with the Snow Queen that scenes from imaginary tales are still more vivid in my memory than the living room of the house where I actually lived. I plowed through the *Arabian Nights*, Rudyard Kipling, and Walter Scott. What seems long-winded and overwritten to me now was never long enough then.

And always my mother would read a story or poem before we went to sleep each night. The music that spoke most directly to me then was a little verse by Robert Louis Stevenson that gave words to the wind that tapped on the window all night. The poem made me long for the English girls pictured in the book, with their empire dresses whipping around their ankles and their black curls flying straight out.

> And all around I heard you pass,
> Like ladies' skirts across the grass.
> Oh wind a-blowing all day long,
> Oh wind that sings so loud a song

These words made me feel that Isak Dinesen spoke the truth when she said, "Longing is itself a pledge that what we long for exists."

There was one story no one told me—the history of the desert where I lived—though that was a tale no less harrowing and improbable than the myths that shaped my perception of things. I don't think many people in Oranjemund (including my father) knew very much about it. The Germans had arrived late in Africa, just as they arrive late everywhere. They employed the classic three-wave strategy deployed by Europeans all over Africa. First came the missionaries (the Rhenish Mission in Namaqualand) to rid the native African of his superstition and idol worship. Once his world view had been supplanted by Christian love and forgiveness, the military was sent in to make sure the lesson stuck. And after the soldier with his gun came the businessman with his contracts. In Namaqualand, it was Herr Lüderitz who played the German Cecil Rhodes. In the 1890s, with their cattle dying of rinderpest, the Herero people tried to raise capital by selling land to the Germans. Another tribe, the Nama, signed away twenty "miles" of desert coastline (measured inland from the water's edge). They were not informed that a German mile measures four and five eighths the length of an English mile. Herr Lüderitz took care not to mention this. When the Nama realized they had lost not twenty but ninety-three miles, the Germans explained that once a legal contract is signed ignorance of European measuring standards is no excuse to back out of it. The Nama were asked to kindly vacate their land and their future.

Fraud on the European scale baffled the African imagination. Stealing a few cattle and some land was only human. But to make off with an entire landscape and then claim moral superiority on the basis of a signature—this was something new under the sun. Commissioner Goering (father of Hermann Goering—head of Hitler's Luftwaffe) was the man who insisted on the letter of the law—a German mile was not an English mile and that was the end of it. When the Nama objected that now they had no land left and nowhere to go, Commissioner Goering said it was nowhere they must go, or they would be shot.

The Herero tribe, finding themselves equally defrauded of land and cattle, declared war on Germany in 1904. General von Trotha fastened his helmet, saw to it that most of the men were gunned down, and drove the surviving Herero women and children out into the hot sand. By 1915, 80,000 Herero were reduced to 15,130 (according to the official figures). Of the 20,000 Nama, fewer than half survived.

When we arrived in Oranjemund in May of 1939, the landscape offered only a few springbok, ostriches frustrated by barbed wire fencing, hyenas, and the occasional cobra slithering through the delicate skulls of the dead. The entire desert was off limits, patrolled by camels, dogs, horses, policemen.

Had anyone drawn a series of concentric circles around Oranjemund in 1940, he would have noticed that violence and disorder increased exponentially the farther out he traveled. The Afrikaners were rooting for the Nazis to whip the British. The South African parliament had gone against Nazi Germany only after a close vote. South Africa's declaration of war against Germany would have been defeated without the influence of Prime Minister Jan Smuts. His influence won him and his country respect overseas. He became an international figure with celebrated friends in London and Washington. And while General Smuts went off to command South African troops fighting the Germans in the Sahara, his liberal deputy, Jan Hofmeyr, worked to give black people more rights at home. "I take my stand for the ultimate removal of the Colour Bar from our constitution," said Hofmeyr in 1946. This statement created such a scandal that Hofmeyr was driven from public life and died in obscurity.

There are few saints in South Africa. Back in the 1920s, General Smuts himself had ordered his army to shoot down the Israelites, an African sect led by Pastor Enoch Mgijima. Declaring their rights to a bit of vacant land and declaring that the end of the world was coming in any case, the Israelites had squatted in Bulhoek and waited. Smuts sent the army. Most of the clan were shot down (183 dead, 129 wounded are the official figures). The survivors were sent into a Native Reserve.

My parents had landed in South Africa during a liberal period. The depression forced Nationalist Prime Minister Hertzog to join forces with Jan Smuts's South African Party and form the United Party. The conservative Afrikaners, led by Daniel Malan, broke away and began to work out a policy of apartheid, the same policy that became law in 1948. It all sounded like nonsense during the war.

We English children all knew about Doctor Malan. We imagined him as a kind of watered-down Adolf Hitler. He represented the comic book side of Afrikaner politics, the clown who'd founded the *Ossewa Brandwag* (Ox Wagon Watch)—a name we pronounced in a wild whisper, rolling our eyes idiotically. Malan's *Ossewa Brandwag* was, like the post-war John Birch Society in America, a gathering place for the nutty and the narrow-minded—tight-lipped old farmers who prayed to a bearded god, and young thugs who wanted a simple world where heads full of liberal ideas would simply be chopped off. During the war, members of the *Ossewa Brandwag* carried out acts of sabotage against the Smuts government. Some were arrested without charge and detained in special camps until after the war. Then Daniel Malan was elected prime minister and initiated apartheid (correctly pronounced *apart-hate*).

To keep Daniel Malan out of trouble in 1938, the Smuts government had put him in charge of the Afrikaner Centennial. Taking his cue from Goebbels, the evil genius of German propaganda, Malan used the Afrikaner celebration as a forum to rewrite South African history. He convinced the world that when the Voortrekkers left the Cape and took possession of the South African interior they entered a virgin land with not a Zulu or Xhosa in sight. "Afrikaners were there first" was the message. Had the Americans produced a Daniel Malan at their World's Fair in 1939, the world might now be convinced that the Chippewa, Sioux, Mohicans, Apache, Navaho, and Hopi Indians drifted north from Mexico around 1900 and had been making trouble ever since.

18

Bliss

WHEN MY FATHER, AGED THIRTY-FOUR, DROVE INTO ORANJEMUND, the African workers noted his prematurely white hair, took him for a man of sixty, and called him "the old one." Among the engineers, mechanics, and clerks were some English, a number of Afrikaners, and a great many Germans. The Germans were sharply divided into opposing factions. The Nazis, finding themselves saddled with an American manager, masked their contempt with sullen respect. The liberal Germans approached timidly, bearing little gifts of fresh cabbage and condensed milk.

My father told me later that he never could adjust to the German habit of cringing in the presence of superiors and then trampling inferiors. The first day he walked into his office, he found himself in the presence of an enormous photograph of Adolf Hitler, staring down balefully. He assumed he was being tested and sent out a memo requesting that all images of persons not directly associated with the staff be removed. A small delegation arrived to confront him. They said images of the Führer promoted morale in the work force. He said that he would not insist that pictures of Franklin Roosevelt be placed in every office. He hoped they could compromise.

My father's unassuming "American" manner tended to undermine the swagger and strut of the more politically advanced Nazis. It is difficult to describe his special blend of affection and remoteness. But except for those hopelessly twisted by politics or monstrous childhoods, men responded well to my father's management. He was reasonable and always ready to listen. Still, I wonder if anyone felt they knew him. Toward the end of his life, he grew even more remote, as if some irresistible current bore him away into the distance. But in Oranjemund he was still young and believed in his future. He had been given a chance to use the skill afforded by intelligence and an American education.

Of course there was no end to the African colonial pecking order, but he tried, in the grand American manner, to bypass all of this complicated European rigamarole. When he wanted to get a ditch-digger's perspective on the job, he simply joined the man in his ditch.

He mentions in a letter to Bess how he spent several hours with the new operator of a stripping shovel (a sand removal rig) to instruct the man and give him some sense of how important his job was. Oranjemund had two or three of these immense dune eaters. They were the size of houses and crept over the desert on broad metal tracks at two miles an hour. At one end, a rotating shovel lifted sand onto a conveyer belt. The broad belt ran through the bowels of the rig and out the other end on an arm twenty yards long, supported by cables. In a day, they could clear an area the size of a football field.

My father's job was complicated by the German victories in Europe. While Hitler's armies overran Poland, then Belgium, then

France, my mother was serving tea to ladies who assumed the future of the world would be dictated by Germany. She had no doubt it was all going to end in disaster, that Hitler was destroying Germany and himself. But she kept her opinions to herself.

When the honeymoon with Adolf was at its height, in October of 1939, she wrote Haroldine in New Jersey: "Well, by gum, all the Nazis here are simply waiting for Hitler to cop off the war so they can belong to the Fatherland again. I wish you could see me going calling on the Nazi frauen whose living rooms are adorned with swastikas, eagles, plaques, and pictures of Der Lieber Führer Adolf in all kinds of attitudes, all fierce. Makes me writhe to see that visage with the 'stawsh' (Patsy's pronunciation of mustache) mucking up all the available wall space. Of course all the families aren't Nazi. There are about eighty families on this mine altogether, and the non-Nazis are pariahs among the others. They even come to fistfights over their durned politics. But most of the people are Hitlerites. They resent the English and Afrikaners like the devil, and they barely tolerate us Americans. It's only because Drury is the manager that they are civil and cringing. But I know what they are thinking all the same. Some of the women I like very much personally, but we don't dare discuss Hitler or I quickly lose my dignified manager's-wife-presence. After being in Germany myself for even a short time and knowing what goes on under that regime I just can't believe it possible that people are made to be such sheep, to follow a man, or I should say a megalomaniac, like Hitler."

Eschewing politics, my parents concentrated on plumbing, electrification, and milk. The first cow in Oranjemund was obliged to get there by foot. When the company denied his request that every family have hot water and electricity, my father did the job by saving money and materials from a warehouse project. He picked up a hundred cheap toilets from a wholesale distributor in Cape Town and blandished the Germans with new bathrooms and running water, movies from Hollywood, and pay bonuses. All over Oranjemund, ditches were being dug, poles erected, wires strung.

He wrote Bess, "The job is going pretty well, but if this place is any example, I sure have lost all belief in that world-famous German efficiency. I've never seen such sloppy methods from the office right down to the shovel boys. Already I've increased the average over-all efficiency on mining over 33 percent and on some jobs have had a 400 percent increase. The metallurgy used in the mechanical treatment process doesn't even pass a freshman rating. There must be thousands of diamonds in the tailings piles, which I propose to test for retreatment early next year. My only regret is that the place is not working full scale so that the improvements that I make would appear larger in the cost sheet. The first month when my figures went into the office, they wired back for correction thinking there had been a mistake." (Production jumped by over sixty percent his first month at Oranjemund.) "I have two stripping shovels in operation (300 cubic yards per hour) and on these I've got increased working time equivalents to three full shifts per month just by careful scheduling . . . and I've increased the hourly rate from 200 to 300 cubic meters (a 50 percent increase) by getting the operator interested in his job. When the second shovel started, the new operator did his best to keep up with the first man. And he's doing it. The only thing I'm worried about now is how to wangle a raise in pay for myself. Due to the war the diamond industry is showing a very poor month . . . It's so bad the directors broke down and appropriated half a million for an advertising campaign in America. . . ."

My mother writes, "These poor people have to send their children away to school at six or seven. I certainly don't think much of the weak-kneed former so-called manager. We are hiring a schoolmaster from Holland."

My father urged his staff to learn Ovambo, the local language. He complained, "These people have never taken the trouble to find out

how to get the most out of native labor. In fact, very few can speak
the native language. And they expect to get them to work when the
poor devils can't understand what they are talking about. Some Africans know a little German or Afrikaans, but they are in the mi-
nority."

Unfortunately, my father had no ear for music and little talent
for language. My sister and I used to make cruel fun of his Afrikaans accent, which we considered hopeless. He spoke the language
all the same, and went on to add Ovambo to his list of foreign
tongues.

A few months after my parents arrived in Oranjemund, my mother
mentions that the Afrikaner children were beginning to lose the
swamp-sour smell that distinguished them from their German and
British playmates. She started a campaign to teach all the kids to
wash so they would not get ringworm and to brush their teeth. Pre-
ferring the local habit myself, I avoided soap and water whenever
possible. I hated wasting my valuable time sitting in a bathtub or
plying a toothbrush. I was irritated by hairbrushes, socks, hats, shoe-
laces. Barefoot and bareheaded, with a scalp full of sand, I roamed
the desert holding a long, smooth stick. I would push the stick in the
sand ahead of me, looking for sand vipers and cobras. Snakes were
my special fascination.

My mother insisted I wear shoes, but I used to take them off, tie
the laces together, and drape them over the neck of my doberman,
Frankie. He would patiently tote them around all day, and I never
lost a pair until after the poor hound was run over chasing the carpenter's truck.

The Nazis in Oranjemund were eager to join in the great struggle
back home. Young men hurried overseas the moment they were old
enough to join the army. And every one of them was killed in the
first few months of the war. (In her letters, mother makes particular
note of this fact.) Nor did the German government make it easy for
their parents to learn the truth. The War Office in Berlin ignored

inquiries from Africa and only after repeated badgering would bureaucrats forward a businesslike letter which ran (more or less): "This is to inform you that regretfully your son died gloriously defending the Fatherland. Heil Hitler!"

The day Germany invaded Poland, the townspeople poured out into an open field and lit a bonfire. They shouted and danced and sang all the songs they could think of, everything from the Horst Wessel song to Schubert's *"Der Lindenbaum."* I had just turned six and loved the German national anthem, *"Deutschland Über Alles,"* and sang along with the best of them.

Years later, while suffering the exquisite pain that only a man with a kidney stone can know, a kind nurse shot a hypodermic full of morphine into my grateful rump. The pleasure I felt at that moment is the only thing in my experience that compares to the emotional high I enjoyed among those ecstatic Nazis. Unbearable reality was replaced by sheer bliss.

I imagine the Blitzkrieg being launched in the same high spirits—Germans dashing across the Polish border with every synapse on full alert. Listening to Wagner's *Lohengrin* may give some dim notion of the vaulting, death-saturated rapture that carried Germany into Poland that September.

Nothing was more fun than a Nazi rally, and I managed to sneak off to a number of their blowouts despite my mother's disapproval. My parents, meanwhile, tried to sustain the nervous liberals. Beleaguered, physically battered, they were enormously relieved to see a couple of unpolitical Americans roll into town.

Doctor Behne and his high-strung wife left surreptitious gifts and a note at our back door. Behne had studied medicine in London and admired the parliamentary system, but the state of his English (I have his note in hand) indicates why we all had to learn German fast. "Dear Mrs. Pifer, if you like to get this cabbage, you can keep it."

Herr Putzi Zeiler was another holdout again Nazi euphoria. He was my father's secretary, a compact, handsome man who resembled the actor Dirk Bogarde. Putzi's wife, Gerda, was a pianist, trained in Berlin and very popular with my mother, who brought a piano in from Lüderitz and took lessons.

Our neighbors were the usual complement of bitter eccentrics, misanthropes, minor careerists, and religious extremists; people who had dreamed of a new life on a better planet and found themselves instead in a perpetual sandstorm. A few of the British engineers were married to Afrikaner women. Perhaps they hoped the desert would put some distance between them and the tribal hatred that corrodes South African society.

My mother was forced to recognize the power of this hatred in Nigel, where some idiot began to call her a "hunky" after she mentioned her birthplace. Too often, any European from anywhere south of Paris was considered no better than a Portuguese—and the Portuguese were perceived as small, dark persons who washed in olive oil and smelled of stale fish. With German armies galloping all over Europe, our local Nazis grew more outspoken and boisterous. The purity of their blood emerged in their swagger. The politically suspect arrived at work with black eyes and swollen noses. My father had to separate two men who began swinging at each other in the office next to his. "All I did was bang a book on the desk," he told me. Privately, he dismissed fascism, communism, and socialism as all equally "impractical" (for him, a term of extreme disdain). Herr Hitler's power over the German mind was a mystery, something beyond my parents' grasp. No matter how they worried the subject, they could never make out how an entire nation waxed enthusiastic over an obvious maniac.

How wonderfully simple he made our world, *unser lieber Führer!* We children knew he had brought hunger and death in our time. He was the cause of all the disorder and most of the sorrow. We knew exactly what good and evil were. Everything was as obvious and bright as a cartoon. "What is the hill that Adolf can never climb?"

we asked each other. "Churchill," we shouted. The world was precisely divided into areas of total darkness (Germany!) and glorious light (Britain!!). And the black-and-white films coming out of Hollywood only strengthened that impression.

I have a strange and very distinct memory of standing, one afternoon, near a shiny, square-bodied airplane out in the airstrip behind our house. A large German woman is giving me a hug. By then I had picked up the language and was chattering away. I much preferred the rich expansiveness of the Germans to the gutteral reticence of the Afrikaners. Why everyone was so happy that afternoon, I don't recall. But I felt myself in touch with a world full of castles and rivers and curious German words that contained dark, winding streets and cathedrals full of singers. I felt the future would be filled with brilliant torchlight processions and great glistening icebergs of drifting time. How was it that the German language and this German woman communicated something so strange, so musical, so complex? How was it that I could feel European history and the European landscape snugly curled in the language we spoke? On that day, hugged by the large German woman next to the square airplane, I felt once again their mad joy running in my blood. For a moment I, too, was a German. I experienced the pleasure they felt—a kind of collective ecstasy which, years later, I recognized at once during the euphoric sixties, in drug-saturated San Francisco.

When history ripens into a rottenness that drives flies to a frenzy, when the end presents itself as a beginning, then something about to die believes for a moment that it is being born. I was, I suppose, tasting history—a shift in the axis of events. What stays with me is no more than a sensation, a sound, the smell of something like overripe fruit. But it is precisely the taste of this fruit we cannot communicate to those born later. The stink of a historical moment is reserved only for those who live there and then. As the whiff of methane gas from a sewer in New York City may remind a survivor of the latrine at Dachau, so the odor of smog in Los Angeles reminds me of Johannesburg, where I once stood on the lawn in winter and was told by my aunt that I must never play with black children. And the odor of aviation gasoline still reminds me of that moment with the German woman when I somehow felt myself saturated by Nazi bliss.

It seems to me that moment in European history got its odor from everything the Nazis were crushing—the cultural accumulation of a thousand years, everything Europe was sacrificing to politics. The Old World was being mulched into sweet, poison gas. And perhaps the thing I smelled on the desert was the end of Europe, the first tiny whiff of death, which may be easily confused with perfume.

Thus it happened that while Europe attacked its civilization with every technological toy science appeared so eager to provide, my parents—like magpies building a nest—salvaged bits and pieces of the discarded old culture to put their tiny backwater in order.

Sir Ernest on his Olympus voiced no objection to the town being lighted at night. Plumbing was fine, if that was what people wanted. My father asked for money for a recreation center with kitchens, billiard rooms, a bowling alley, and an auditorium where American movies were shown on weekends. My mother set up her library there. The schoolteacher from Holland arrived just in time to escape the invasion of his country. The children of Oranjemund were soon learning to read in two languages and sing in four parts.

Parkinson flew in from Kimberley and was full of praise. Sir Ernest was so pleased about the production figures and the quiescent Nazis that he spoke openly about making my father the next general manager for the entire southwest mining region—a territory that stretched from Kleinzee in the south to Angola in the north. And then, after Park replaced the present general manager, Donald

McHardy, my father would move into the assistant g.m. slot back in Kimberley.

My mother wrote Bess, "We are so excited about all of this recognition that we couldn't sleep for two nights thinking about our future prospects. Eventually, of course, Gus will become one of the De Beers directors. So far everything I have slated for him has come true, and that will too. I fully expect him to be one of the directors before he is forty."

19

The Sea and the River

I DON'T KNOW WHERE MY MOTHER LEARNED TO RIDE, BUT SOMEHOW she'd picked that up too and took to galloping across the desert on her Arabian, Loki—the most powerful horse in Oranjemund. Occasionally, she'd galumph around town on one of the police dromedaries. I was heaved onto my first horse at the age of six. I weighed the equivalent of an overnight bag, so my horse, Hans, could outrun everyone except Loki.

Every Thursday, the company groom, Rudolph, came for me and we would canter off to the river or the beach. Rudolph was an ancient Hottentot, with skin the color and texture of a dried apricot. His eyes were sunk deep in the furrows of his face. He wore a floppy hat and *velskoen*—boots with rolled uppers worn thin as mouse skin. Our common language was Afrikaans, and I did all the talking. He spoke only when I was in danger of killing myself. *"Was op!"* (watch out!) was the usual extent of it. He assumed complete charge of my

training, and my mother was not allowed to interfere. If she complained that we were two or three hours late, he would calmly inform
her that "it is necessary."

Rudolph liked to gallop along the river over the short grass. I
preferred the beach and would work myself into a kind of ecstasy
dashing along the margin of the sea, in simultaneous contact with
earth, air, and water. (Years later, flying a helicopter a few feet above
the surf along the beaches of Southern California and Alaska, I experienced something of the same sensation.)

My mother reports a fall I took when my horse tripped in a sand
hole, tossing me over his head, but I don't remember it. I do recall
plunging over his neck one morning when he stumbled in the surf. I
was aware of flying, then swimming with my mouth and trousers full
of sand and salt water. When I stood up in the cold waves, spitting
and snorting, I saw Rudolph sitting still as a statue on his orange
nag, observing without expression, while Hans rose glistening wet
behind me and gave himself a shake. Rudolph beckoned me with a
twitch of his head and checked me over as I staggered toward him.
Evidently all my bits and pieces were still in working order, and
hoisting me by my belt, he dropped me back in the saddle.

I usually mounted the horse by climbing our fence and dropping
onto the saddle from above. In the desert there was nothing to climb,
so I depended on Rudolph to get me back on the horse. He was a
tiny man and very old, but strong as steel cable. He didn't mention
to my mother that I had tumbled into the sea, and I thought it wise
not to say anything either.

On bright mornings, the sea was benign as I pressed Hans through
the shallow waves with the wind in my face. But most afternoons the
ocean off Oranjemund grew hostile. The waves picked up a black,
frozen sheen as they bore the cold Antarctic current to shore. I imagined mermaids riding their crest, creatures who have no souls and
end up as sea foam blown about by the wind. My father repeatedly
warned us about the powerful undertow along those steeply sloping

beaches. Stand in the surf on even the hottest day, you were soon as cold and slimy as a fish. Swim out and you might never come back.

Sometimes we picnicked on the beach at night, hoping the wind would die down. Usually it only changed direction. If there was ever a perfectly calm day on those beaches I don't remember it. I remember huddling behind blankets stretched over driftwood, burrowing into the sand that still retained some of the day's heat while the sea crashed and hissed, spitefully flinging gravel up and down the beach, and the wind laid its cold fingers on our backs.

In the fall of 1940, a fishing boat was blown into rocks off the coast of Oranjemund, the men on board drowned. We discovered the wreck in the cold morning light, beached like any other sea skeleton, bits of torn sail flapping against the mast. I could feel the presence of the dead still lingering in the sogged mattresses and waterlogged Afrikaans bible drying in the cabin. The deck was scrubbed and sanded clean. The sea is a scrupulous housewife. Troubled by a vision of dead bodies sinking down in the black water, I felt wildly alive, standing on the steep deck in an icy wind and burning sun.

At night, too, walking on the cold sand, I would find my thoughts drawn away from the land, out across the waves, and I would imagine myself sinking beneath the surface, floating in the horrifying, lightless silence, breathless among the drowned fishermen who stared at me with their luminous dead eyes.

The river seemed less hostile than the ocean, and it was positively friendly in the dry season when it dwindled to a benign trickle. Then the crumbling clay bottom would crack into thousands of geometric platters. When we eased one of these plates from its damp bed, insects would dash for cover—centipedes, spiders, bright orange scorpions with priapic tails. In summer we crossed the Orange on foot, splashing through muddy shallows on our way to Alexander Bay. Then the river was so orderly that even my tiny sister felt bold enough to leap into the long ponds that lay only a foot or two deep between grassy banks of mud. But during flood the river overnight transformed itself and showed a more treacherous face.

I have no idea how many times we crossed the Orange River mouth to Alexander Bay. I remember vividly our first crossing, because it had rained all night and when we arrived on the river a stiff wind was blowing from the sea, and the water had put on a dark brown, foreboding look. The Orange, having crept up the banks to the edge of Herr Kuhner's orchards, had transformed itself into a series of broad streams running between islands of sludgy mud. The surface was chopped into white caps the color of creamy coffee.

We were visiting the Groblers for the weekend. It was always the Groblers we visited in Alexander Bay. Mr. Grobler managed the mine on that side, and my mother had taken a fancy to Mrs. Grobler (who seemed to us much older than her slim, sporty husband). She was generous, kindly, intelligent, and overweight. My mother had adopted her as a parent.

Mr. Grobler was an Afrikaner graduated from one of the British universities in Cape Town. Having picked up cricket and soccer and adopted the English colonial style of life, he liked to wear trim white trousers, neatly pressed, and brilliant blazers with elaborate emblems embroidered on the breast pocket.

On our first encounter with the river, we reconnoitered early that morning with two glum Afrikaners sent over by Mr. Grobler. It was the Afrikaners' job to ferry us across. They hoped to perform this feat in a light kayaklike canoe glued together from narrow strips of wood and canvas. Having just battled across in the powerful wind, they were no longer sure this kitelike little craft was sturdy enough to float a family of four with all their luggage across the Orange in a high wind. No one had said there would be a woman with children. The large one said he wouldn't do it. The small one said it was up to the American manager. My mother said she had no objection to giving it a try. My father said he would try it first with the baggage. If he made it, the three of us could follow.

Because this was his first social call as the new manager of Oran-jemund, my father was all spiffed up in a suit, vest, and hat. But as he rather grandly descended the muddy bank to the boat, the soft mud suddenly gave way and he sank down in slime to his crotch. My mother began rolling about on the grass, laughing helplessly. Her merriment made a profound impression on the Afrikaners who had never seen the wife of a manager laugh at her husband before.

Besides several suitcases packed with formal wear designed to get my parents through the long weekend, our luggage included golf clubs, tennis rackets, tins of homemade cookies, and a large fish caught the night before. All of this fine paraphernalia was packed in around my father who had meanwhile removed his trousers, rinsed the mud off in the river, and laid them across the gunnels to dry in the stiff breeze. The Afrikaners pushed off grimly with our luggage and the new manager of Oranjemund, who was clad in a jacket and underpants. The large pale Afrikaner splashed on ahead, hauling on a rope, while the small red one pushed behind.

The kayak was visible for a while, but it soon disappeared behind the mud islands. My mother thought we should go up to the Kuhners' house and change out of our good clothes. The Kuhners lived above the river on a hill. Kuhner ran the pumping station that supplied water to Oranjemund. He was a hydraulics engineer who had come from Berlin twenty years before looking for a better life. Frau Kuhner grew most of the town's vegetables and fruit in gardens and an orchard that ran down slope to the river. Kuhner liked isolation. His wife hated it. Like my mother, she longed for city life. She hated the desert. She hated the Nazis.

Fifteen years before, the Kuhners had lost their four-year-old son when he went out to look for his mother one afternoon in a windstorm. His small body was found a week later a quarter mile from the house in a slight depression, face down, his little arms clasped over his head. He had died trying to shield himself from the stinging sand. Another Kuhner boy had fallen from a horse and badly fractured his leg, which was then amputated by an incompetent doctor who couldn't deal with a compound break. But this bad luck turned into a blessing after Hitler started the war. The Kuhner boy, attending university in Berlin, was unfit for cannon fodder so they parked him in an office. Among all the young men from Oranjemund who found themselves in Germany that year, he alone survived the war. Frau Kuhner's third boy had been conscripted in August of 1939 and was dead before Christmas.

We sat on Frau Kuhner's veranda watching the river until, an hour later, we saw the kayak working its way back through the mud islands. Rejoining the Afrikaners on the riverbank we found the large one shouting at the small one, who was giggling helplessly. They had been swept down current half a mile, and the big one was blaming his partner. My mother had removed her dark silk dress and put on a seersucker skirt and raincoat. I had folded my good blue suit away in her knitting bag. My sister still wore her white party frock and straw hat with artificial flowers. She had absolutely refused to dress down, river or no river. Wedged on the floor of the kayak between her mother's legs, she stared at the hurrying brown waves with an expression of grim foreboding. The fat Afrikaner handed me a rusty tin can and told me to bail water for all I was worth.

The Orange River is shallow, but there are sudden potholes and nasty underwater surprises. Every few minutes the Afrikaner up front would suddenly disappear. This vanishing was marked by a splash and a floating hat driven rapidly upriver by the wind. Surfacing, he would thrash after the hat, shake it, slap it, settle it limply on his large, pale cranium and then stand up. But these exertions had caused his beltless trousers to descend to his knees, and he was obliged (in full view of the manager's wife) to pull his trousers up over his large, dead white bottom. He wore no underwear.

My sister, sitting in a good two inches of water, complained that I was not bailing fast enough on purpose. My mother, struggling not to laugh out loud, pushed her nose into my sister's neck. The large, pale Afrikaner was exhausted and extremely irritated. After another dunking, after once again losing his hat and tearing the fly of his trousers, he came back spitting water and said the wind was making it impossible. We would have to go back. The widest and most windy stretch still lay ahead and the wind was rising steadily.

My mother said it was impossible to go back because she had not come this far to give up. The large Afrikaner said it had nothing to do with giving up. It would be irresponsible (*"nie goed nie!"*) to take children farther out in such a gale. We were all soaked by then, especially my poor sister who rested her chin on her mother's wrist and wore the weary expression of one past caring.

My mother now assumed command and asked the rebellious Afrikaners to kindly put us ashore on a mud bank. I was obliged to translate. "When we are on shore," she said, "we can empty the boat and rest for a bit. After that we'll all feel better. And when we get across, we'll get you some nice hot tea."

"I am very sorry but we must go back," said the large, pale one. "There is no other way."

"Well, you may do whatever you like," my mother said. "But I am going across with the children."

Because they could not very well shout at the wife of a mine manager speaking through a six year old, the two men went off to the far end of the mud island and shouted at each other for a while. Then they plunked the kayak back in the water and we continued across.

And hours later (so it seemed) there was our father waiting in his suit and tie, and Mr. Grobler in his natty white blazer with the Springbok emblem embroidered on his breast pocket. Arriving at the Grobler house was like arriving in paradise. There were hot baths. There were dry clothes. There was a heavenly green garden full of asters and roses, protected from the wearing wind. Flowers bloomed year-round in the desert as long as you watered them.

Breakfast was served in a glassed veranda. The women sat on

wicker chairs with a light breeze stirring the hems of their pale dresses. My sister and I played with some new puppies on the lawn. In the afternoon we joined the Grobler children for tea in the pantry, where we had our own china cups, serviettes, and silver. Children in that part of the world were treated with a formality that matched the grown-ups'.

It was impossible to spend Sunday in Alexander Bay without going to church, because the Groblers were intensely religious. My mother didn't mention her lapsed Catholicism, or her aversion to organized religion. We ourselves had no idea she had been brought up a Catholic. She planned to send us in another direction entirely. Only in deference to the Groblers would we all dress up in our Sunday best and go to the Dutch Reformed church together. But the moment we showed the least sign of restlessness our mother would order us out with a display of impatience. "If you can't pay attention and behave, please go outside!"

When we left Alexander Bay on Sunday afternoon, Mrs. Grobler loaded us down with fresh sausage, cookies, biltong (dried springbok), cakes, flowers. There was no way we could get it all across the river. So we munched on the cookies while waiting for the kayak. The cake fell overboard. The flowers floated away. Once home, we washed the sand out of the sausages, and after dumping us in the bathtub to wash the sand out of our hair, my mother praised Mrs. Grobler, saying "She really is a wonder." It was a phrase I heard her use often. We grew up assuming wonders.

20

Lessons

On the night of June 26, 1940, the Germans in Oranjemund vanished. When I stepped outside our gate with the arbor and trellis curving above it and stepped into the white dust outside, no one was there. Empty houses stared back at me. The British army had arrived the evening before. The men had been stabled in a big room in the new recreation hall overnight. At dawn trucks arrived and our Nazis were driven away to a camp somewhere in the interior.

My father took me that morning to see the room where the men had spent their last night in town. The walls of the enormous room were covered with slogans and swastikas. He had let them have all the beer they wanted, and the room reeked of stale hops. They had spent the night bellowing patriotic songs and praising the Führer. And many of them, moved by a rebellious impulse, or some obscure desire to record their moment in history, penciled their names with the date on the walls, though they must have guessed the walls would be painted over in a day. My father snapped a picture of the littered room. A penciled swastika and a single name is visible—Bradmann 27-6-40. Who Bradmann was I have no idea. But his name at least has stolen a short march on oblivion, secure for a brief lifetime in the pages of our family photo album.

By September, people from Kimberley had replaced the German staff and my mother was transformed from the manager's wife who never discussed politics to an enthusiastic supporter of Winston Churchill and everything British. "We are busy knitting for the soldiers," she wrote Bess. "Tomorrow night we are giving a dance in aid of the Wool Fund for the women's auxiliary of the British Empire Service League. We get wartime recipes over the radio. The announcer is now female. Quite a number of the men here have been called up." And with a touch of that mysticism that she usually suppressed in herself, she adds, "If that medieval prognosticator, Nostradamus, is to be believed, this war will only end in 1944, the final battle to be fought near Poitiers, and Hitler to wind up in an iron cage. I hope this won't mean another four years. But it is quite likely at that."

My father had objected to the British hauling away everyone with a German passport and insisted that persons who were anti-fascist should not be put in the camps. He knew perfectly well who the liberals were: those few families and one or two single men who had been snubbed, insulted, beaten, or spat on by the Nazis for being politically degenerate. Among those spared incarceration by the British was Putzi Zeiler and his wife, the only pianist in Oranjemund. And, of course, Doctor Behne, born in Namaqualand, so young, so pale, so tentative and scholarly. Doctor Behne's smile, his quick nervous speech expressed a sensitive nature. He had grown so ashamed of being German, so repulsed by his countrymen and their beloved Führer, that he could never bring himself to speak that contemptible name. If the subject of Hitler came up in conversation (and it always, always came up), he and his wife averted their faces, as if their countrymen had inexplicably served for dinner the contents of a sewer.

Gerda, his wife, a one time surgical nurse, was even more fragile than her husband. They had met in Heidelberg, where he was finishing his studies after taking a degree in London. Because she had married late and was decided on a family of seven children, she set about having them at once in assembly line fashion. Frau Behne often spent long afternoons with my mother, who was very fond of her. The Nazi women had made her life miserable, snubbing her in public, pecking at her in private. She and the Herr Doctor felt a great weight lifted from their spirits on the morning our "good Germans" were trucked to the interior.

Frau Behne was nonplussed by my mother's control over her children. She complained that her girls not only ignored her, but maliciously did precisely what she begged them not to do. She was baffled by our family, which apparently got on without any rules or ideas (*mit keinen ideen*). How exactly was it done?

"Well," my mother said. "They behave because they don't have any other choice. Unless, of course, you believe they know better than you."

Astonishing, to Frau Behne, was the way my sister and I ate up whatever appeared on our plates. She would stand in the doorway and watch while we stowed away our potatoes and spinach. Her children threw their food on the floor, or at each other. Possibly we were especially well behaved around Frau Behne in order to make her more miserable.

Most perplexing of all was the way we marched off to bed at eight sharp. Even in the hot season, with the sun high above the horizon, we listened to the evening reading and dropped off, no matter how bright it was outside. Frau Behne's eldest flatly refused to go to her room at any hour. The mad child would dash about, frantic with fatigue, until she fell asleep at some ungodly hour, dropping to the floor like one of those ancient citizens of Pompeii preserved by falling

Elizabeth Chalmers Newman (Bess) with Louis Newman. 1940

Picture of my mother and me taken by Nick in Nigel. 1936

The alluvial diggings at Kleinzee. Jack Carsten stands stolidly at right, pipe in hand. 1937

(From the top) Kleinzee from the air, circa 1938. Of the four buildings gleaming in a low sun, our house is the one at the far right. In Oranjemund, our house is among those at the top of the picture, above the tiny single men's shacks. The power plant in Oranjemund was the tallest building for hundreds of miles around.

My parents sailed from Cape Town to Genoa in April 1939.

ORANJEMUND:

*My father's
company photograph;
the desert landscape mined;
(opposite top) vital
equipment—a sand mover
the size of a house;
(opposite bottom) Evambo
laborers digging into bedrock.*

TRANSFORMATION
IN THE DESERT,
ORANJEMUND, 1940:

*(Top) The house as we
found it; (middle) the
garden fenced and laid out;
(bottom) the trellis and
bedroom addition;
(opposite top) the four of
us around the new pond;
(opposite bottom) myself
with an Afrikaner friend in
the garden, the pond packed
with water lilies and goldfish.*

CHILDHOOD:

(Top) View from our back door—my sister and I constructing a small city in wet sand after a rain; morning instruction with my mother.

My father with Van Zyl, the diamond security officer in Oranjemund and a close friend of our family.

SOCIAL LIFE IN ORANJEMUND:

(Top) Field day organized for the town children; (bottom) my sister's birthday party with some of the German women who would soon be placed in special camps by the British Army—Frau Behne (next to my mother) was allowed to remain in town.

On the road to Cape Town, circa 1940; the kayak that we used to cross the Orange River.

BIRTHDAY, 1940:

My sister insisted on taking a picture of the party; a new book from Bess.

A dance group from the costume pageant organized by my mother shortly before we left Oranjemund. My sister is in the front row, at left.

ash from Vesuvius in attitudes of final exhaustion. "I don't have your words," said Frau Behne. "I must learn your words."

Frau Behne made a great effort to always look lovely for her husband. She wore long dark skirts and crisp white blouses with starched collars. Her long, black hair she pulled back to show off her high forehead and small ears. She made a point of wearing no makeup because the doctor preferred her natural. To me she looked like a young witch with her long face and long nose and long dark skirts.

Late in her fourth pregnancy one morning, she felt a stabbing pain in her abdomen and hobbled out immediately to the hairdresser's to have her hair set "so she would look charming sitting up in bed," while she gave birth. Hours later, when the pain resolved itself into a case of indigestion (my sister and I had been saddled with babysitting her children all day), Frau Behne tottered into our house and collapsed in tears.

"She wanted seven children in seven years, she's completely worn out," my mother wrote Bess. "Fancy being an incubator for three children in twenty-seven months! I've been keeping an eye on the two eldest. Now their mother is in the hospital with a nervous breakdown and no darned wonder. The youngest is in the hospital where the nurses look after him. . . .

"Patsy and Lou [my sister and I] are heroically helping to entertain the two other children, but after the kids are gone they both breathe a sigh of relief and say they're glad we haven't any babies permanently in the house! They aren't used to screaming children."

Though Frau Behne loved our mother, she avoided us. We were, after all . . . children. And though we were disgustingly well behaved and even helped our mother to serve tea, Frau Behne never said more than a word to us. It was my impression I frightened her. So I approached only when my mother insisted I pay her the respect due any visitor, poking out my hand and showing all my teeth.

We were expected to show our faces when there were guests. We had to shake hands and sit for a few minutes to answer polite questions. We might even become interested in the conversation and join in. And afterward our mother would tell us what a good impression we had made and let us know all the nice things people had said about us. We were left with little doubt that good manners were a primary commodity. But then life in Oranjemund demanded a considerable formality and being the manager's children upped the ante. I suppose we bore almost no resemblance to American children. When we arrived in the States all of our artifice, oddly enough, gave us a measure of power over grown-ups that most kids our age didn't enjoy. Getting rid of my good manners was, like forgetting Latin, easier than picking them up. I was to find American manners baffling and complex—layers of easy spontaneity masking stern puritanical expectations that I simply could not penetrate. So I would settle for silence or outrageous behavior.

When the Germans were driven out of town their euphoria and their language departed with them. I felt that a wonderful technicolor cosmos had been replaced by something black and gray. The town had lost its third dimension. Worse, my mother now packed me off to the village school and expected me to wedge myself all day behind a desk with a crowd of Afrikaner children—small boys like myself with dirty bare feet and shaved heads, skinny girls in tiny frocks, and big girls with budding breasts and sullen expressions. Aged six through sixteen, we were lined up in rows before Mynheer Meyer, who had come all the way from the Netherlands to deal with our collective ignorance.

During the Easter break, I let it be known that I was through with school. I was bored. I wasn't learning a thing. I wanted to read *Oliver Twist*, not an Afrikaans primer. My mother explained that no one quit school. It was unthinkable. It was impossible.

I argued that I must be the great exception. This notion of mine put her in a very bad temper. She said she didn't want to hear any more about it. So I dropped the reasonable approach and went for it directly. On the morning that school resumed, I refused to leave the house.

My father had gone to work so mother and I faced off alone. She ordered me out the door. I stood my ground. She said, "I am ordering you to go to school because you have to learn just like everyone else. And you will go, Drury. Now walk out that door." I refused to budge.

It was the first time I had confronted my mother on an important issue. Furious, she went for the horsewhip. I was perfectly willing to be whipped. I was willing to be whipped every morning rather than put up with six hours of boredom every day. She gave me a good whack across my bottom. I emitted a yelp and prepared for another. It was delivered smartly. I prepared for another. She glared at me, suddenly flung the whip into a corner and said my father would know how to deal with me.

She wouldn't look at or speak to me the rest of the day. It was a wretched situation, but some monster in me resisted even the misery I knew I was inflicting on her. I slyly guessed my poor father would be unable to deal with me. He was simply too reasonable while I had darker forces on my side. Whatever he said that evening made so little impression on me that I don't remember a word of it. I could see that my pigheaded behavior had made an impression on my mother. I heard them arguing in the bedroom. She was doing most of the talking. And in the end she sent off to the Calvert School in Baltimore for a correspondence course that her friend Haroldine had told her about. She had decided, over my father's mild objection, to go on teaching me herself.

This, I realize now, was the most important victory of my childhood. It changed the way I would live my life. From that time on I was suspicious of classrooms, lectures, information, textbooks. The rebel in me won his first battle and recognized himself in the freedom he had won. Like the Afrikaners, like the Irish, like provincials everywhere, I would be ill prepared for the century where I would soon find myself. But there is something to be said for arriving late on the scene with baggage imported from another time.

My victory made me far more stubborn than I might otherwise have been. I began to imagine that if I wanted a thing (even an impossible thing) it would be possible—provided I was willing to suffer for it. And when I consider the briefness of my mother's life and the few years we had together, I see my pigheadedness as a kind of wisdom. I was wise to defy her because I have had only three or four great teachers in my life and she was the first and the most important.

She taught writing and history and arithmetic with a kind of graceful inadvertence. Casually raising a question, she would then wander off into the kitchen or out into the garden. I would get the impression that the answer to her question was out there in the world—outside somewhere, circling the house. And sure enough, after a few moments it came drifting toward me.

"Yes, that's it. Good. That's good enough for now," she would say with a sigh.

"Can I go out now?"

"Write your essay first. It won't take long."

"Awww! Essay on what?"

"How about the duck?"

"The duck! Why the duck?"

"Because you are trying to duck out."

"Is it about ducking out or the duck?"

"You're writing it. You decide."

She taught the subjects; people at the Calvert School did the grading. My work was sent back to Baltimore in little brown packages across the submarine-infested Atlantic. For some reason my highest scores were in math, a subject that discomfitted me. I have no clear idea of how she managed to fix my mind to numbers. Mathematics seemed to me a language without substance. My father pointed out that numbers could gloriously account for sheep, stars, grains of sand, and pounds, shillings, and pence. He admired mathematics because (he claimed) nothing could be more trustworthy. "The only precise language," he said. But I felt this famous precision as the flip side of a deathly vagueness. Write "a duck flies south" or "a white goose lays a golden egg" and you've got something for the imagination to work with. Write "100 trees divided by 100 trees equals 1 tree" and you've murdered a forest. Words lived in my mind. Words evoked a world I could respect—damp England and a blind pirate; frozen Lapland and the Ice Queen; yellow American forests and Chingachgook in beaded moccasins.

For me, words had a rich precision far beyond the empty magic of numbers. Words were intricate and slippery as eels. They resisted you. They dropped wriggling off the end of your pen and hatched one out of the other in unpredictable combinations. No wonder my best scores were in arithmetic! Numbers were so obedient, so easily trained, all heading in the direction of zero the way ants head toward their hole.

My sister was too young for school and sat with me each morning doing her watercolors or practicing her letters. Her intelligence always amazed me. Three years my junior, Patsy seemed to me my equal in everything except laziness. While our parents were in Europe we had come to depend on each other. At two and a half she was already wordy, bright, irascible. When I bullied her, she pinched and bit me. Our mother told Bess she was not worried about Patsy surviving an overbearing brother. A natural empiricist, very little escaped her sharp bird's eye. I, on the other hand, was master of the inspired guess, the intuitive crash landing. I would long remain a noddy boy with my intelligence curled up tight in the amniotic fluid of unde-fined emotions. Patsy gloried in precision. When she painted a red circle it was a bull's-eye. When I painted the same thing it was liable to turn purple, droop on one side and develop a drippy nose on the other. My shoes and bed collected sand. Fleas liked me. During our sojourn at Minx Carstens's house, I overturned a bowl of oatmeal on the floor because I missed my mother. Minx shamed me by cleaning up the mess without losing her temper. It was left to Patsy to tell me I was behaving like a pig. In one of the two letters Minx wrote Bess, she says she can hear my sister in the next room ordering me "to stop your silly nonsense." However I would remain dedicated to silly nonsense, and my loyalty to it remains firm to this day.

The games my sister and I invented reflect the time. "Yesterday Lou and Patsy played ambulance the whole afternoon," my mother wrote Bess. "Patsy had on her Red Cross apron which came with the toy doctor's set we got from Montgomery Ward. Lou fastened a sort of dog box painted white on top of his wagon with a door at the back. He made a stretcher and they conveyed wounded dolls to the garage, which was the hospital. Finally, they must have had an epidemic because they turned the ambulance into a hearse and had a mass funeral."

Only reptiles and long novels totally absorbed my flickering attention. In my first letter to Bess, I brag about killing three snakes in two days. I dreamed about scorpions, sand vipers, and cobras. I longed for puff adders and mambas, the most dangerous snakes in Africa. Puff adders were fabulously poisonous. Mambas were reputed to attack on sight. My parents could do nothing about my obsession with poisonous things. "He apparently has mongoose blood," my mother wrote Bess. She is probably referring to my favorite Kipling story where Rikki-tikki-tavi, a mongoose, saves a child from a cobra. Whenever my father drove me anywhere in the car, I would take his snake-bite kit from the glove compartment and examine the fascinating contents—a white linen tourniquet, the bright little scalpel with which you sliced through the double puncture wound left by the snake's teeth, the red rubber suction bulb used to extract the poison, the pills you swallowed to keep your nervous system from seizing up.

While touring the town dump one afternoon, I saw a cobra emerging tail first from its hole next to a worker's bare foot and was briefly celebrated for having killed it before it bit him. Later, in Kimberley, a large cobra came into the bathroom while my sister and I were having our bath. As the reptile wriggled into the dirty-clothes hamper three feet away, we raised a cautious shout. Sitting naked in the tub, knowing this particular snake squirts poison into its attacker's eyes from six feet away, I was wise enough not to challenge it in the nude. My father soon arrived wearing dark glasses and riding boots, armed with a riding crop. He began to lift the clothes from the hamper one by one until he uncovered the snake. But before it could draw and strike, he crushed the head with a single blow—impressive for a man who insisted he was no good at sports.

The most exciting present I ever received in Oranjemund (aside from a bike which I preferred to my horse) was a German air rifle given me by Putzi Zeiler on my seventh birthday. My mother was afraid I would put out my sister's eye and hid it away. But I made her life miserable until she let me have it.

The gun fired pellets that were neatly packed in a round tin box painted blood red. Each pellet was molded in the form of a tiny lead shuttlecock. With the war on, Berlin was no longer supplying Oranjemund with ammunition for airguns, and no matter how I hoarded them my pellets were soon gone. So I was reduced once again to a stick and caty (catapult)—a slingshot made from the Y of an almost-impossible-to-find tree fork, and rubber strips cut from tire tubing.

Walking in the desert with three Afrikaner boys one afternoon, I pretended a sand viper had bit me and lay on the sand howling and holding my leg. The boys were so frightened that they ran away in tears to find my father. I jumped up and shouted that it was all a joke. But nothing could stop them.

Twenty minutes later (there was nowhere to run and hide) I saw my father's Chevy bounding across the desert like a mad thing, spewing sand in every direction. He leaped out of the car and came running toward me with an expression that terrified me. I had never seen him in such a state and had to repeat that I was a liar, a liar, I was lying, before he understood it would not be necessary to slice me open with the scalpel he was holding.

He drove me home without a word. I was too ashamed to look directly at him, but I could see his hand trembling on the steering wheel. When we pulled up next to the corrugated metal fence in front of the house, he switched off the engine and passed a hand over his face. Looking straight ahead, he said, "Please, don't ever, ever do that again!"

Both my mother and I took piano lessons from Frau Zeiler, who had wonderfully curved wrists. When she played, her fingers seemed hardly to touch the notes, and I decided that piano playing was a kind of magic, a gift that lay thousands of miles beyond the little arctic circle of my talent. The pieces I was given to play lay dead on the page. Frau Zeiler could bring them to life in an instant. I was astonished to find they stuck in my head, and I could pick them out by ear. This was extremely pleasant because it meant I didn't have to learn notes. So I immediately gave up the attempt. Instead I craftily got Frau Zeiler to play through all my pieces and used my ear instead of my brain to reproduce them. Her correction of my approximate renderings took the place of actual note reading. I could even improvise bits of pieces on my own and thus earn praise for doing nothing whatever. When I arrived in America five years later, I still could not convert the written symbols 3/4 and 4/4 into an internal sense of stressed beats. I was confined entirely to the music tintinnabulating within.

My mother confided to Bess that I was growing up "a complete backvelder" who spoke more Afrikaans than English and cared only for cobra killing. She tried to extend my interest in music by bringing home from Cape Town a child's gramophone. The records that came with the machine were mostly Mother Goose verses set to music. The awful thing is, I can still sing them today. These verses were performed by a pop singer of the time, a tenor with a thin, sexless voice—one of those lightly lipsticked young males who appear opposite marcelled blondes in Marx Brothers movies. This crooner was occasionally joined by a chorus of children squeaking in the background.

In Oranjemund, the desert wind sang a better kind of music. My father had installed electrical wiring in all the family houses, and every afternoon the wind turned the town into a giant aeolian harp. The sound expressed a desolation and longing, a plangent song that evoked worlds I imagined must exist in my future, the long life I had yet to live. I would press my ear against selected poles in town because each pole produced a unique hum, drone, or babble that rose and fell over the dull pedal point of the wind. The poles were brand-new and you had to be careful you didn't skewer an eardrum when you pressed your cheek against the yellow, splintered surface. But once your face was flat against the pole, the wind sang a song terrifying, sad, and full of yearning.

As for the little gray record player, it was not the total loss it seemed at first. Hidden among the Mother Goose records were a pair of disks of a different order. In one, a chorus sang "Land of Hope and Glory," which struck me as rich and gorgeous. The other was a puzzle, titled "Journey." It consisted of nothing but violins played in what I imagined must be total darkness. For some reason, I could never get enough of this strange music. I played it so often that the record soon wore out and the violins retreated into a hopeless, disorganized hissing.

This brief moment of music, these dark notes, assured me that somewhere in the world existed possibilities beyond my power to imagine. These sounds were like the promise of an inheritance, something I could count on. But the feelings the music raised were so far removed from conscious expression, so deeply buried, that it never occurred to me to ask my mother to bring me more music of this kind. And only now do I struggle for words to express emotions that were inaccessible then, like a fabulous city at the bottom of the sea.

A dozen years later, a few months after my mother had died, I went alone to a concert. When the conductor launched into the third movement of Brahms's Third, I knew at once what I was hearing and the music returned me in an instant to our house on the desert where I had squatted on the blue carpet and wound the handle on the gray gramophone. Again my mother arranged snapdragons and asters in a bright green vase on the table by the door, and again my small sister advanced with an armful of white flowers, which she held up. With the familiar welcoming smile that we took for granted, my mother bends to take the flowers. Behind her, through the glass panel in our front door, I see the tall bamboo in the garden tossing wildly in the afternoon wind, and the unnamed theme starts again. *Poco allegretto,* C minor: C,D,E-flat, and off we go, yes. Off we go.

21

The News from Cape Town

DID WE EVER GET ALL THE WAY TO CAPE TOWN BY CAR? WE MUST
have made the trip once at least. But no, my mother's letters never
mention it. And all I remember are breakdowns in the desert, tires
bursting, generators burning out, fuel pumps shattering, engines quitting, radiators vomiting jets of red rust and white steam. Temperatures were in excess of a hundred degrees, unless you drove along the
coast over broken cliffs that fronted the freezing black sea. Inland,
drifting dunes and roads slashed by corrugations doomed our trips
south. We never passed another vehicle.

There remains fixed in my mind the suspicion that no vehicle can
be trusted, that journeys aborted by breakdown are normal and every
trip may end in extreme discomfort with a moon bright as an interro-
gator's light keeping you from sleep. Equally fixed in my parent's
minds was the American dream of a family zipping along over smooth
highways on a carefree holiday. They were never quite ready for the

steam geyser under the hood, the thump of a broken axle, the car jerking to a stop. We would all gather around and stare at the sick machine while the sun banged on our backs like a fist. Did we really have to sit helpless in the breezeless heat while my father walked ten or twenty miles to the nearest garage or phone? No question.

Tying his handkerchief around his brow, pressing his good city hat in place, my father would disappear over the rim of the desert while my mother and I shoveled a foxhole under the car. It was the only shaded spot anywhere, unless you cared to bake to death in the backseat. And how cool those horizons looked with their heavenly blue mountains set in lakes of shimmering air! And how marvelously relaxed the vulture floating high overhead with his eye fixed hopefully on us.

Traveling at night made more sense. The car was less likely to overheat. In the road ahead, strange creatures suddenly appeared— mesmerized rabbits, jackals, the humpback shapes of hyenas with enormous eyes alight, like the reflectors on a bicycle. But soon the road would degenerate into a boulder-strewn track, and when the car no longer cared to move, the sudden silence would gradually fill with the sound of insects. After my father had trudged off, we would try to sleep, sitting like Egyptian effigies among our suitcases. Overhead, the moon edged into position and shone its light directly through the windshield into my mother's eyes. In the backseat, the fruit boxes tortured my sister and me. Unable to sleep, we at last unloaded everything out on the sand. My sister would then fit herself neatly on the shelf under the back window while I curled up on the backseat. My mother would once again wedge herself under the steering wheel to escape the moon, but the vile satellite would sail into perfect position and shine like a searchlight against her lids. Forced to get away from its light, she stretched out on the shadow side of the car to sleep in the sand, muttering, "To hell with snakes."

Around first light, a vehicle would arrive to pick us up—a grease-saturated garage truck or a motorcycle with sidecar. And somehow we wrestled all our baggage to the train station. The car would be abandoned. We'd board the train because no carburetors for Lincoln Zephyrs were to be found anywhere in Springbok, Nababiep, Okiep, Bitterfontein, Komkans, Vanrhynsdorp.

My father usually drove a company Chevrolet with balloon tires, but the car I remember best is Van Zyl's Lincoln Zephyr. Van Zyl was the Chief of Police, a tall, kindly man with a magisterial nose. Years later, my sister told me she was in love with him (aged six). He was a fine horseman and I remember him once mounting a horse that had just thrown my father into a pile of rocks and riding the bucking animal until he wore it out.

In my view, the most attractive thing about Van Zyl was his pet monkey. But why he had bought that Lincoln Zephyr none of us could figure out. The machine had been designed to hum through the suburbs of Connecticut or Bucks County, Pennsylvania, on silky smooth concrete. Our desert soon showed the miserable machine up for what it was—a concept, not a car. The frustration and extreme discomfort Van Zyl's Zephyr caused us has permanently scarred my appreciation of cars in general, and I have been unable to look at any Lincoln since without feeling a certain irrational contempt.

It was this worthless art object of Van Zyl's that my father borrowed to cross some of the worst roads in the world. And he borrowed it not once, but three times. The Zephyr not only broke down; it made sleep absolutely impossible. The molded seats, the fashionable curves, the extruding door handles, every internal detail was beautifully designed to support the human body in a bolt upright position. My mother (we all learned to hate it) said it was an automobile created "for show-offs." And while she tried to find some comfortable position under the steering wheel, she cursed the thieves in Cape Town who had unloaded this torture chamber on a naive South African policeman.

After abandoning the Zephyr in a sand dune, we traveled to Nuwerus in a motorcycle sidecar. From there we took the train to squalid Bitterfontein or Garies to wait for someone to fish the car out of the desert for repairs. To while away the hours, we read to each other, or blew bubbles in the courtyards of sun-baked hotels. I flew balsa wood airplanes while my sister toddled off with my mother in search of fruit stands. Parts for a Lincoln Zephyr were no more available in the real world than in dreams. It was necessary to phone Johannesburg, Pretoria, or even Léopoldville in the Congo. Then we lugged our suitcases back to the station and took the train south, having lost at least two days of our precious twelve-day vacation.

Once, after loading our baggage on board, we were told there would be a two-hour delay. So we wandered off for a ramble around the town. But the train suddenly felt better and lurched off without us. My parents treated the whole thing as a joke and two days later we finally caught up with the baggage in Cape Town. There must have been moments when my parents lost their tempers, but I don't recall any. I remember no shouting in public, no bellowing in private, no embarrassing scenes in hotels, railway stations, or isolated roads. Only later, after my mother's death, did I realize they were the exception, hardly the rule. My mother's temper grew short when her allergies flared up, or her eyes were infected, or the cyst on her tooth caused her pain. But she never made us feel her discomfort was our fault.

As for my father, when I was older and knew enough to be confused, he would seem to me remote. But I do believe he was the most even-tempered man I have ever known. I recall seeing him flare up only half a dozen times. Engines exploding in the desert, twenty mile hikes under the furious sun, weekends in Bitterfontein or Garies were simply aspects of the inevitable, and he knew nothing came easy.

My sister and I had no clue that families are so often prison cells of repression and fury. I had no clue about how profoundly her family in Seattle unsettled my mother. We were aware that her brother Nick and his pretty wife, Rene, had impressive tempers, that she hurled china plates at him. But we knew that kind of thing could never happen in our family. Like many people with a highly developed moral intelligence, my mother's judgments somehow carried no guilt. She didn't approve of the way Nick ran his life, but it was his life and she had done what she could to improve it, so there it ended. Trust conscience, don't listen to guilt.

We were still in Oranjemund when Mari stopped writing. My mother fired off letters to Nick, to Leslie, to John, to Emil, who was now seventeen. She got no replies. So she asked Bess to investigate. She guessed that something terrible was happening to her mother. She had expected it. It had been a relief to have Petar festering away on the other side of the planet, but the thought of her mother living with the little monster always nagged her.

Growing up with her stepfather, my mother learned disobedience early. She discarded piety and humility and the Catholic church. She plumped for energy, wit, elusiveness. She wrote Haroldine soon after my sister's birth, "Yes, I think our daughters will have more fun than either of us did, always being repressed and suppressed. I never had any unalloyed fun till I got away from home and got married." For her "fun" was linked to being expressive; it was allied with art.

It was her strategy to feed us the disorder of the world in carefully regulated amounts, a spoonful at a time. When we were grown and had to take the poison straight, then our systems might withstand the shock. We would presumably not shrivel into romantic escape artists or moral cripples. So it was as if each year of our childhood she drew a circle on the surface of the world. And within that circle we had perfect freedom to toddle about and bump our heads. Outside that circle lay the great Terra Incognita of the future. My mother's genius lay in knowing exactly how much to expand the circle and how to convince us that within that ring we already had more work than we could handle.

I see my childhood from this present distance as a feast of reason, the opposite of her life with Petar. After our glorious last Christmas in Kleinzee, the toy supply dried up because she saw no reason for us to have more than the Afrikaners in Oranjemund. So we made our own playthings from sticks, rags, rubber bands, abandoned wheels. Books were the great exception. Our advantages were plain. I could ride a horse. (Only one other boy, Phillip Broughton, had a horse.) Once, when I behaved in a lordly manner with some other children, she took me into the bedroom and gave me a dressing down I will never forget. We might look and sound English, but we must never forget we are American.

My mother had the freedom of a disobedient daughter, but her freedom was controlled by a very sharp intelligence. She often picked up people who interested her. She collected them in hotel lobbies, on trains and boats. Signs that said Keep Out attracted her. Police-men were helpless around her. She bought packets of strawberries and shared them with us behind the backs of museum guards. Make your own rules, but only if your rules are more stringent than the rules you break. If you eat strawberries in a museum, leave behind less mess than those who do as they are told.

In 1940, cannibal Europe was disintegrating while everything seemed to be coming together for us in the desert. I could gallop about on Hans all day without getting tired. My sister had stopped mixing up her languages and had decided she was English after all. My father was told repeatedly how much Ernest Oppenheimer approved of his progress. The possibility of a glorious future was discussed around the dinner table. My sister and I might possibly be educated in America and live as citizens of the world, like the Parkinson children. My parents were frustrated by the blind American isolationism while Hitler calmly gobbled up one European country after another.

Having secured Oranjemund and dealt with the Nazi problem, having raised the efficiency of the mine to levels the people in Kimberley at first refused to believe, my father assumed the best. But fate once again shunted my father off on a branching line going nowhere.

It was, for some reason, in Cape Town that my parents always got the worst news.

I well remember the total eclipse of the sun that took place in October of that year in Namaqualand. I peered at the fading star through a piece of smoked glass while the town and all its houses turned a sinister burned brown. Two days later Pietjie Bloom, child of one of the poorest families in town, threw a peanut butter jar in my sister's face and killed her two front teeth. The teeth began to turn black a few days later.

That same month, while we were getting ready for a trip to Cape Town, my parents got word that Nick and Rene in Rhodesia had lost Peter, their son. The baby was given another patient's medicine by mistake and died in an hour. I began to grow very quickly, like Alice in Wonderland, lost my coordination, became anemic, and picked up a cough that wouldn't go away. My mother added vitamins and orange juice in cod-liver oil to my diet. But the chest problem turned into whooping cough. My loyal sister immediately picked it up so we could whoop together.

We had some of the hottest days ever recorded in Namaqualand that November and my sister got better while I grew worse. The cyst in my mother's eye bloomed. She had to see the specialist in Cape Town and decided we must go with her. So we all piled into the Lincoln Zephyr and drove south. The Zephyr gave up after three hundred miles on a road that consisted mostly of boulders the size of human heads.

Arriving in Cape Town after the usual hikes, phone calls, and hours waiting for trains, we signed into a pleasant hotel in Fish Hoek. Our room overlooked a beach with white sand and palms. But the weather had turned cold and a vicious sky was filling with rain. Still whooping away, I was made to drink ever taller glasses of juice and cod-liver oil, a concoction I grew to hate and to associate with sadness, love, debility, and death. My mother insisted I spend my first day in bed. From the window I could see the waves below our hotel seductively sliding across the beach. The next day I said I felt wonderful and wobbled down to join my sister in the cold breeze.

I felt shivery and heavy-headed, but stayed in the water all day, even after my sister sensibly marched back to the hotel, after warning me that I had "a bad chest" and should keep warm. My mother was at the doctor's and then went off with my father shopping for a musk-rat fur. Arriving back just before dinner, she took one look at my blue face, said "You're a fool!" and bundled me into bed.

By morning I had a fever that rose ever higher while my parents ran around looking for a thermometer and tried to phone a doctor. But it was Sunday and the town was closed up tight. All the doctors in Cape Town were at church or having lunch or playing golf or inexplicably elsewhere. By noon I had lost consciousness.

I was dimly aware of my father wrapping me in a blanket and lugging me down to a waiting taxi. They drove me to the Simons-town Naval Base, where a Doctor Lowenthal (the twentieth person they had phoned) had agreed to interrupt his lunch and take a look at me.

Meeting us at the security gate in order to get us past the guard, he looked puzzled. "They told me you were Coloured people," he said. "It must have been the accent."

I was carried to a room high above False Bay. Through a wide window I saw a flotilla of gray ships stretching to the horizon. The British fleet had chosen that moment to get away from the war and prepare for the coming battle. For some minutes I clung to conscious-ness, wishing to gaze out at the dark ships dotted about under pale clouds. But my lungs were full of liquid and my chest rattled like dice in a box.

I was dipping in and out of sleep when the red-haired nurse led in an alcoholic cockney with a long, veiny nose and unsteady legs. He was delighted to find himself rooming with a child and immediately began to entertain me by imitating a bagpiper, pinching his nose tightly shut and simulating the nasal drone while he smartly whacked his adam's apple with the side of his free hand. Marching up and down next to my bed with a tottering step, he wheezed out a highland battle song until the red-haired nurse wrestled him into bed, and as she tried to disentangle herself from his embrace, he gave me a conspiratorial wink and faded away with my consciousness.

When I opened my eyes seventy hours later and asked for my mother, her smiling face appeared immediately and I felt her hand on my wet forehead. When I asked for the bagpiper the nurse said he was dead. And I would have been dead, too, had it not been for the British fleet anchored in the bay. Those warships had brought one of the first consignments of the new sulfa drug to South Africa. Hearing that there was MB693 available out in the bay, Dr. Lowenthal had somehow got his hands on enough to keep me from joining the cockney bagpiper on his march to the underworld.

On the journey home, we picked up the Zephyr in Bitterfontein, but it broke down around midnight. My father walked fifteen miles in brilliant moonlight to the nearest town, accompanied by a chortle of hyenas. Back in Oranjemund he found the work force full of complaints. The war had siphoned off the young, and those left were "becoming truculent. I just about have to let them have their own way in everything," my father complained to Bess. "A couple of days ago I narrowly averted having ten or so quit in a body by doing a bit of fast log rolling."

Two weeks after our return, my dog Frankie was run over by the carpenter's truck, and with Frankie no longer around to carry them, I lost the new shoes I'd brought back from Cape Town. And shortly after that a sweater my mother had hand knitted. (The moment you put an object down it disappeared under the blowing sand). In those days, what you lost could never be replaced without sacrifice, and my mother vowed never to knit for me again.

A dentist in Cape Town had extracted my sister's two front teeth and for the next two years, every time the little girl smiled, my mother would be reminded of that detested "little savage" Pietjie Bloom. Patsy then compounded Pietjie's slight to her beauty by gashing a hole through her upper lip. Standing upright in a rocking chair and violently hurtling back and forth, she lost control and flew face first into a bedboard. Her shrieks brought my father running. He assumed I had pushed her and was furious. My poor sister had to protest my innocence with her mouth full of blood.

Her fall had forced an eyetooth out of line, and it took twelve stitches to sew up the gash. She was no sooner patched up than I slipped and almost fell into a cauldron of boiling water while playing tag on the rooftops of the outbuildings behind Phillip Broughton's house. I had the brilliant idea of taking a shortcut across the laundry boiler. The lid tipped and I saved myself from total immersion by employing a combination of brute fear and forward momentum. Seizing the roof overhang, I hauled myself out. But my left leg had been immersed halfway up the thigh and turned a bright pink while I howled for my mother. Mrs. Broughton, meanwhile, poured cod-liver oil over the leg. I demanded that my mother slop unguentine over me as well. She used to mix the stuff herself, and I regarded it as a magic elixer. But only Doctor Behne's morphine finally dissolved the monstrous pain.

A month later, digging in a dune, my friend Theo Fourie almost put out my eye with a shovel when I leaned over to see what he was doing. Five stitches closed the gash. I was back with Doctor Behne a month later, after jumping off a shed and driving a large spike through my bare foot. A series of tetanus shots followed. "Every time I go out of town he has another accident," my mother complained to Bess. "By the time he's grown, he will resemble the hunchback of Notre Dame, but what can I do about it?"

After pneumonia had nearly carried me off, our stay in Cape Town was extended until I was strong enough to make it back through the desert. On the day we finally left, my mother received a letter from

Bess with news that Mari had lost her mind and been institutionalized. My mother was furious with her brothers for not writing. But
the family had long since disintegrated. John, the eldest, was in a
submarine. Seventeen-year-old Emil, the youngest, was soon to head
for the South Pacific where he would survive the Battle of Truk Island. Leslie was embroiled in a divorce and no longer spoke to his
father.

My mother wrote Bess from Cape Town: "I've only just two
minutes to spare, writing this at a counter on the day we're leaving
here. I wanted to get this off to tell you that if my letters from home
seem stilted it's because I know the censor, and they know us, so
naturally any family business, anything pertaining to Mom, I want to
keep out as much as possible. I like our family affairs to be kept
strictly among ourselves. You may write whatever you like, as your
letters are censored here in Cape Town. Please give me all the details
of Mother's condition. What nursing home is she in? Is she improving? When did you last see her? Please don't have anything to do
with Petar. He has lost his mind long ago and is not responsible for
what he does or says. I'm terribly sorry for Emil. I wish he was away
from home.

"I'm glad the USA is in it boots and all [America had just declared
war on Germany], but this development has put a monkey wrench in
our plans. So I don't know when we shall see you. We got quite a
fright when we heard about Jap bombers over San Francisco. We've
had a lovely, short holiday, leaving tonight. The damned car broke
down again."

Back in Oranjemund, my parents found a letter from the consul
in Cape Town in their mailbox. My mother was informed that she
was, technically speaking, an immigrant to America. Congress had
just passed the new Nationality Act. With war finally declared, the
congress was enthusiastically packing off Japanese Americans
to camps and declaring every naturalized U.S. citizen five years
absent from the country a permanent alien. Having arrived on Ellis

Island, aged six, she was now informed she must either go home or join the throngs of other stateless persons who traveled without passports.

That same week came the worst news. Park told my father that, despite earlier promises, he was no longer being considered for general manager of the west coast region. Sir Ernest had decided to put another man in charge, the younger brother of Kimberley G.M., Donald McHardy. The younger McHardy was a mechanic by trade. He had been with De Beers forty years. He appeared a few weeks later, a listless, shifty-eyed man who sniffed before he spoke. He moved into the company office in Lüderitz, and the office staff soon began referring to him as "Mac Hardly."

My mother wrote Bess, "He's about as charming as plug tobacco and he's moving to Oranjemund next, so Gus was asked to build him a house. He has absolutely no ideas on how he wants the place built. He just picked out a plan from several drafted and says, 'Do this one.' No alterations, no additions! So Park and Gus got together and put together a darned good house for him. I suppose he'll complain about it once it's done. Behind Gus's back he complains that he's never shown anything. Yet when he comes out here, once a month, he just walks around and never opens his mouth, never asks a question. We aren't the only ones who can't stand him. He's never been known to keep his word. Makes a lot of promises, never says no directly. Since he was going to Cape Town to see the company agent, we asked him to get us a new hot-water heater. Six months, and not a word. Finally, I asked him about it. 'Oh, yes, I've just got the quotation,' he says. But when I saw the agent in Cape Town a few weeks later the man didn't know a thing about it. McHardy had never asked for a quotation, much less ordered a heater."

My father had no reason now to remain loyal to De Beers, but he was always more liable to blame himself when others let him down. Why hadn't he seen this coming? Why did he always discover too late that he was gullible, blind, foolish? He was worried about my mother's status with American immigration. In six months, the consul said, she would probably be denied entry into her own country. So they made plans to return to America in May 1942.

Before we left Oranjemund, my mother drew together the strands of her accomplishment there and with the schoolteacher and Frau Zeiler, the pianist, put together a stage show that involved every child in town. The new recreation building my father had designed was easily converted into a theater with a large stage. The billiards rooms and conference chambers were turned into dressing rooms. The evening included a three-act play depicting the victory of a good fairy over an evil witch, and a series of dances drawn from various nations of the world. My mother choreographed the dances and helped Mrs. Fourie design thirty costumes. Every afternoon, children came in after school to learn their steps and rehearse lines. The first rehearsals began in late August.

Small English boys with twig legs danced with buxom Afrikaner girls twice their size. The carpenter's son learned the trepak, a Ukrainian dance, and my sister was the smallest in an ensemble of Japanese. That Japan had just attacked the United States didn't seem to affect my mother's choice in the matter. Many of the children spoke very little English, and getting an Afrikaner of any age to loosen up and flow with the music was, as my mother said, "like getting Mohammed into a church."

The most difficult child in town was Pietjie Bloom, infamous for having knocked out the teeth of the manager's daughter. Even though my mother had described him as "a little guttersnipe" and "a barbarian," she included him in the program. But Pietjie remained elusive. So she went to visit his mother.

The Bloom house on the south edge of town had degenerated into a kind of wind-blasted skeleton structure, with cracked windows and a door that would not close properly. Vrou Bloom was a gaunt, narrow-eyed woman with a body like a tree in winter. Her husband drove a truck, as I recall. Whatever the case, he was seldom in town. When Pietjie misbehaved, his mother stuffed him into a gunnysack and hung him on the clothesline. If the offense was rank, he was left to dangle all night. The diggers would amuse themselves by shouting "Pietjie, the sack!" and laugh when he sprinted away like a terrified rabbit. I visited his house occasionally and was offered lukewarm coffee laced with condensed milk and stale brown bread spread with yellow lard.

Vrou Bloom told my mother she didn't want Pietjie involved in the theater pageant. He would only make trouble. She didn't want his big sister, Myra, on stage either. But Myra went secretly to my mother and begged her to go back and speak again to Vrou Bloom. So my mother told Vrou Bloom that she needed Myra badly. In fact, the success of the play depended on Myra. Thus fortified, Myra was allowed to appear in the play. She was given the part of the evil witch and stole the show.

My sister and I were handed minor roles. I was cast in a group of six boys serving as messengers of the good fairy, played by the lovely Myra Fourie (another Myra). My fellow owls were all Afrikaners, and we wore owl masks which made us anonymous. In the dance part of the program, Myra Fourie and Myra Bloom appeared in the morris dance with two other big girls. In their bright green, yellow, and blue silk Victorian gowns, they looked like creatures from Oz.

Beside the Japanese dance and the Russian Cossack dance, there was a gypsy dance, an Eskimo dance, and a Scandinavian dance. I was given a chance to show off in the Dutch dance, but I had never felt less inspired. My partner was a frail Afrikaner—a tiny blonde who looked even skimpier after she donned her heavy wooden clog shoes. Her name has been erased from memory. We never smiled, we never spoke, and I was obliged to palpate her goosefleshy, pale arm and hold her cold, bony little hand as we wobbled and circled unsteadily in our enormous wooden shoes. I was no less distasteful to her. The moment rehearsal was over we turned our backs on each other and clumped off to opposite sides of the room.

There is a 16mm shot my father made of the little blonde Afrikaner and me at the afternoon dress rehearsal. I kneel in a bright shaft of sunlight waiting for my partner to turn and acknowledge my existence. She is dressed in a brilliant yellow dress and lace collar and chats with a friend just long enough to let me know how unimportant I am. The shy smile on my face belies the irritation and shame I feel.

So our dance, despite all my mother's patience and goodwill, was a spiritless sham. I had already mastered the art of making lazy recalcitrance look like hopeless ineptitude. Not even my mother's genius for wringing water from rocks could enliven our spiritless clodhopping. What remains crystal clear in memory is the music, and the words of the Afrikaner song we danced to. "Jan Piriwit, Jan Piriwit, Jan Piriwit stand still [repeated] / Good morning, my wife, here's a little kiss for you / Good morning, my husband, there is coffee in the pot."

Mrs. Fourie, the costumer, loved fine detail. The Japanese had black wigs and kimonos. The three Eskimos wore real skins from the slaughterhouse. On the evening of the performance, my mother made up every child's face herself. The whole town turned out and the hall was packed. Only Mrs. Bloom stayed away although everyone agreed her daughter was the hit of the show. I doubt Oranjemund ever saw the like again. Facing a live audience, we all did our best to break through the totemic mask that substitutes for the human face in persons denied access to the power of make-believe.

Some of the magic did rub off. For weeks after it was over I saw children executing queer little skips and jumps on their way to school. Myra Bloom came to our house and went into the bedroom with my mother, where I heard her weeping bitterly. She was furious with her mother. She hated her father. She was ashamed of her brother. She felt caged, trapped. She wanted to be somebody. She wanted to be an actress. But she knew it was impossible. Did Mrs. Pifer think it was possible? Could Mrs. Pifer make it possible?

I don't know what my mother said to her. During the rehearsals,

I saw her embrace Myra often. I remember her praising Myra Bloom, letting people know Myra was the most talented young woman in Oranjemund. Perhaps Myra reminded her of herself. But she had lived in Seattle where, no matter how provincial the city, there was still hope. It was already too late for Myra. The Americans were leaving.

When my parents drove out of town, all the children had books they could read and fresh milk—if their parents were willing to ask for it. My mother's hen house was taken over by the company kitchen. The four thousand books she had accumulated for the library were handed over to the schoolteacher to administer. I wonder if three or four of those volumes still remain out there in the desert today. My father knew all he had accomplished. But he considered himself a fool for having ever taken Sir Ernest seriously, because the chairman had sent a fool to replace him.

He wrote Bess, "I now take all [the company's] promises as just so much soft soap to keep me on the works. I am the only senior mining engineer in the group outside of the Consulting Engineer's Office. But you know how it is when a family gets control of a firm. I can see I am stumped in my present position for the next five to ten years. I am not satisfied to remain here that long. This is the time to make a change."

In Cape Town, they looked for a ship that would get us home before my mother's citizenship rights were revoked. But the Atlantic was infested with German subs and the American Navy would not allow women and children on any American ship. The only ships available were slow Portuguese freighters, booked a year in advance. America was in the war, as my mother put it, "boots and all." So my father found himself unemployed, stuck in Cape Town, and unable to get out of Africa.

We spent weeks in Cape Town living in an airy hotel with a view of Table Mountain. My sister and I played all day on a stony hill under eucalyptus trees. Residential streets sloped toward the sea, bearing pale houses and long lines of palm trees downhill. We visited beaches and bookstores and never dreamed that father was spending his days vainly attempting to find some way of getting home before we ran out of money and options. Our parents never let us know that our mother was on the verge of losing her citizenship. They had by then developed the art of the possible to its utmost refinement. My father's letters express some anxiety, but it was just one more holiday as far as my sister and I were concerned.

The anxiety in Cape Town was of a piece with the calm that continued like fine spring weather throughout our childhood. As long as we downed our spinach and got to bed at eight, there was nothing to get upset over. My mother took us out to the beach at Muizenberg. We visited the old Dutch wine plantations at Stellenbosch. My father used up what was left of his color film.

Meanwhile, back in Kimberley, the gentlemen who ran De Beers woke up one morning to find they had no mine managers left. It had not occurred to Sir Ernest Oppenheimer that the war might leave him short of experienced men. Park said later that Sir Ernest never really planned for anything "more than two weeks in advance." He respected markets, not engineers.

Ziervogel, the only man in Kimberley capable of running a large diamond mine efficiently, had suddenly gone off with his reserve unit to fight in the Italian campaign. Park was obliged to inform Sir Ernest that he was now stuck with the two biggest diamond mines in the world and no one to run them. There was one person, yes, but he was leaving for America as soon as he could find a Portuguese tub that would allow his family on board.

Sir Ernest told Park to cable my father and ask if he was willing to take a job in Kimberley.

When he got the telegram, my father was more pleased than he wanted to be. He had become very reluctant to book passage on a Portuguese ship and cross the Atlantic at seven knots with ships sinking every day off Gibraltar. For the first time in his life, he found himself in a bargaining position, and he demanded a higher salary than he thought the company would agree too. His demand was met by return telegram.

Later, after raising production fifty percent in Kimberley and watching the wartime inflation eat up his savings, he would conclude that he had miscalculated again. He would say that while he made millions for the directors and stockholders, his salary was pegged to a dead letter. He would wish he'd had the sense to link his income to the rise in production. But once again he had played the fool, and he would arrive in Seattle without money for the down payment on a fifteen thousand dollar house. The feeling that he could never get ahead, the feeling that he never knew enough to outfox the crowd he longed to join, a sense of almost-but-not-quite would dog him to the end of his life.

22

Nick

On the trip to Kimberley, we paused for two weeks in Johannesburg to visit Nick and Rene. Nick was the same—handsome, loose-limbed, jovial—but Rene's beauty had faded. She was changed. I had always thought of her as the Rene I knew on the day of her marriage, when my mother had pressed me (aged four) into service as a page. Dressed in white shoes and a silk shirt with two enormous buttons that held up my velveteen shorts, I followed the bride down the aisle hoisting the train of her silk gown.

Later, she came with Nick to Oranjemund for a visit to show us her new baby, Peter. Again, it is Rene I remember and not my uncle. I discovered her in my bedroom feeding her infant, with the blinds drawn against the glare and wind outside. She told me to go somewhere else, but I heard the little cricket sounds of the child feeding at her breast. Peter died eighteen months later.

All through the war, her parents' letters to my mother lamented their daughter's impatient, fidgety nature, her inability to settle for something sensible. She looked to them like a material girl, but I think she never really recovered from the death of her child.

That year we paused in Johannesburg, Rene was still haunted by Peter's ghost. A volatile mix of fussy affection and abrupt irritation, she discreetly sipped scotch whiskey to get herself through the long mornings. Afternoons, she shopped with money Nick claimed he didn't have. She longed for a life that was affluent and merry. But her existence had lost its center. She would walk into the middle of a room and forget why she had come. She chain-smoked, with jerky little motions, blowing the smoke out the side of her mouth and darting distracted glances out the window. Nick's aggressive good cheer aggravated her. He didn't want her brooding over Peter's death. He believed in putting the past out of mind and getting on with life. Each had blamed the other for their child's death, though neither was to blame. They had said terrible things to each other. Peter had been in the hospital for a little fever, nothing serious.

Rene could not forget how a careless nurse had casually killed her child by administering the wrong medicine. Not long after Peter's death, she was told she was barren and could not have another baby. An early photograph shows Rene looking at Nick adoringly while he poses, barrel-chested and mighty-armed, in front of a little waterfall. She no longer admired him. Five years had turned two beautiful people into a bitter, middle-aged couple.

There exist a few feet of film my father took of Rene about this time. She sits puffy-faced and plain, absorbed in a book. Aware suddenly of the peering camera, her eyes and mouth fly open in a kind of clockwork horror. She screams with laughter and slaps the book over her face. And Rene vanishes.

She and Nick adopted a little boy to make up for Peter. They named him John. But no one could replace her own golden child. During one of their quarrels, Rene furiously smashed her fist through a window and severed an artery. Bitterness and fury overwhelmed the marriage, which dissolved in a rain of flying dishes and hurled chairs. Fifteen years after the divorce, John was killed in a traffic accident.

My ninth birthday was celebrated with Nick and Rene the July we left Oranjemund. After the dry heat of the desert, the winter cold entranced me. Each morning the lawn was covered with a carpet of ice crystals that glittered fabulously in the first light, and I would go out to turn on the faucet in the yard and shoot long dowels of silver ice from the garden hose. Johannesburg was swathed in a blue haze with a fruity, penetrating odor. It was my first whiff of smog. I found it as exotic as fine perfume and associated the smell with freedom and far horizons.

My mother organized a birthday party for me, and Rene invited over some of the neighbor kids. They sat around the table wearing paper hats, stuffing cake in their mouths, staring at me, too shy to speak. The washerwoman's son was much more interesting. He was a boy my own age who could walk on his hands. He had a sly sense of humor, and his acrobatic skill seemed to me admirable and useful. He taught me the trick, and we practiced under the kitchen window where, from time to time, Rene's face appeared upside down.

When she could stand it no longer, my aunt came out and told me she would very much like to see me in the house. She informed me that I was not to play with the children of servants. She did not want to see me near that boy again. I don't recall my reply. I do remember stealing a big handful of her cigarettes from a silver box on the mantelpiece. These I took to the washerwoman's son, and we smoked them all at one go in the back alley. He felt fine. I lay down under a bush to recover.

Rene didn't miss the cigarettes but caught me down the alley walking on my hands with the washerwoman's boy and asked my mother to deal with me. I was requested to join them in the living room.

My mother wore her attentively listening face, her lips slightly pursed, eyebrows slightly raised, eyes slightly down, not focused on anything in particular. "After all, we do have the neighbors to consider!" said Rene, twitching and blowing smoke.

"Of course you do," said my mother.

"He should be told it is not done," insisted Rene. "Because it is not right, and I assume you do not want him playing with nigger boys, do you?"

"He's listening," said my mother, laying her hand lightly on my shoulder and pulling me slightly toward her.

My mother's slight smile said the opposite of what Rene may have thought. So I went right on playing with the washerwoman's son until I could walk on my hands—a skill which proved far more useful than most of the things I would soon be asked to learn.

Because my friendship with an African child seemed to her a scandal, Rene now stands out in my memory more clearly than Nick, whose cheerful optimism I experienced as a kind of absence. In the old days when he lived with us, Nick's affection for me (my mother's letters report) was intense. But after his marriage, he lived far away. We were told that Rene hurled pots and plates at him. This made them objects of intense interest. In our company, however, the couple were disappointingly well behaved.

Nick would be father (or stepfather) to seven children. Only two survived. I think this uncle absorbs me because he so passionately refused to admit the existence of darkness that he drew its attention to him. He insisted on a life that unrolled like a Hollywood film where disasters never affect the hero and death is little more than a smooth glide into the next scene. Nick banked on hard work, perpetual motion, and making his own luck. He was an exemplary survivor. But, somehow, those left in his care did not survive.

After his screaming divorce from Rene, my uncle married Peggy, an expert swimmer and tennis player. She was sweet tempered and graceful. But, after some years, she suffered an aneurism that affected her ability to speak. She was teaching herself to use words again when Nick came down with cancer in 1972.

His death was long and hard. My father had died the previous year. A lifetime had passed since our last glimpse of Nick, but his death seems to me emblematic of what happened in the years after we left. Nick had moved to Rhodesia shortly before the roads were besieged by guerrilla fighters and the country was renamed Zimbabwe. Living in Salisbury (Harare), Nick transformed himself from a mine manager and prospector (hired by the presidents of spanking new African nations) into the wealthy owner of three liquor stores. His most profitable establishment (in the poorest section of black Salisbury) was managed by a boisterous South African, Ivy Joliet.

Visiting Nick in the hospital, Ivy found found him dying. A severe surgical procedure had left him unable to digest hospital food. She saved his life by feeding him papaw fruit. He recovered, started up an affair with the woman, and moved her into his house with her two children, big Mike and little Kim. Peggy was still there with her children by Nick, Patricia and Leslie.

Ivy was outspoken and greedy for life. Peggy's children detested her. Peggy, who could only speak with great difficulty, begged Nick to make Ivy leave. Nick ordered the two women to work out their own domestic arrangement. He was concerned with beating his cancer and would not waste energy on settling female squabbles.

Driven away by Ivy's loud vulgarity, Peggy fled to Cape Town with Patricia and Leslie. The children refused to have anything more to do with their father. Ivy, with her booming voice and powerful thighs, demanded that Nick divorce Peggy and marry her. Failing that, she expected to be written into his will. She had saved his life; he owed her everything. She was, moreover, still taking care of him and wanted a reward. She kept after him; but the harder she pressed, the more jovial he became, as if her rapacity and angry opportunism gave him energy to go on.

Nick busied himself writing long letters home full of apocalyptic foreboding. These missives were carefully filed in boxes by his brother Leslie, back in Seattle. "I have seen Africa which is a beautiful country brought to ruin and nothing but tragedy for the African people of the future. This has all been caused by Russia . . . playing on the ignorance of the African uncivilized people."

Living in a mansion that once had housed the West German embassy, my uncle was troubled by visions of childlike Africans handing the keys of their jungle kingdom to wily communists. It depressed him that American politicians refused to see how South Africa alone was staving off the Russian wolves circling Africa.

"The Africans in South Africa have gained considerably since I first entered the country. I am of the opinion that the only hope to save the West and the Free Countries is for the United States to support South Africa and move into Simonstown Naval Base."

He adds, "Apartheid may not be a good thing in the eyes of other countries, but this is purely a domestic policy and is not doing the Africans any harm."

Like Joseph Conrad's Kurtz in *Heart of Darkness*, Nick came to believe that the people least suited to control Africa were the Africans. He harps repeatedly on the inadequacy of the black man: "The African Negro just has not the I.Q. or intelligence to learn skilled trades. In my opinion it may take another 1 or 3 centurys [sic] for the African mind to develop."

Thirty years earlier, my uncle had lived with us in Nigel and observed African miners under my father's instruction take more readily to advanced mining techniques than their white Afrikaner overseers. He had watched Fleisher try to destroy my father on that very account. But the lesson had never registered. And, just as superstition twisted the medieval mind, so racism darkened the perception of my modern uncle. His world was an imaginary one where he tilted at windmills.

In 1956, Nick had been hired as manager of the Modderfontein Gold Mine. I have one of his reports, which lists the wages of Europeans versus Africans for a gold milling and clean-up job: 77 Europeans earn £4,891; 522 Africans earn £2,400. Thus the African earns

£4.60 versus £63.52 for the European. The African wage is 7 percent of the European. The effect of such disparity on motivation was never a part of Nick's analysis.

In 1978, the doctors informed Nick he would be dead in six months. He lived on to endure chemotherapy and thirteen major operations. His thick black hair fell out and grew back pure white. He outlived three of his doctors. He thrived in Ivy's energetic hectoring. When John, his oldest brother, visited him in 1980, he heard the big woman bellowing from a window upstairs, "Write your will, Nick! Write your bloody will!"

Nick's will became such an obsession with Ivy that she went to court and had her name legally changed to his—Joliet to Martincevic. But all she had done was saddle herself with a name that no one could pronounce or spell. Her furious greed grew greater as he weakened. Near the end, Les's daughter, Joan, came for a visit. She arrived after Ivy was gone, and it was Joan he wrote into his will.

After ten years of frustration, sure that he would never make her his wife, Ivy drove a rented truck up to the house while Nick was in the hospital and, with the help of Helen, her shrewish daughter-in-law, moved out every stick of furniture (five bedroom sets included), all the silverware (save for six cocktail forks), and everything else she could lay her hands on. When Nick returned he found nothing except his clothes. Nick went out with Ashwell, his old African servant, to buy new furniture.

An ileostomy, and then a colostomy, kept him going. Ignoring the cancer that was removing his vital organs one by one, he flew around the veld in his little airplane with Ashwell. Then about forty, Ashwell had been with him since the age of fourteen, longer than any wife or child.

When Nick was dying, his brother Leslie jetted from Seattle to Salisbury and found the house taken over by a retinue of parasites. He compares it to a Hollywood film. He arrived to find them all at dinner while, upstairs, their absent host writhed in his own excrement. Included around the festive board were Helen, Ivy's charming but bad-tempered daughter-in-law, and her phlegmatic husband, a local cop. Though Ivy had carted away everything Nick owned, her son and his wife had mysteriously returned and were occupying the bedroom that housed the best new furniture. A pair of German women who shopped for Nick were there, and a minister of the church, who said he was present to administer spiritual comfort to the afflicted.

The minister (Les later realized) had calmly funneled American dollars mailed to Nick into his own bank account back in America. Leslie cleaned Nick up and made him as comfortable as he could, then took a turn around the vast rose garden. The garden struck him as paradisial. He walked back into the house and found Helen on the stair hoisting a chair. She was moving all the furniture in her room into a van parked out back. Leslie insisted that she return it, that she move everything in the van back into her room. She bared her teeth and hissed at him, but complied when he lost his temper.

During his last weeks, Nick's brain was affected by the disease. He had wrestled for twelve years, had been told three times he had only six months to live, had outlived three of his doctors, and had dodged death at every turn. He became abusive, leaped from his wheelchair and stumbled up and down the halls of the hospital threatening the other patients. The hospital staff said he was more than they could handle. He must die somewhere else.

When Leslie came for him, Nick was handed over naked. The hospital staff had lifted his wallet, glasses, watch; his small change, coat, trousers, shirt, shoes and socks; his underwear and the night-shirt off his back. My uncle was driven home to die wrapped in a filthy sheet.

23

Kimberley

The grand approach to our house on the Dutoitspan Road descended on its way from Kimberley through the Beaconsfield slum. Once across railway tracks, you put behind you the dingy streets of Beaconsfield and cycled easily across a waste of red dust overlaid with gray tailings dumps. Across from the barbed wire that enclosed the mine property, our house crouched behind a corrugated iron fence. Five acres of property were divided into four spaces separated by either the same corrugated metal or stands of bamboo. These four divisions were four worlds and they replicated in miniature South African society, with its caste system and compartmented bathrooms, theaters, parks.

There was no question who belonged in the garden with its airy flower beds, fishpond, and tennis court. Green lawns extended from a line of tall fir and cypress trees to the tennis court and garden house. Passing through a vegetable garden on the left side of the house, or rows of citrus trees on the right, you entered a backyard where my father was busy constructing a chicken house. In Kimberley, chickens would become one of my father's obsessions, and I would dissect their cadavers with so much interest that my mother concluded my future lay in surgery. She, of course, was familiar with chicken coops. Her family always kept chickens and a cow. As a child she had lived in a chicken coop while her stepfather constructed the house in South Seattle.

Our backyard in Kimberley had the puritanical look of a servants' world where clothes were laundered, eggs gathered, chickens butchered, and African visitors lounged in the shadows of the eucalyptus.

The fourth yard was secreted behind a transverse fence raised against a tall water cistern under shedding eucalyptus leaves. A small house for the servants had been constructed under the trees. When the summer heat was most intense, my sister and I would climb the tower and sit cooling our feet in the dark water, reading or smoking acrid cigarettes made of dried eucalyptus leaves rolled in newspaper.

Our house had seven small rooms and came with three servants, including Paul, a gardener; Lucas, a "houseboy"; and Josephine, the cook. Josephine was about to marry and gave notice the week we arrived. "The document is being drawn up tonight where the number of cattle for her dowry is to be decided upon," my mother wrote Bess. "So dinner is early."

As for Paul, he was responsible for the disappearing silverware, china, sugar, flour, my father's underwear, and Lucas's good suit. He had installed a shadowy woman from the city in the servants' house and he brought her food from the garden and fridge. My mother said she thought it might be best if he moved on, and Paul was replaced with Willie, a benign, bandy-legged little man with a clouded left eye.

Lucas was an eager cook. In Oranjemund my mother had found

the native Ovambos as untalented as English housewives. But Lucas had a true gift and became deeply absorbed in the niceties of sauces and bread crusts. Within six months he was serving everything *en croûte* and garnishing the meat course with nasturtiums. But he soon realized that my mother had transformed him into a valuable commodity and he took off for Cape Town to market his new expertise.

After Lucas departed, she found Stephen Gute, the last in the long series of servants my mother hired during her thirteen years in Africa. Stephen was a gentle, middle-aged man, who loved children.

While I still have a clear mental map of the garden and yards, the only room in the house I can visualize completely is the bathroom (where I walked in on Maria taking her bath when she visited us a few months later). The bedrooms remain more vague than dreams. The living room is defined by a single object, the small, bright piano my mother bought brand-new. While she worked on a red-and-white volume entitled *The Climax Album,* my green book featured small ink drawings of great composers. The pieces had been selected randomly so the very easy were lumped together with the very difficult beneath the grim visage of Beethoven or of Rachmaninoff brooding. It was exactly this crazy mix of easy and impossible that piqued my interest while undermining my technique.

Our house was protected from mosquitoes on three sides by a screened veranda. It was there we slept during the hot season. The war had swallowed up every electric motor in the world, and the great age of appliances lay far in the future, so fans were nowhere to be found and air conditioning was unheard of.

During the long mosquito season, a good night's sleep required enormous expertise. The first trick was to slip under the mosquito netting as quickly as possible. Even so, there were always one or two of the enemy inside, waiting to make a meal of you. They hid in the fragile netting until you were drifting off, but soon the whine of a tiny motor would alert you that the fun was about to begin. With the light fading fast, you had to pick out a tiny form among the cloudy folds of the netting and clap him between your hands before he descended to gorge on your face. Successful executions were marked by a spatter of bright blood on the palm. If it was dark, the best technique was to pull the sheet up to your chin and wait for the light tap of his landing on your exposed skin. You waited a fraction of a second as he settled into place and prepared to plunge his proboscis in your cheek, then killed him carefully with a pre-positioned tap. Only perfect timing ensured his death before he poisoned you. It took self-control to crush a mosquito parked an inch from your eyelid without at the same time poking out an eye.

Confident that you had executed them all, you sank back and closed your eyes. But, just as you were falling asleep, another whine in a different key brought you to full alert. You hoped the vampire was outside the netting, trying to get in. Then how pleasant it was to lie with your face an inch or two from the netting while a frustrated mosquito went insane trying to get at you. You felt that at last you were inflicting on him something like the irritation he usually inflicted on you, and his furious whining would serve as a kind of perverse lullaby. But, once asleep, you inevitably rolled against the netting. Feeding through the skein, the enemy left your face a patchwork of stinging welts.

There were summer nights when storms came rumbling in and poured tons of water and hail on the tin roof with a hellish racket. Having just arrived from the desert, I assumed that every mosquito within a hundred miles had been drowned. But as soon as the flood was over, and even before the trees in the garden stopped dripping, a familiar whine would ring out of the dark, like insomnia or the memory of an enemy's face, and the war would resume.

Nevertheless, Kimberley was heaven after the desert. The landscape was littered with objects. Even the tailings dumps struck me as not unattractive. There were streets, tramlines, gardens, and faces I saw only once. I could hardly imagine better weather. My mother's letters remind me that the wind and rain were violent. The temperature dropped below zero in July and she records 146 degrees Fahrenheit in the December sun. But I recall Kimberley as a kind of Shangri-la. And there was no comparison between our small garden in the desert and the Kimberley grounds where I wandered from two lines of orange trees, through flower gardens set in a broad lawn, past the carp pond, to the tennis court.

At the far end of the tennis court was a high wall covered with pomegranate vines. When you pulled the leathery skin off their fruit you discovered angled pellets packed densely together. These gelatinous seeds yielded an illusory sweetness that soon turned starchy and bitter in the mouth. A dozen years later, I was reminded of those tightly packed seeds when the U.S. Navy introduced me to the atom bomb—the implosion device, kernels of high explosive, packed with the same cunning precision as a pomegranate fruit—death imitating nature.

"Kimberley is a small town of about ten thousand," my father wrote Bess. "But now we're just part of the mob instead of the focus of all eyes. It is a pleasing relief to me. But the move has been very expensive and our ordinary expenses have doubled."

"Kimberley is a sociable town, more so since the war," my mother adds. "My callers have begun coming in, and numerous cocktail parties are being given for us. Park's sister is giving one tonight. Our doctor gave one last Thursday. And Friday, the Becks. Saturday we will have a party here and show our movies. Wednesday, I'm entertaining a woman from Oranjemund." She also tells Bess about a high-toned cocktail party laid on by the legendary Sir Ernest Oppenheimer and compares her diamonds to those of other managers' wives.

Although my parents saw him fairly often and were entirely dependent on his whim, Sir Ernest remains a dim and distant figure in my parents' correspondence. He was to remain inscrutable, unpredict-able, as difficult to assess as some pagan god. His word arrived from on high, filtered through Dickinson (the director), or McHardy (the G.M.), or Park (alias Mercury). When my father says scornfully that he regards the company's promises as "just so much soft soap to keep me on the job," he takes care not to mention Sir Ernest's name, though it is Sir Ernest he means. My mother, conscious of her past, knows that a word in the wrong ear can spell disaster. My parents had come too far since their first frozen year on the Rand not to practice a little silence and cunning.

In Kimberley, the little émigré girl who had once milked the fam-ily cow on Beacon Hill in South Seattle was hobnobbing with people who owned the earth. My father was persuaded that the enormous jump in production under his management was too impressive to ig-nore. My mother feared his status was an illusion. Sir Ernest had more important things to worry over than the casual promises he made to keep his engineers happy and hopeful.

Luckily, we were Americans so we always had America to fall back on. As wings to angels, so was American citizenship to our family, the promise of escape to a more pleasant place. And there was good news! The consul in Johannesburg had got word that the new immi-gration act would not turn my mother into a non-person because her husband now managed the three biggest diamond mines in the world, and the U.S. government considered him part of the war effort.

What my father wanted most was to sit on the board of De Beers, where he knew he could change the way mining was done in South Africa. He wanted to alter the relationship between African and Eu-ropean. He had rapidly raised the output of the Kimberley mines to the highest level in their history. He could hardly believe that Sir Ernest would ignore that kind of efficiency.

His hopes were raised further when Sir Ernest invited another American onto the board—John Morrison, a diamond dealer. Morrison was close to powerful business interests in the States, and Sir Ernest cared a lot about markets. Park, having brought John Morrison to Sir Ernest's attention, went on to introduce his wife's sister, Ruth, to Morrison. They married soon after.

Ruth became my mother's best friend in Kimberley. Unlike her sister, Margaret, Ruthie was neither musically talented nor darkly beautiful, but she had a heart the size of the sun. A large-boned woman who worried about her weight, she never worried enough to pass up a good slice of my mother's cake and homemade ice cream. My mother describes John Morrison as "brilliant." She probably means "successful." Morrison was "responsible for those ads you see in *Life* and *Time* for De Beers diamonds." My mother adds, "The company [i.e., the chairman] gave him a £500 check [roughly $25,000 today] for his wedding present. He started as an office boy. . . ."

Besides the check, Sir Ernest personally gave Ruthie a diamond as a wedding present. This made a great impression on my mother, who would have been bowled over had he sent her a Christmas card, much less a five-carat rock. John, it seemed, was Sir Ernest's kind of man—extremely able and well connected to important markets, a perfectionist, a self-effacing workaholic fundamentally unsure of himself.

To my ten-year-old eye, Morrison was short, pudgy, and owlish— a kind of middle-aged Charlie Brown. His plump tummy and kind manner didn't make a strong impression. According to my mother's letters, John's father had been a religious fanatic who ended up in an institution for the insane. John's brother and uncle she describes as "distinctly odd." John was one of the few Morrisons not yet institutionalized.

Ruthie and John loved children, but were unable to have any of their own. They were always ready to look after my sister and me when our parents traveled. My mother remarks in several letters that every time she goes away I either fall sick or do myself physical dam-

age. I'm sure I would have given Marcel Proust a run for his money
in the neurotic-attachment-to-mom department. My attachment and
dependence on her remain firm to this day, and she has been dead
now for over forty years.

I remember lying dog sick in my bedroom at Ruthie's house staring
at the walls, the sumptuous furniture, the wall paneling, and heavy
curtains. Everything glistened with a kind of feverish shine I'd seen
only in films. My parents' furniture had been battered by constant
moving, and only my mother's skill at placing and combining odd
pieces gave visitors the illusion they were in a living room and not a
used furniture store. I found John and Ruthie's house a little stifling.
And I missed my mother, who could turn even a fever into a lovely
day.

Not long after he joined De Beers, John Morrison was sent to the
States on "an important mission." He was charged by Sir Ernest with
using his personal contacts on behalf of the company. It was all so
hush-hush that my mother suppressed the details. But whatever it
was Sir Ernest wanted him to do, John Morrison came back to South
Africa sure that he had failed and let down the demigod. It was,
moreover, the first time in his life he had failed, and perhaps Sir
Ernest had made this abundantly clear. In any case, John fell into a
deep depression. He sat huddled in a dark bedroom with the curtains
drawn, moaning and refusing to come out. He wouldn't speak even
to poor Ruthie, who had no idea what to do.

Margaret blamed Park for getting her sister involved with a mental
case. Park went to see John and somehow talked him out of his dark
room and into the car. He then drove the miserable man to Johannesburg, where a doctor gave him radical insulin therapy. Either this
(or Park's irreverent conversation) snapped John out of it, and he
was soon back among us, smiling his kindly smile, as benignly unem-
phatic as before.

My father had come to Kimberley extremely skeptical of Sir Ernest
and his promises. But when the production figures began coming in,
reason asserted itself and once again the chairman was singing his

siren song. My father was told he was next in line for Park's job as assistant general manager. It all followed as the night the day. Donald McHardy, the retiring G.M., would be replaced by Park. And there was simply no one else in Kimberley with enough experience to step into Park's shoes, especially since Ziervogel had been killed in Italy. My father was the only candidate around.

He tried hard to preserve his skepticism. He continued to plan to leave Africa as soon as the Atlantic was safe for travel. He bought one or two diamonds at a discount through John Morrison. My mother found herself loaded down with two big rings (about eight carats in all), earrings (slightly yellow), a brooch (six carats), and a ring for Bess (two carats). The entire family fortune was tied up in these rocks. The plan was to sell the stones back home and buy a house. That was all my mother cared about—getting back. At the same time, she wanted my father to succeed.

Finding himself now in line for a seat on the board of directors, my father realized how deep was his attachment to Africa. He had spent too many years, he had tested too many techniques, he knew the terrain too well to quit once given a chance to make company policy. He knew the mines were the most practical place to demonstrate the high cost of racism and the best place to upgrade the role of the African was underground. The movement away from racism could be masked by the need for efficiency.

He had repeatedly demonstrated a system of bonus pay and personal prizes that appealed to both Afrikaners and Africans. These prizes were handed out separately. At the Saturday morning tribal dance where the African miners unwound by dancing until they dropped, he came to distribute cash awards and praise the best men. When he moved through the crowd, there was a lot of laughing and joking. He combined a certain awkward distance with a kind of benign immediacy. Hands reached out to touch his arm or shake his hand. He was enthusiastic about men who did the dirty work. He had been there himself not so long ago.

He wrote Bess, "Probably in two or three years I will be assistant to the general manager as the present G.M. is about to retire and Park will take that job. Very attractive, but we are not that anxious to stay here. Just the same, I am the only man in the group who has had the experience of managing all of these mines at one time or another, and the job is a certainty if I want it."

The dinner parties in our garden grew more sumptuous, more vivid. Evening after summer evening the lawn spilled over with grown-ups and children. We children washed down slices of triple layer cake and scoops of my mother's famous ice cream with inconceivably delicious Coca Cola. Life was good, but my mother was ever more conscious of time passing. Eleven years and she'd had enough sun, enough heat, enough dust, enough of the caste system. She had adapted to the British; she had even put up with the Germans and their politics; but she was American. She longed to get back to something essential that had been arrested, broken off—the promise of her youth. The Parkinsons were so concerned about getting their kids into American schools they'd chanced the U-boats. Now the war dragged on forever while her longing for home grew more acute. Her mirror told her how Africa was gobbling up her life. Now it was going to work on her children. We were her best excuse for returning home.

Yet each week brought better prospects for my father. He was offered a high-paying job in an iron mine up north, but turned it down. His future had never looked brighter, and my mother's dinner parties in Kimberley evolved into elaborate and elegant occasions. The long table was laid with a Madeira lace cloth and silver. There were tall candles and glass bowls with flowers. The butter patties were rolled into little balls between serrated wood boards and put on ice. The rolls were fresh, the vegetables and fruit came from the garden (after my father had learned to protect them from the mousebirds). For the first time in their lives, my parents found themselves overweight.

Their guests would talk from six to past midnight with the enthusiasm of college undergraduates, and among the best memories of my childhood is their laughter in the living room, the tinkle of someone playing the piano as I was falling asleep—sounds I mistakenly took as a promise that adulthood was a richly amusing world where people always had something interesting to say, where words were pure affection given form. I had no clue that my mother was practicing an art. Only after she was gone and we fell into cultural poverty did I understand that living without grace, without a touch of irony, existing without beauty makes life nasty, brutish, and boring.

My sister, meanwhile, fell in love with the chickens and would not permit anyone to butcher them. So it was necessary to chop off their heads in secret. Stephen taught me the technique. He also showed me how to wring their necks. Seeing a chicken run across the yard without its head, I experienced a kind of double vision. The awe that I felt in the presence of death was mixed with a terrible curiosity. The transformation of the bird from a feathered creature with a vague, idiotic gaze to an enticing main course with a lovely glazed skin—this was a change too mysterious to bear much contemplation. The headless chicken with crimson spotting its feathers joined a category that included the accident of birth, the contents of a coffin, the origin of blood, and the mystery of Adolf Hitler—questions without answers.

One day in spring I found a baby chick, cold and still under a pile of scrap metal. My father pronounced the ball of fluff dead. I thought I detected a heart beat and warmed it over the stove while forcing a few drops of milk on it with an eye dropper. The revived chick took me for its mother and began to follow me everywhere. The moment I came back from school it would make a beeline for me. But darting in and out of the chrysanthemums with my sister one afternoon, I stepped back from the bush and felt the chick's warm little guts gush out under my bare foot. I had saved it; now I had murdered it and would have to live with the image of my tiny companion running away from me to die on the bright grass. The terrible sensation of that step back out of the chrysanthemum bush would stay with me for good.

Late afternoons I spent reading, comfortably wedged in the upper branches of a tall eucalyptus that grew in the corner of our backyard. I had complicated relations with certain favorite trees. Sometimes I stretched out in the sticky branches of our front hedge; the odor of pine induced a sense of powerful well-being. In fact, the odor of every plant, it seemed to me, induced differing states of mind. The eucalyptus had a kind of consciousness, which I thought I could sense by rubbing my cheek or forehead against its smooth gray-green bark. The rustling of the leaves in the breeze induced a mild ecstasy. For a long time, I preferred my trees to most people.

Each summer, the peppertrees in the yard with the water cistern were festooned with papery wasp nests. I found them stuffed, like some kind of complicated French pastry, with sticky, pale larvae. To knock them down, I climbed out on the branches where they were fastened. I was allergic to their poison, which upped the stakes and increased my pleasure. A good blow with a stick did the job. When the nest fell, the insects swarmed angrily, and, leaping down, I would run for it. One did drive his sting beneath my left eye once, and the effect was so bizarre that my father insisted on taking a snapshot. I looked like two people joined at the nose—on the right, myself; on the left, a grotesquely fat person with a slit eye.

I climbed these favorite trees so often that reaching the top seemed no more difficult than mounting a stair. One day, darting up a familiar route, I reached out and almost seized a dark little snake curled around a branch. My body's reaction was so violent that I fell out of the tree, bouncing helplessly through the branches and landing hard on my chest. Paralyzed, unable to take a breath, I thought, *This is death, and I can't even call for my mother!*

But soon I was sucking in air again and aware that I would go on living after all. When I peered up into the trees, looking for the snake, I couldn't make out its shape, and I wondered if I had imagined it. But the image of its glistening black eyes with yellow pupil slits was so sharply fixed in my mind's eye that I decided it must be real. It seemed prudent not to mention the snake and the fall to my parents, and I never swarmed up a tree again without making sure the branch above was, in fact, a branch.

My sister and I had moved so often and traveled so much that the only longstanding friends we had were each other. We thought of America as home—no matter we'd never been there. Africa was a temporary aberration—no matter we'd been born there. This world of ours would soon vanish, and real life awaited us in Oz. So the present seemed always a kind of transparency through which an ideal future was visible, no further away than wishing.

As we grew up, our games became more elaborate. We invested our favorite collection of dolls with complex personalities. Doc (one of Disney's seven dwarfs) was gruff and laconic, a Humphrey Bogart-like character. His sidekick was Doggie, benign and ironic. Doc had long since lost his red cap and spectacles, but we made up for the loss by sewing patches and odd buttons on his jerkin.

Doggie was a small, orange-and-white mutt with round black buttons for eyes. A nonstop talker, he kept losing his stuffing until finally he collapsed. I sliced him open and packed his belly with cotton wadding, then sewed him back up again. My mother knitted him a small orange sweater to cover his scar.

Occasionally I scribbled down some dialogue and we put on a play for our parents. Doc, Doggie, and my sister's Raggedy Ann got equal billing with us. The only title I remember is *One for the Other*, where we played an Englishman who can't speak Afrikaans attempting to teach a Boer how to drink tea without hiccuping and burping. I was probably the Boer.

One evening, our parents went out about bedtime, leaving me to tuck in my sister. Rain had soaked the garden and the sun came out an hour before twilight so everything outside was glistening with jewels of light. That didn't stop us from dutifully taking our baths and putting on our pajamas. Just as we were getting into bed, my fox-faced friend, Kenneth Boxall, knocked on the door. It seemed polite to invite him in. It seemed polite to join him outside. Soon we found ourselves with a small flotilla of toy boats on the tennis court. The heavy rain had turned the court into a muddy lake. The exciting thought of pulling a boat through all that creamy mud had overcome my sister's usual sober judgment, and she joined us in the red swill.

It was glorious puddling about in that rich goo, until I looked up and saw two very still figures observing us from the shadow of the syringa trees. It was not a good moment. Kenneth discreetly popped through a hole in the fence and vanished. Seeing my small sister through my mother's slitted eyes, I grasped the full measure of my immorality. They had left me with a little girl, fresh and pink. Now she resembled something hatched in a swamp. Her pajamas were composed of mud. There was mud on her face; there was mud in her hair. My pajama trousers were soaked through to the knees and flecked to the shoulders with spots, drips, trails of brown.

We were made to stand on the lawn while my mother hosed us down with very cold water. We then repaired to the bathroom where I was told to wait, shivering and naked, while she selected a suitable instrument of punishment. I have no idea what my father did while all of this was going on. She used to call him "old softie," because he always turned over the hard discipline to her.

She came back to the bathroom with the fragile slat from an apple crate and whacked my rear end. The thin wood broke after a couple of passes, and I don't remember feeling a thing. I had failed her. God knows, I would fail her again. But this failure was worth the price, because that evening fixed in memory the twilight sun reflecting pools of light into the grape arbor beyond while Patsy sloshes merrily through the sienna mud dragging a toy boat on a string, and my parents stand under the syringas—she with her arms folded, he leaning casually against the tree—and then, my worried sister peering up at me, hoping I will somehow (genius that I am) produce an explanation that erases the ignominy of her appearing there, two hours past bedtime, completely covered with mud.

24

The Agony of Ian Hogben

I WAS NINE, WOULD SOON BE TEN, AND HAD SPENT ONLY THREE months in a classroom. With a sigh of relief, my mother turned me over to the brothers at CBC (Christian Brothers College), reputedly one of the best schools in South Africa. Founded by an Irish Catholic teaching order, it was organized on the British public school model, and the teachers there were the toughest bunch of men I ever encountered. After CBC, I would find Navy boot camp easy sailing.

My sister was six and could hardly wait to start school. Thus both of us were first institutionalized in the same year. Outfitted in gorgeous uniforms emblazoned with school colors—splendid striped blazers, striped caps, matching socks, and sweaters with stripes—we fell in love with our mirrors. Every morning at eight sharp, Patsy marched through the garden gate and was whisked uptown in the De Beers station wagon with other company kids her age. A few minutes later, I peddled out the back gate on my bike.

My sister immediately developed a passionate devotion to her teacher. "She thinks Saturday and Sunday are just a waste of time," my mother wrote Bess. "And everything the teacher says is gospel. Even to cleaning one's nails. Such a brushing and scrubbing and cleaning goes on now, I wonder how long it will last. She went off this morning complete with a big bouquet of flowers she picked herself for dear teacher. She's as orderly as can be. So everything is ready to hand at the crack of dawn next day for school. She even puts her blazer and hat on before she sits down to breakfast."

The road I peddled to school ran between dusty red marching fields and gray tailings dumps. Grotesque in their sterility, these hills, brought to the surface from the sunless center of the earth, lay strewn across the land like the bodies of decomposing dinosaurs. Rainwater had sliced steep ravines in the slimy clay, and each spring torrential downpours cut the grooves deeper. Along their shadowy bottoms grew stringy weeds. Water that boiled down these gray slopes during cloudbursts left a thin layer of gray sand, the bones of reptiles, and an occasional decaying dog.

In the hard ground near our back gate, a thorn tree had forced its way into the light. Just beyond the tree, a streambed worked its way past rocks and red sand beneath a culvert. Travelers used the concrete walls of the culvert as a public toilet, and once someone dumped a truckload of used Kotex napkins. I assumed they were bandages, dumped by the Cape Coloured Regiment bivouacked across the road. When the rainy season arrived, all of this waste was flushed away in the flood. Crossing the little bridge after a rain, my mother once remarked that she now understood why God had found the Flood convenient.

The Cape Coloured and Malay regiments provided most of our local excitement. The authorities had organized the Coloureds (people of mixed blood from the Cape) and Malays (men from the Indian subcontinent) into separate regiments and set them directly across from each other in a compound. The question of racial superi-

ority surfaced immediately, and the two regiments developed a mutual hatred more potent than anything felt for the Nazi enemy in
imaginary Europe. Weekends were bloody, and the military police
were kept hopping.

One Saturday night in early winter, the regiments began beating
each other with rifle butts; then some fool fired a shot and soon everyone was shooting. They must have fired in the air, because no one
was killed. Or perhaps some were killed, but we were never told
about it. The police arrived in force and organized a battle line in
front of our garden gate. One of the officers was so terrified by the
gunfire that he fainted and was carried into our yard where they laid
him out on the grass. My mother brought him a glass of water, and
he recovered as soon as the shooting stopped.

When the police line charged, the Coloureds and Malays stam-
peded around the perimeter of our yard, hurling their rifles over the
fence. Being arrested with a loaded gun brought with it a charge of
mutiny. The police took half the night rounding them all up, and the
paddy wagons drove back and forth till morning. Before breakfast, my
sister checked the bushes and announced the yard was clean. "Last
week she was hunting easter eggs. This week it's rifles," my mother
wrote Bess.

I sensed that our new world was less benign than the desert where
one had only cobras and sand vipers to worry about. Skimming past
the houses of poor Afrikaners clustered behind scraps of fencing,
crossing the train track that ran through Beaconsfield, I felt vaguely
uneasy. Downtown Beaconsfield consisted of a few poor shops under
a corrugated tin arcade. There was also a bioscope (movie theater);
one afternoon, a stranger with a soft voice and fawning manner got
off at my stop and offered to buy me a ticket. I declined, because it
seemed a perverse waste of good sunshine to sit in a dark theater.

Beyond Beaconsfield the road to Kimberley broadened and developed sidewalks and overhead tramlines. This pleasant boulevard ran
uphill into the posh districts where the Morrisons, the Becks, and

the Grays lived. European gardens were carefully laid out with red brick walls, jacaranda, and box hedges. Peddling through these tree-lined byways, with their sculptured shrubs and gardens crowded with flowers, I felt the acute satisfaction of the desert dweller arriving at an oasis where water plashes.

I avoided the rutted, dusty streets of lower Beaconsfield, populated with resentful Afrikaners and the nervous Africans who lived in adjacent neighborhoods. Venturing through those potholed streets, I heard shouts of "*Voertsek!*" *(foot-sak)*—a term of abuse reserved for dogs, stray Africans, and Englishmen. Strictly translated it means "Get you gone, I say." But the phrase is loaded with venomous resentment and expresses the contempt felt by a born underdog for the arrogant overlord.

At first I was puzzled. What had I done to merit the hostility of these ragged kids, with their shaved heads and dirty elbows? I believed that I was an American. But everything about me was English, from my chirpy accent to my unconscious assumption of privilege. I might live below Beaconsfield across from the mine gate, but all the people my parents invited over came from the district beyond—those tree-lined boulevards where English civilization asserted itself. Naturally the Afrikaners saw me as the British enemy, flaunting my bright CBC uniform in their dull streets, and their hatred was like polluted air, palpably oppressing the lungs.

My first real school was an imposing pile of institutional brick, set well back from the boulevard, across a wide field where the cricket teams played in the hot season. A loggia run along the side of the building and overlooked the chapel. There was also a clock tower with Big Ben chimes that sounded every quarter hour.

On my first morning, I walked nervously onto the field and found the place crowded with boys in blazers and gray flannel shorts energetically shaking hands or knocking each other over. Brother Ellif, a young man with a bright red face blooming above a clerical collar and cassock, advanced to shake my hand.

"This is the American!" he announced to the group who ran up to inspect me. I found myself shaking hands with twenty or thirty boys who were clearly disappointed that I didn't look, sound, or smell like their idea of an American. I was pleased to be an American while remaining indistinguishable from my schoolmates. It was the first time I had been around so many boys my age, and I was a little overwhelmed by their collective violence. To establish yourself it seemed you were obliged to knock someone flat. I spotted my old friend, Michael McIntosh, who had grown up in Pomona, a desert spot near Oranjemund. He had arrived at CBC that same day and looked as bewildered and lost as I felt. Aping the others, I dashed over and tackled him so hard that we both fell on the ground.

"Good lad!" cried Brother Ellif. "He's a tough one!" he added approvingly. Thus I established myself from the first moment, although I knew perfectly well that I was a sham and felt secretly ashamed for taking advantage of Michael, whose dreamy, vague nature echoed something in my own. We had both grown up in one of the most remote places on earth, and the wind and silence had turned us inward. Sent to be civilized, we found ourselves surrounded by savages.

In the classroom, the savages behaved with amazing self-control. They were more accustomed than I to sitting all day behind a desk. It took me weeks to stop twitching, and I never could stop doodling. My first teacher, Brother Cook, was a nearsighted young man with a round, pale face and pink hands. He looked like a grown-up version of Michael McIntosh. We started off the year by lining up in a shoving mass to buy books at the store under the loggia—arithmetic texts, an Afrikaans grammar, English grammar, European history. No South African history. African history was taught only in second-rate schools to children relegated to second-class citizenship. CBC was organized to instruct the ruling class. Aged eleven, we would be required to think in whole earth terms. Vasco da Gama's face was prominent in our history, along with Sir Walter Raleigh, Lord Nelson, and Clive of India. We would pick up algebra early, immerse ourselves in Latin. We would memorize pages of poetry and write long essays.

I was issued six varnished pencils, a wood nib holder with a cork grip, and three steel nibs. Each desk was supplied with a glass ink-well, and each well was filled every morning with a glutinous black substance stored in a large bottle. It was comforting to sprawl in the seat of my battered old desk, which was bolted to the floor and carved with the initials of previous generations. Brother Cook had thirty-seven boys to deal with, so he was always busy, and I took full advantage of his kindly nature to do as little as possible.

My mother had outfitted me with a stiff leather backpack. Soon the rich odors of sandwich spread, peanut butter, and Boveril had been liberally worked into the lining. That smell contained the inde-finable essense of everything I loved about CBC—the quality of its stone architecture; the Big Ben clock-chimes every quarter hour; lunch sandwiches wrapped in crinkly waxed paper; the backfields where the bagpipers practiced; the rapid ride home, zipping downhill in the late afternoon with the wind cool in my face.

I was unable to read textbooks, and my writing was sloppy. But I found myself strongly attracted to books, paper, and ink. It was the objects themselves I loved, the quality of the binding, the different kinds of print, the oilcloth odor of the skinny, dark green booklet that contained the multiplication tables. I learned multiplication be-cause I liked the shape and color and smell of that book with its slick, green oilcloth cover. But most satisfactory of all was scraping a nib full of ink across a sheet of paper, turning the nib this way and that to vary the line. Even when I didn't understand a word, a sen-tence, a paragraph, I still grasped the meaning, I had no idea how. This odd sixth sense allowed me to lollygag and relax. It was as if strange words marched up and offered their meaning with a smile. But when I tried to use them in sentences, they often flew through my mind in such swarms that it was impossible to settle on a line of straight reasoning. Overwhelmed by an overload of possibilities, I remained more or less unintelligible. My arguments ran in mad spirals up an espalier of cross-purposes. "Keep it simple," said Brother Cook. He may as well have said, "Get into that ink bottle."

On the other hand, I loved the sensation of writing, the feel of a flexible nib scraping across a paper surface. The compositions I struggled to write provided mostly an excuse to absorb myself in the formation of shapes. Curious, then, that my handwriting was so spastic, my notebooks so blotchy. I distrusted boys who drew perfectly neat lines around the titles of their assignments or used rules to underline salient points. I was mysteriously dedicated to mess. My notebooks filled up with odd doodles, secret codes, airplane shapes, monsters, botched sketches of various schoolmates and Brother Cook. I sketched profiles of people wanted by the police in my diary. I gave them names and invented crimes for them.

Yet I was infinitely fussy about the surface of the paper I used and no less fussy about the quality of my nib. Nothing was quite suitable. I have spent a lifetime looking for the perfect nib, hoping that the right point will lend me the power to conjure some magic form from the paper surface.

My mother said that I lost everything except my hands and feet and she was quite right, of course. I was forever pestering her to buy me another fountain pen. I would then take the treasured writing instrument with me everywhere—even to bed. But precautions were useless. I lost all my pencils, my sweaters, my shoes, my coats. My mother never had to wonder what to get me for Christmas or my birthday. She had only to buy exactly the same thing she always bought me. And there under the tree, or beside my breakfast plate it lay, as always, nestled in its slim box, and I would always feel an identical thrill when I opened it and vow, as always, never to lose it.

To guard against myself, I developed precautions so elaborate that anyone observing me would have thought I was either the most eccentric ten year old imaginable, or mad. I would not leave a room without tapping the pen. I would never put it away without reopening the drawer to make sure I had put it where I knew it had to be. Before getting out of a car, I would take out the pen, then put it away again. I sat with my hands in my pockets on couches to make sure the pen did not slip behind a cushion. But all my worry came to nothing. Within a few days or weeks the pen was gone. (And, not long ago, I left my laptop computer on the overhead rack in an airplane.)

I was so feebly engaged with the world of actual objects that I even left my new bicycle standing outside the grocery store in Beaconsfield and walked home without it one evening. Not once did it occur to me that, having arrived on wheels, I should depart on wheels. I wish I knew what daydream I was laboring over that afternoon.

Only hours later, at dinner, did I remember my bright new bike, which I'd left leaning against a post on the main road to Kimberley. I sprinted the half mile into town. Of course it was gone, and I cursed the Afrikaner (who else but an Afrikaner?) who had stolen it and spent the worst night of my life, unable to sleep, hating my slipshod, dream-clouded brain.

The bike, however, was too big to slip into the odd dimension where all my pens had piled up. My mother phoned the police the following morning. They had it. The Indian store owner had taken it in for the night and turned it over to them first thing.

In the final years of the war, fountain pens disappeared entirely from the world. My mother searched every store in Kimberley without success. I had just lost a pen with the smoothest nib, the most even ink flow, the most flexible line of any I had ever owned, and I regarded myself as the greatest ass in the world. I suffered self-loathing and anguish, wondering what I could possibly do to save myself from myself. Nor could I help note that while I lost whatever was not attached permanently to my body, my little sister lost nothing at all.

My schoolmates were unaware of my odd obsessions and regarded me as more or less normal. They had come to CBC from all over South Africa. Many of them were boarders who saw their families during holidays only. We all spoke a quick, twittering English that played itself out in complete sentences—the sy.itax of a lost age. We assumed (the class system is rich in examples) that shabby speech indicates a lower order of being, and I am sure our public school English would have made the average American politician sound tongue-tied. We soon possessed a fair amount of Shakespeare, Wordsworth, and Walter de la Mare by heart, and we quoted them in conversation, if only because our heads were buzzing with their phrases.

It never occurred to us to be hostile to learning although some of us were hostile to hard work. We had only to look down the street to see how dangerous ignorance was, how it condemned children not so different from us to hatred and dirt. The Afrikaner boys our age provided a constant example.

I had no trouble with Afrikaans literature and grammar because my playmates in Oranjemund had been Afrikaners (a benign lot compared to those I would soon meet in Kimberley). Arithmetic was its usual vapid self. European history promised more substance, though I preferred *The Count of Monte Cristo* to the *History of France.* Still, the dense fatness of our history text made you feel that history was important. The no-nonsense engravings in black-and-white, the maps that showed the engorging British Empire in blood red, the grim portraits of famous sea captains in bearded profile, the small print and crinkly thin paper—this sort of thing made clear that history was a serious business. When I arrived in America and saw the cute textbooks with their plummy interiors and snatches of cereal-box prose, I was greatly relieved. I knew that life in the New World would be easy because it was not possible that anything difficult or important could be packed in such frivolous packages. Robespierre and the guillotine had been replaced by social studies and Mickey Mouse. I sensed (without quite knowing it) that these happy-go-lucky textbooks were condescending to me, trying to make out that learning all about the difficult and bloody past of our species was somehow analogous to a tour of Hollywood.

At CBC, we were in over our heads from page one on. It was like being tossed into a stormy sea, and the prose had the uncompromising quality of salt water. No one pretended that learning can be fun. It was hard work. No one intimated that we had plenty of time. We had to grasp the stuff and pass or repeat the whole year again.

Though I had some aptitude for learning, I was ignorant of this. I employed my little talent in order to do as little work as possible. But my sloth was cruelly disturbed when those who had passed the nasty year-end tests found ourselves in Standard Three. Kindly Brother Cook was replaced by fiery Brother Ellif, a firm believer in original sin. Brother Ellif didn't expect us to be one bit better than we were. He assumed that, left to ourselves (with one or two neurotic exceptions), we would gradually sink and cluster around a miserable average, which he set at seventy-five. His job was to offset the entropic power of Adam's curse. His technique was simple. Any student who dropped below a seventy-five on a weekly test earned one cut (on the outstretched palm). Scores below sixty-five got two (one on each palm, or two on one palm—our choice). Scores below fifty-five were dealt three, and anything below fifty got you four cuts and an hour after school, during which you took the test over and wrote a composition describing your study habits and moral character.

Brother Ellif had a broad red nose, sandy hair, and an alert expression. His idea of fun was to join the senior varsity rugby team during afternoon practice and roll in the mud with the rest of them. I have an indelible memory of him in a pair of white shorts and a school rugby shirt, dashing down the field at full tilt, his lips compressed, his face alight with the unholy joy of combat, rugby ball held lightly in both hands as he prepares to boot it downfield in full flight.

We may have seen Brother Ellif a little annoyed once or twice, but he was never in a bad humor. He liked children and he found everything about us amusing, except dishonesty and cowardice. Brother Ellif was so supremely male that, looking back, I find it impossible to imagine him without a woman. Yet some arcane Irish emotion had led him to choose a life of chastity and obedience. In the chapel, he put on piety. Everywhere else, he was cocky and self-assured. "Beat yourself and you can beat anyone," he said.

Brother Ellif's punishment periods on Friday afternoons were the high point of our week. Our class of thirty-seven miserable souls looked forward to these rituals with a thrilling mixture of sour dread and secret pleasure. The (so-called) average score of seventy-five was almost impossible to achieve, and when our test papers came back twenty-seven of us, more or less, lined up for cuts while the geniuses sat on their desk tops and enjoyed the spectacle.

The business began somberly, with a kind of dispirited shuffling as we formed ourselves into a line. No one wanted to be first, the theory being that even Ellif's arm grew tired after a while. As the cuts were meted out and the muffled yelps sounded, the thing took on a strangely festive atmosphere. Having absorbed your cuts, you were free to enjoy the misery of those who came after you while you blew and sucked on your sore palm to draw out the pain.

The strap was a flexible weapon, three thin strips of dark leather sewn together and rounded at the business end. The pain began with a blinding flash that electrified the whole body, followed by burning (as if the hand had been thrust into a furnace), tapering off in the half hour that followed into a stinging sensation, devolving in degrees of discomfort from wasp, through bee, to mosquito.

Some took their cuts without expression. Some paled slightly. Some turned bright red. One or two wiped their eyes. Some shouted, some whistled, some laughed. There was only one rule. Never cry, snuffle, or whimper. Sob aloud, you were finished.

The whole business was made into high comedy by the clowns among us—boys who turned our Friday afternoons into hilarious bacchanals where we staggered around, drunk with laughter. Our genius was Ian Hogben, a slight, pale boy with tufts of white-blond hair that fell limply over his ears and high forehead. His eyes were puffy and pink with pale lashes. His nose was enormous and red and he tended it carefully with a damp handkerchief.

He began by marching to the front of the punishment line, but he then invented excuses for slipping back. Each time a cut landed on someone else, he would grimace, or emit a tiny squeak of terror. These starts and squeaks were real and, at the same time, entirely artificial and absurd. The shorter the line became, the more despairing became his whinnies of suppressed fright. The funniest thing about him was his deadly seriousness. We profoundly offended him; our amusement hurt him deeply. But the more he objected to us, the harder we laughed.

Soon, he was the only boy left, and the whole class stood in the aisles or perched on desks to take in the show. Brother Ellif, ignoring us, seemed only faintly amused by Hogben's anxiety. Hogben always bargained with Brother Ellif. He was sure there had been some mistake in the test score. He had the test with him and insisted on disputing over certain fine distinctions that he was sure Brother Ellif had missed. He claimed the whole class would benefit from such a debate, ignorant lot that we were. He wanted to work something out that would be of mutual benefit to his classmates and their teacher. He made wild promises, with a serious face. He promised to get a perfect score next time and, failing that, take eight, ten, twelve cuts. He would get a perfect score or be sent down from school.

Brother Ellif stood with his forearm raised, the strap drooping back over his right shoulder. "Come now, Hogben! Stop dancing around like a meercat and be a man!" Brother Ellif reached out to position the hand. Finicky as a cat, Hogben withdrew his arm and rubbed his palm with frenzied vigor, first against the other hand, then on his bottom. He put the hand between his thighs and squeezed it.

"Come along, come along now," said Brother Ellif. "It's only one cut, for God's sake, man! What kind of a convent girl are you?"

Hogben got his hand open by blowing vigorously on the clenched fingers. He offered the palm, but twitched it back when Brother Ellif brought down the strap. He even got Brother Ellif to strike himself on the knee. Hogben was making high-pitched sucking sounds. "Give me your hand!" ordered Brother Ellif. Hogben forced his hand in Brother Ellif's direction by seizing the right wrist with his left hand and pushing it forward. Brother Ellif took a firm grip of Hogben's fingers, but Hogben was in such an agony of anticipation that he leaned over emitting shrill hissing and whistling sounds and inter-posed his head between the strap and his palm. At the same time he performed a little broken-leg dance. Brother Ellif brought down the strap. And that was it, all over in a flash.

But Hogben wasn't finished. He exhibited a slow-motion agony that included some of his most brilliant moments. He was astonished by the pain. He had never dreamed that anything in God's good world could hurt so terribly as Brother Ellif's cut. His mouth hung open in agony. His eyes glazed and wandered in his head. The in-jured hand rose slowly like a hot-air balloon, and he blew on it with the exquisite tenderness a mother shows for an injured infant.

Some of us had collapsed on our seats, some of us lay across our desks. Our stomachs ached, our cheeks were wet with tears. We were beyond help. Hogben's glance was full of reproach. Brother Ellif stood in the door, his cheerful face bright red above the black cas-sock. "I will see you all on Monday morning, gentlemen," he said. "Now kindly take yourselves off."

25

Siamese Twins

I WAS UNFORTUNATE ENOUGH TO WIN THE FIFTY-METER DASH ON Field Day. It had never occurred to me that I might be of some practical use, but Brother Ellif informed me that I was to play on the junior varsity rugby team. He was the coach. I was issued a pair of skimpy shirts; a long-sleeved shirt, brilliantly striped in gold, green and blue; and a pair of cleated boots. My afternoons thereafter degenerated into a melee of flying fists, kicks to the shin, and slaps to the head.

To my way of thinking, these squabbles in the mud were redeemed only by the school bagpipers who marched just beyond a green line of peppertrees. When, as a child, you catch the sound of pipes in the wind, the sound fixes itself in your imagination as firmly as a face you have loved. The insinuating whine, irritating in a closed space, is transformed by distance into something ethereal and delectable. The drone evokes an underlying harmony—the music of universal longing. This is the music that sustains men in battle.

So when I found myself pinned under a heap of squirming bodies, my nose and mouth pressed into a brackish puddle, it was the sound of the bagpipes I clung to. When I was unable to breathe, the music sustained me. As long as I could hang onto that bright thread of sound, I was all right. The bagpipes promised I would not always lie under a pile of sweaty, kicking schoolmates with my snout full of muck. Their steady song assured me that even the most desperate moments, the moment of death itself, fall within the circle of a greater order.

My mother's letters report that my team that year won the regional championship. I had completely forgotten that. I was more involved with the particular sensations of being alive. The collective enthusiasm we must have felt has passed me by like a shout in the breeze. There still exists a reel of film my father shot of small figures running haphazardly across a field in the game that decided the regional championship. There is even a short take of the triumphant Brother Ellif grinning up at the movie camera. By then, I was dreaming about America, where my real life would begin. Americans, I believed, were too civilized to play games where people trampled each other in the mud.

Those bagpipes remain more real for me than the mud and the blood. Their song and the sound of the night train passing through Beaconsfield is what I recall best. Odd how such insubstantial stuff can trick the memory into clear comprehension while a hundred downfield runs and a dozen games won fade completely. I still feel with my entire being the trundling sound of the train passing through Beaconsfield with its long, mournful whistle. There was something in that far off clickity-clack that woke up my imagination while the rest of me was drifting off to sleep.

When the hot season came, we exchanged mud for dust and played cricket under the big clock in the front field. Cricket requires—in equal degrees—a contemplative nature, a nice athletic skill, and an appreciation of cucumber sandwiches. These soggy tidbits kept us going as the long, hot afternoons wore on. The game made me appreciate even more the bike ride home in the late afternoon heat, my back sweaty under a leather backpack full of heavy homework, the houses flying past, the breeze drying my damp face.

Passing through Beaconsfield, I bumped across the railway track, and then peddled by Yaapie Hendricks's house on the mine road. Beyond Yaapie's house, peppertrees were planted in a line. Africans camped in their shade, waiting for sign-on day when the mine offered nine-month contracts. My mother writes Bess that when these men moved on they left almost no trace behind—only a little gray ash from their camp fires, contained by a discreet circle of stones.

During our first months in Kimberley, I biked through Beaconsfield blissfully unaware that I was the object of hostile scrutiny. Sometimes I spotted Yaapie and one or two of his fellow Afrikaners lounging near his back fence. I had grown up among Afrikaners in the desert, and Afrikaans was my second language. The Afrikaners in Kimberley were not used to an English boy with free access to their lingo. When I spoke to them they looked disconcerted, sullen, as if a dog were suddenly addressing them in full sentences.

Yaapie, who was about fifteen, affected total indifference when I called out to him. I stopped to introduce myself (he was our nearest neighbor, after all), but he turned his back and slouched off behind a fence. I grew more cautious. I tried waving airily as I cycled past. I may as well have been invisible. Once, finding myself faced with him in a Beaconsfield store, I began chattering away in Afrikaans, telling him who I was and where I was going to school. He stared at me with his pale blue eyes and chopped me off with a curt, *"Wat makeer met jou, kaffer?"* (What's wrong with you, nigger?)

Yaapie lived with his mother, a baggy shapeless woman who appeared to have many small children and no visible husband. The children played quietly behind the corrugated metal that shielded their door from the wind and dust. Yaapie wore *velskoen* (gray, shapeless boots of scrap leather) without socks. Few of the Afrikaner boys in our end of town wore socks or underwear. My schoolmates swore that Afrikaner girls never wore underwear either, but it hardly mattered, since you never saw an Afrikaner girl in any case. Prisoners of their puritanical society, they were confined to their homes or glued to a parent in public. Where poor Afrikaner girls went to school, or if they were educated at all, I had no inkling.

To mark my status as a CBC boy, I wore the school colors on my cap, my jacket, my tie, and my heavy wool knee socks. The socks had been designed for the cold English damp. We wore them proudly in the South African heat. Comfort is not English. In Oranjemund, I had walked on burning sand without discomfort, and I had developed an intense dislike for shoes and socks. CBC changed all that. As my feet softened in school shoes, I felt the wordless regret of a wild creature domesticated.

When I bicycled off the mine road to talk to the African miners down from the north, I was aware of Yaapie observing. It was the dancing that attracted me. Beside blackened cooking pots and a small bundle of clothes, they often carried tiny instruments—one-string violins or pluck pianos. Much of their music was made by beating tin cans of varying sizes and shapes with sticks. Each tin produced its own tone, and the musicians would improvise congeries of cross-rhythms to set up a pattern for their dances. The performers fastened strips of black tire tubing to their ankles and slapped these with their hands, or struck their ankles together to add another line to the rhythm. The drumming was alive with change, one pattern of beats shifting through another, like dyes dropped into swirling water.

Generally, there were one or two dancers in the group who could perform the impossible. My fascination amused them. They urged me to join in so they could have a good laugh. I had nothing to lose, I thought, so there I was, hopping about in the dust in my school uniform. Had I heard what Yaapie Hendricks and his family said while all of this was going on, I'm sure it would have considerably repressed my exhilaration.

I had no idea how little it took to offend an Afrikaner. In Oranjemund my friends had all been Afrikaners, and I had looked at whom I pleased. In Kimberley to look at an Afrikaner was to insult him. It was a point of pride not to acknowledge an Englishman. It was correct to pass by as if you passed no one at all. So my open use of their language, my smiles, my waves were merely provocations as far as Yaapie and his friends could make out.

I understood that I was supposed to pass by in silence. But I considered it ridiculous. I looked at whomever I liked. But soon a grimy fist was shoved in my face. Some boy I'd never seen before stopped me on the sidewalk and threatened me. "What do you think you're looking at, boy?"

"What? Nothing!"

"You call me nothing? Come over here, I'll show you what nothing is. Then we'll see who's nothing."

My father explained that Afrikaner pride had been rubbed raw by British success. A nod, a smile, even a lifted hat might be taken as arrogant doublespeak. The Afrikaners were like men without skins. In fifty years—less than a lifetime—the English had stripped away their status, their homeland, their pride. The mere sight of an Englishman offended them. The grown-ups swallowed their pride and got along. The Boer War was continued by their children.

Yaapie Hendricks's family couldn't afford to send him to school. He had been put to work, and while we studied European history and read Wordsworth he threaded pipe in a cramped mechanic's shop in Beaconsfield. I used to spot him trudging home after work, a small, depressed figure in brown overalls several sizes too large.

The gray tailings dump had been vomited out between the Boxalls' place and my house, a half mile away. Kenneth and Vaughn Boxall lived across the road from Yaapie, one of the few English families in lower Beaconsfield. On weekends, they joined me on the eroded dump. There were narrow paths four inches wide snaking along the crest of the dump, perfect for biking. On each side of these paths the blue ground fell away steeply. The trick was to ride these paths without skidding over the edge. A single misjudgment and you slipped down the steep wall, battered by your bike and losing skin on the sandpaper surface. We carried lengths of clothesline to drag our machines back to the top. Fear quickly turned us into experts at negotiating the narrow track.

On occasion, I had gone into the tailings alone with a book. One day, I saw some Afrikaner boys running along the gully below me and realized these dumps were a no-man's-land where anything might be possible. I went back to reading in the tops of eucalyptus trees.

For three years after the pneumonia almost carried me off, I had lung problems, and a doctor in Cape Town detected a defective valve in my heart. In Kimberley, I caught every cold and flu going and was made to drink orange juice laced with beastly cod-liver oil. My tonsils were removed, and my mother was convinced that had done some good. But I remained a very odd amalgam of respiratory breakdowns and witless athletic skill. I was dimly aware of myself as a mob of disparate powers that it would take a lifetime to boil down into something with a definable shape and aim.

As my health problems faded, my body began growing too quickly. Although Yaapie and his friends were five years older than I, we were all more or less the same size. Compared to them, I felt as soft and limp as a rabbit's ear. The Afrikaner boys were stringy and hard. Among my own all-English schoolmates, I admired boys who were all of a piece, cut from whole cloth—boys with definite identities and simple goals. Mighty Fredericks was the most impressive among them. He is still present in my mind's eye in fine detail, the narrow, freckled face, reddish, short-cropped hair, white eyelashes, pale blue eyes, and fists like small stones. I remember, too, broad-faced Bartram, the top boy in class, mysteriously benign and calm, as if he'd been born aged forty. My best friend was the bespectacled and freckled Bill Byerley, who managed to come in right under Bartram without ever sacrificing the free play of his imagination to cramming.

Besides the nervous Boxalls, the only other English boy near my end of Beaconsfield was George McDonald, the gap-toothed, sweet-natured son of a pipe fitter. This lot all had a talent for fading away when the Afrikaners came out in force, and it was soon evident that the Afrikaners were always looking for an excuse to start something. They were easy to spot, those small, tense bodies and cropped heads. They never so much as glanced in our direction, so we knew very well they were observing us narrowly, tracking every move we made, calculating, forcing us to worry.

Their hostility, which had seemed to me so idiotic at first, was something I soon took for granted—like the violent weather or the thick clouds of red dust drifting through our garden every time the Cape Coloured Corps marched in a north wind. Arriving in Kimberley, I had assumed life would be more pleasant. It was disturbing to find anxiety inevitable.

I wished to make myself appear as benign as possible. But I was English. My accent, my attitude, my privileges were all English. Like the English, I secretly assumed Afrikaner inferiority. These were the people who supported Adolf Hitler. That alone we all knew gave England the moral duty to snatch South Africa from them. Often, passing some Afrikaner, with his cold, impassive face, the thought of our victory over the Boers comforted me. What would they be doing to us if they were in charge?

They inhabited inferior houses; they went to inferior schools. Their inferior books, with simpleminded inferior poems and stories, were printed on inferior newsprint paper. Their language was superior to English only in its power to express hatred and contempt. Thus, my friends preferred their *kak* to our "shit," their explosive *voertsek* to our "go to hell." Even the school colors of their best public school were inferior—an ugly silver, black, and red, if I recall correctly.

The mutual detestation we felt for each other reached its height when our rugby teams met their boys from Boshof. I watched our senior varsity beat their outfit, and it was sobering—the flinty hatred in their eyes and the fury with which they attacked. When our junior team played their junior team, it was no less desperate. The Afrikaners from Boshof had come not to win a game of rugby, but to pay us back for generations of injustice. Their eyes burned into ours (at last we were actually looking at each other!), and when the opening whistle shrilled, we flung ourselves at each other with contemptuous abandon. In the scrum, we kicked shins and punched faces. Someone booted me in the stomach, and I saw the looks of satisfaction on their faces as I rolled gasping in the dust.

We respected their desire to murder us. We reveled in the chance to humiliate them. They played like suicides with nothing to lose. Their fear had been anesthetized by loathing, but Brother Ellif had turned us into a better team, so we beat them anyway. I have forgotten the score. I remember that no matter how they dashed themselves at our line, elbowing, grunting, bellowing with fury, the ball was always somewhere else. They limped off after we won, elbows bleeding, knees gashed, and for a moment they seemed almost human to me—boys fighting back tears of disappointment. As for our wounds, they felt wonderful. The cheers each team sent up for the other rang even more hollow than usual. And when we shook hands, they looked into the distance. Once again, we English had ceased to exist.

In Oranjemund, I had read only poetry, myth, and fiction. In Kimberley I began to read all I could find about the European war. I fell desperately in love with the British Spitfire and knew its Merlin engine better than the multiplication tables. My father shoveled scientific books my way. Among my favorite was one that detailed nature's worst mistakes. Especially fascinating was the case of Siamese twins. Two individual creatures forever bound together—it seemed to me that nature here had collided with a Greek myth.

I had no sooner learned that such a thing existed than I was privileged to observe a pair of Siamese twins with my own eyes. Walking home from school one evening, I was astounded to see the freakish thing appear on a dusty lot in front of Yaapie Hendricks's corrugated metal fence. I could hardly believe my good luck.

In this case, the twins were dogs, understandably unhappy. They clearly wished I would go away. Strangest of all, the twin behind was much larger than the twin in front, and they even seemed to belong to different mongrel strains. I made quite a fuss. This was, after all, of some scientific importance, this freak of nature right in front of the Hendricks's house.

Yaapie was skulking about in clear view. The pedagogue in me took over, and I ran over and insisted he come and see the dogs. I felt it was too significant a discovery to let silly national differences stop him from joining me. (I even hoped the thing might bring us closer together.) I explained in rapid-fire Afrikaans that he was unlikely to see such a thing more than once in a lifetime. I even took him by the arm and tried to move him toward the dogs. He gave me a very hard push, so I gave up on the poor clod and returned to examine the dogs at closer quarters, squatting in the dust beside them.

But now Yaapie's mother came running out of the house and ordered Yaapie into the kitchen. Then she began to scream at me. I had never said a word to Vrou Hendricks before and I wondered if she hadn't lost her mind. (The afternoon was full of wonders.) I tried to explain what a Siamese twin is. She was shrieking, pointing up the road, calling me a bad boy, and ordering me to get on home immediately. Across the street, some Africans with wide grins stood enjoying the show. Perhaps they had never seen an Afrikaner woman go stark raving mad before.

I have no memory of who enlightened me, whether it was my parents or some dim realization of my own that fornicating dogs sometimes get stuck together. That I finally got my biology right hardly matters, since it was too late for me to feel embarrassment or to apologize or to show up with a little gift (flowers? a tin of lard?) and repair the social fabric now ripped to shreds. I knew Vrou Hendricks would always see me as a perverted, monstrous English boy. And whenever I passed her house after that day, I was vaguely inclined to see myself that way. The affair of the Siamese dogs marked the beginning of some very bad days in Beaconsfield.

26

The Handsome Boy

MY MOTHER, WHO COULD NOT LIVE WITHOUT A PIANO, HAD NO sooner installed her new spinet than I found myself taking lessons from the highly regarded Mrs. Lloyd. Mrs. Lloyd was full-bodied, to say the least. I was impressed by her black, flowered dresses, her perspiring double chin, the black-rimmed spectacles, and the magisterial creak of her corset. I took in everything but her instruction.

Mrs. Lloyd's studio was a narrow back room in downtown Kimberley. The grim upright piano reserved for her students stood with its back to the wall, less a musical instrument than a torture rack. On Saturday mornings, I studied music theory. On Thursday afternoons, the upright had its way with me.

For someone so addicted to the sound of music, my sloth is difficult to understand. Mrs. Lloyd, who would never learn a thing about me, put me to work on the usual Bach and Beethoven. She belonged to the "by rote" school of pedagogy and either had no imagination herself or assumed that small people one fourth her weight did not. She would point to a note on the page, point to its referent on the keyboard, then dab her damp neck and sigh. I stared at the notes and saw blackbirds sitting on phone lines. These birds bore no resemblance whatever to the sounds jangling in my head. Mrs. Lloyd (wearily beating time) didn't notice that I was not bothering to connect musical sound to patterns framed by staves. She went on naming notes, and I continued in my ignorance. As for music theory—sitting at a table and writing out the Phrygian or Lydian mode or sorting out diminished and augmented chords on a perfectly good Saturday morning—this was simply to waste my favorite day in the week.

Mrs. Lloyd, with her noble double chin and impressive bulk, fanned herself vigorously while I sat with an idiot's dull eye, staring at the leavings of genius. At home I improvised. But somehow Mrs. Lloyd gave me the impression that playing "by ear" was immoral, so composition became my secret vice. My own music was devised from a spectral scale of five notes that sounded, I thought, Chinese.

I composed a number of little pieces, but continued to show up for my lesson prepared only to desecrate Beethoven exactly as I had the week before. Mrs. Lloyd would shake her head, sigh, and wipe her red face with the large handkerchief she laid out to dry on the top piano keys. My favorite piece was the Chopin Waltz in F-sharp because it employed these high keys. This gave me the chance to flick her handkerchief to the floor. Too fat to lean over and pick up the article herself, my poor teacher would wait patiently for me to do so. Even this little pause in the excruciating effort of mental work was a relief. I have never understood why I avoided the small effort it took to memorize notes. I knew perfectly well that one day I would play the piano, no matter how much work it took. Perhaps it was the crushing sense of inevitability that I kicked against, like an overloaded mule that sees ahead the length of the road, the height of the mountain, the day just beginning.

My sister, meanwhile, learned eight new pieces in eight weeks (reported in a letter to her grandmother) and played a duet at Mrs. Lloyd's annual students' recital in Kimberley. I had also been lined up to play a duet. My fellow artist was a pallid, trembly girl who resembled, I thought, an asparagus. She regarded me with equal distaste. Perhaps our mutual detestation undermined her health, because she came down with the mumps the day before we were scheduled to exhibit ourselves, and brilliantly saved us from public humiliation. So I sat in the audience like a man transferred from death row to an ice-cream parlor, and listened to my sister twinkle her way through "Climbing the Stairs."

Everyone always said Mrs. Lloyd was the best teacher in Kimberley, but we were not made for each other. We both secretly agreed I was a lazy dunce, and there our agreement ended. She made it clear, by sign and by sigh, that I would never be Rachmaninoff or Rubinstein, but she was willing to go on training me as one might a recalcitrant chimpanzee.

Mrs. Lloyd never learned about my fascination with music. I never mentioned my own pieces. I would wake up in the middle of the night to the sound of African singing or to music blossoming in my mind's ear. But my musical talent was more than matched by my genius for resisting rote mental work. And whatever came easy to me, I somehow distrusted. I am sure it was never Mrs. Lloyd's intention but, with my support, she helped me to cancel myself out perfectly.

Again, it was my mother who saved me. After tucking me into bed, she often sat down at the piano. On a certain summer evening she played Beethoven's little Minuet in G with such perfect simplicity that the music took on immense meaning. The orderly notes filled me with a joy that ran along my spine like an electric charge. Her playing contained, in its wordless design, the meaning of my childhood. The love I felt for my mother was there, gathering life from the music, the rich shadows of my room, the silver tricks of water running in the garden, the click and crash of the door opening and closing as my father came in late from work. She laid bare for me the passionate design of the world.

However, even the most ecstatic insight didn't contain enough dynamite to raise me off my bottom. As lazy and distracted as ever, and still unable to identify a D above high C, I failed to notice that triplets are everywhere the same, for all eternity. I had decided that whatever appears on a musical stave was magically beyond me. I was dedicated to idiocy and made nothing of the music burbling in the sump of my imagination. Written notes belonged to people with talent. The rest of us were doomed to improvisation.

It never occurred to Mrs. Lloyd to delve into my murky nature, to question my motives (if any), to identify whatever was musical in the tropical swamp of my psyche. There was a musician hiding out in there, God bless him, but it was not poor Mrs. Lloyd who flushed him out.

To get to Mrs. Lloyd's studio, I lugged my music books past Yaapie Hendricks's house to wait for the bus that ran up the Dutoitspan Road, past the botanical gardens, to downtown Kimberley. But one Thursday afternoon, shortly after the Siamese dogs incident, my way was blocked by a group of Afrikaner boys. They formed a line across the road as I approached. Yaapie hung back and said nothing, but this was clearly his party.

A boy I had never seen before came forward and spoke to me. He was a handsome boy with smooth skin and perfectly even features, better dressed than the others. His hair, cut in the English style, angled across the forehead. He was so even featured that I found him unpleasant to contemplate, as if beauty were the beginning of corruption. Looking back, I would say he resembled one of those pretty Hollywood actors who somehow transform good looks and a tiny talent into the appearance of perfect self-assurance. He wore a clean white shirt with a softly rolled collar and dark navy shorts. His gray knee socks were ringed with the colors of the Afrikaner school we beat that season in rugby. His family was clearly better off than Yaapie's, but where he came from, where he lived, who he was, I would never find out.

He walked right up to me as if we were old friends and we stood more or less eye to eye, though he probably had five years on me. His smile was direct and easy. He knew exactly what he was going to do, and I knew exactly what he was going to do. But since he had not done it yet, there was nothing I could do to stop him.

The handsome boy had a born leader's self-possession and good timing. I had only my damnable intuition, which let me know everything that would happen without giving me a clue what to do about it. The other boys closed in around me with the alert, expectant air of dogs in a hunting party. *"Hoe gaan dit met jou vandag?"* (How are you today?), the handsome boy asked with a smile.

"Baie goed. Wat maak jy hier met Yaapie?" (I'm fine. What are you doing here with Yaapie?), I returned.

He had assumed I wouldn't understand his Afrikaans; he had expected to embarrass me. Now he pretended not to understand me and switched to English. The whole encounter was an elaborate act and would have seemed silly had I not been so afraid.

"And what are we carrying there, if I may ask?" he went on, reaching for my books. His English had the artificial precision of a good student's. He was a clever lad, the handsome boy.

"Music," I said.

"Ag, so we play music do we?" he said, taking the book from my hand and flipping the pages, faking interest. "Very nice. May I borrow this from you?"

"Waarom?" (Why?), I continued in Afrikaans. He persisted in English, affronted by my rude question.

"That's my affair," he said, handing the book to one of Yaapie's friends, who dropped it in the dust.

The ring of boys had tightened around me. The handsome boy

reached out and fingered the other books I held. "I want these too," he said.

"*Waarom?*"

"Because I have asked politely," he said. "Didn't your parents teach you good manners?"

"I'll be late for my lesson," I said, persisting in my Afrikaans.

"That's your affair, not my affair," he said, and suddenly he yanked the books from my grasp, dropping them in the dust between our feet. I knew better than to try to pick them up.

"When was the last time I hit you?" he asked, stepping closer.

"You've never hit me," I said, knowing I should not have said it.

"Today," he said.

I found myself flat on the ground, lying among my books. When I stood up, he genially knocked me down again. They all wanted to knock me down. They were all dying to get into it. I felt hopelessly limp and oddly absent, as if this were happening to someone else.

I decided not to get up again and sat there looking up at their eager faces. The handsome boy clicked his tongue; he was disappointed in me. The drama had gone slack. He pretended he was going to kick me, then broke stride and walked away, full of amused contempt. The rest shambled after him, taking care to trample over my music. I gathered up the filthy books and went to my lesson, pausing at the Indian greengrocer's to wash my face. I told the owner I had fallen down. It seemed more noble to lie than to tell the truth.

My afternoons were now full of anxiety. Every week or two, the handsome boy and his gang would bar my way, detaching themselves in a group from the shade under a peppertree or swarming up from under a culvert. It would have been smart to turn my bike around the moment I saw them and peddle back into Beaconsfield. But each time they showed up, I rode slowly toward them, stopping as if for their convenience when they blocked my way. My passive refusal to back down contained at least the ghost of resistance.

Each time they stopped me, I would politely answer the handsome boy's idiotic questions. Then, after a bit of bland dialogue, he would knock me to the ground. Once, when I blocked his arm and grabbed his hand, one of the others spun me around and pushed me over an outstretched leg. When I refused the handsome boy's invitation to stand up, he came over very slowly, shook his head sadly at the sight of me, half turned as if he were leaving, then suddenly, with exquisite timing, kicked me in the chest. "Never hit an Afrikaner, *kaffer-jie*. Do you understand what I am telling you?" he said and spat in the dust near my head.

To avoid these little get-togethers with my Afrikaner neighbors, I took alternate routes home. I would slip past the Boxall house and take the back road behind the tailings dump. My bike was my best protection, and I made sure the tires were hard, the chain well oiled. The trick was to move past Yaapie's place in a businesslike way, but not so quickly that I looked afraid. More than a fist in my face, I feared looking like a coward.

Once they ran out of a gully after I had passed by, and I could hear them thinly crying out that I should come back. They had something they wanted to tell me. With a luxurious sense of power and ease, I ignored them and rode on without haste.

Because I now sported bruises and black eyes, I had to admit to my mother that I had got into a fight with some boys. My mother didn't question me closely. She could see I was hiding something, and I could see that she could see. I knew she had a way of waiting for me to confess, which made it impossible not to confess. I felt that she already knew what I would say, that she already sympathized. And I wanted nothing more than to break down like a big baby and ask for help. But I knew that doing such a thing would change me permanently for the worse. One morning, when I came to breakfast with two black eyes, she said I was not to go to school unless I told her what was going on. I told her but hotly insisted it was my business.

She thought something could be said to Yaapie's mother. My father agreed with me that it was best for kids to sort these things out for themselves. When I came home with a tooth loose, my mother insisted that something be done. It was, she argued, a second tooth, and nature would not issue me another.

Still, I objected. I was sure my parents' interference would be the end of me. My father let it ride until I woke up one morning with the right side of my face turning black. That afternoon, when I got home, he was waiting for me. He told me to get into the car, no arguments. We drove directly to the Hendricks's house.

"I'm going in. You can stay out here if you like," he said. But I felt idiotic sitting alone in the car with the small Hendricks children staring at me, so I went with him.

Our Chevrolet looked embarrassingly out of place parked against the rusting metal fence that straggled around the Hendricks's property. My father knocked gently on the door. When Vrou Hendricks appeared, she gave a start. My father suggested we all go inside to talk. The interior was clean and spare, no pictures, no photographs, no carpets or rugs. Chipped enamel cups had been placed on the bare wooden table.

Two small girls came in, and Vrou Hendricks sent them scurrying out with a sharp word. She closed the door, and we stood around the table while she and my father stumbled about in two languages. She knew hardly any English, and my father's bad Afrikaans was just one more ghastly embarrassment as far as I was concerned. He wanted me to translate. Vrou Hendricks wouldn't look at me, however. How could I explain to my father that Vrou Hendricks thought I was a filthy little beast who actually enjoyed watching dogs stuck together? That I had called her out of her house to come and share in my perverse pleasures?

My father said he didn't think it was right for a lot of older boys to beat up on a younger boy. Vrou Hendricks stared at a corner of the room and said she knew nothing about it. Then Yaapie himself came shambling through the back door and stopped dead, eyeballing me as if I were a ghost. His mother looked at him, and he quickly slinked away.

Our visit to Vrou Hendricks conveyed a confused message. My father was being his usual kindly, genial self. She was too upset to respond. How could I tell her, no matter how able my Afrikaans, that this slightly awkward, rather elegant man was one of the most reasonable people on earth?

Having said he was pleased that the beatings were now a thing of the past, he led me outside, and we drove grandly away in our great, expensive American car. I would have felt more comfortable, and less conspicuous, crawling away in the dust on my hands and knees.

For some weeks after that the Afrikaners disappeared, and all I saw was the rusting fence around Yaapie's house and, beyond that, the thin line of peppertrees where the Africans sat patiently and the Cape Corps drilled, raising great clouds of dust that dropped a fine red sediment on the leaves of our orange trees. Time passed, perhaps a month or two. I began to relax.

Then one twilight, after a long afternoon with the Boxall boys, as I nosed my bike along the back route behind the tailings dump, the gang again materialized. The back road was a rock-strewn track beside a ditch. The tailings hill rose steeply on the left, and halfway up the cliff face was the entrance to a great cave shaped like a howling mouth. An apron of earth spewed from this mouth, forming an incline that reached all the way to the road below. Working my front wheel around the rocks in the road, I glanced up and saw a crowd of boys running silently down from the cave, taking up positions on the road directly ahead. The stab of fear I felt fixed in my mind forever the low sun over Beaconsfield on my right, the friendly road ahead that I would not take, the sour, dusty smell of the gang surrounding me when I drew to a stop.

The handsome boy, with his sinister, friendly smile, came up and laid his hands on my handlebars. The gang had grown in number, but Yaapie was gone. This group of white Afrikaners had allowed a single black African to join them. It was clear the kid was a stranger to their rules. He didn't understand that the handsome boy must do all the talking, that he must stand silently, with an alert, wolfish expression, ready to leap if his leader nodded. The African boy pushed his way to the front and tried to show off by giving me a push. I ignored him. He seized my arm. I knew the rules and struck his hand away. He took a feeble poke at me. I caught his arm and twisted it.

The handsome boy had indulged the black boy enough. He gave the African a look. The African boy immediately understood that he was out of place and faded back with a bobbing, groveling motion of his head. I was the handsome boy's toy, not his.

The handsome boy was so pleased to see me that he rang my bicycle bell gaily to celebrate our reunion. "I thought you were running away from us," he said. He always spoke to me as if I were an idiot, and answering him always made me feel stupid. But saying nothing seemed even worse. It was only long after our encounters that I knew what I should have said, the sarcastic, witty, condescending remarks I might have used. I loathed my own well-bred politeness, the fastidious distance I preserved, which earned me nothing but a fist in the eye. "I wasn't running," I said.

"And are you going home to your nice dinner then?"

"Yes," I said.

"Are you so sure about that?"

"I don't know what you mean."

"I think you know very well what I mean."

"I don't think so." (Feeble!)

"Do you want me to show you what I mean?"

"No," I said. (Too quickly.)

"This is a very nice bike," said the handsome boy, ringing the bell again. "May I have it?"

"It's mine," I said. (Stupid.)

He began to rock the bike gently from side to side, smiling at me, testing to see how long I would hang on to it. I let him have it. He gave the bike a flip, and it rolled down into the ditch and bounced off some boulders.

The African boy had worked his way forward again and was still looking for a way to show he belonged. "Go and get it," he said to me and looked gaily around, trying to catch their Afrikaner eyes. No one reacted. His presence among the Afrikaners struck me as the most mysterious thing about that evening. Had he been brought along to make some point with me? Like a breeze passing over still water, a look of mild irritation passed over the handsome boy's face. "Piss off," he said. The African boy moved back as if he'd been slapped. I stood like an ox, waiting for the hammer blow. The handsome boy stepped closer and stared into my eyes.

"Bang?" (Afraid?), he asked in piteous tones, hanging his head.

The switch to Afrikaans was intimate and ominous. It was, I realize in retrospect, the unholy intimacy of torturer and victim. He brought his hands up slowly to my chest, pretended to play with a button on my shirt, then gave me a sudden, hard shove. I flew back into the ditch and landed on my fallen bike. There was a pain in my side where the peddle thrust into my ribs. I untangled myself from the crossbars and stood up. The handsome boy lounged on the edge of the ditch looking down. He had picked up a handful of small stones. He began to throw them at me gently. "Listen, I want you to do something for me," he said. "I left my jacket in the cave up there. Fetch it for me, and we'll let you go home to your nice dinner."

"You'll steal my bike," I said.

He said I needn't worry. I refused to leave without it. He pretended to fling a stone at me as hard as he could, and everyone laughed when I threw up an arm. "Take your bike then," he said. "But do as I say. Hear?"

I straightened out the handlebars and started up the slope to the cave. The sun was setting beyond Beaconsfield and shone directly on me. The boys, ranged along the ditch below, were in deep shadow. I had no intention of bringing the handsome boy his coat from the cave and considered him foolish for allowing me to leave with my bike. I planned to climb to the top, then push off and shoot down the incline to the right. Unless my tire skidded on gravel and I took a spill, there was no way they could stop me. The ride down over loose stones was treacherous, but I had done it before. The demand that I fetch the handsome boy's coat was, I thought, just another of their pointless games. They were letting me go because my father had visited Vrou Hendricks and they knew better than to beat up the mine manager's son.

It took me about five minutes to push up the incline to the mouth of the cave. The boys in deep shadow were still standing by the ditch, still as statues. I took the bike into the cave, out of sight so that I could turn it around and take off downhill. Like every cave in that part of the world, this one had been used by transient Africans. There were sleeping ledges cut in the wall and a circle of fire stones with ashes. The cave curved around out of sight.

I swung the bike around and suddenly someone came out from the interior of the cave, moving from shadow to sunlight. I saw the knife, then the face. Not a face I had seen before. One of those pinched, undernourished Afrikaner faces—narrow nose, shaved head, light blue eyes. He was up there waiting to strike me with the knife. I stared stupidly at him and, had he attacked me then, I may well have stood quietly while he buried the knife in my body. Perhaps the bike between us, or my stillness, or something in my face, or the fact that I had a face, made him pause. Perhaps he had imagined some other face entirely. An anthropologist might link my stillness to the reflex in certain African baboons who are so overcome when they confront a snake that they faint dead away.

The boy said, *"Voertsek!"* and kicked the crossbar of my bike. He wanted a moving target. Or maybe he was giving me a chance to run for it. I stood staring at him. My most powerful inclination was to speak with him—"We have lives, we have mothers"—but I was afraid, unable to speak. When I stepped back from the bike, he hefted the knife. I pushed off, standing on the left peddle.

There was a flat space that seemed to go on forever. Whether the handsome boy and his gang had disappeared, I took no note. I was headed down another track and had just reached the incline when the Afrikaner came for me. I raised my right hand, releasing the handlebars, and the bike went out of control, shooting downslope as I tumbled after. The tip of his knife slashed through the end of my fourth finger, but I felt nothing. It was only after he had scuttled away down the far side that I saw the blood.

The sun was still hanging fire on the horizon and perhaps twelve or fifteen minutes had passed since I first spotted the handsome boy fanning out from the cave as they ran to intercept me. No segment of South African time is better preserved in my memory. The stones, the sandy ditch, the bitter face of the boy with the hunting knife, the sun over the Beaconsfield slum, my bleeding hand wrapped in the tail of my shirt as I ride.

27

Brother Keene

THE IDEA OF ONCE AGAIN VISITING VROU HENDRICKS WITH MY FA-
ther fronting for me was intolerable. So I bandaged the finger tightly
and said I'd cut myself with a pocketknife. I'd slashed and punctured
and ruptured parts of myself so thoroughly over the previous three
years that my mother didn't question me. In this way, I got my private life under my own control. But the handsome boy's bestial smile
still plagued me.

Lying in bed at night, I ran through scenarios, evasion tactics, killer attacks. Each afternoon, peddling nervously past the tailings dump, I looked for Afrikaners to swarm out of every ditch. I
confided my fears to Kenneth Boxall, but he had no reason whatever to stick his neck into my noose. He said the handsome boy's
name was Jan. Useless information. Every third Afrikaner's name
was Jan, and an Afrikaner's name was useless to an English person. They lived in a separate universe, and came out only when

they wanted revenge. The sensible thing to do was to look for a weapon.

I had always been attracted to knives—hunting knives, pocket-knives, slim straight knives, curving knives, stilettos, and scimitars. This attraction now developed into hot passion. After school I went looking for knives the way teenagers look for girls. I was soon well acquainted with the two or three cutlery shops in Kimberley. The best was down the street from Mrs. Lloyd's studio. I searched for a knife neither too heavy nor too light, a knife that would not snap back on the fingers, a knife that would slide unobtrusively into my pocket. I wanted a knife with a lovely, slim blade that flicked open on touch and was sharp as a snake's tooth.

Ralph, one of my classmates, told me he knew just the knife for my purpose. The most interesting thing about Ralph was his webbed toes. Whenever a new boy arrived at CBC we would ask Ralph to take off his shoes and show his feet. Ralph said he had an uncle who had brought three switchblades back from France before the war. I insisted on seeing them, so Ralph took me to his uncle's house. It was cool and dark and a clock was ticking loudly. Three identical knives glittered in a drawer. Press a button and they sprang open like reptiles striking. Their blades tapered in a subtle curve to a needle point. They fitted my pocket perfectly. The French term was *couteau automatique* and on each blade was inscribed *Laguiole Extra*.

I told Ralph I would do anything to get one of those knives. After days of backing and forthing, he finally agreed to introduce me to his uncle, a weary, diffident, balding individual who said, "Yes, yes. Take it."

Was I hearing correctly? Was he actually handing over this price-less object, no questions asked? I tried to thank him. He didn't want to hear about it. He gave one to Ralph too. The knives created a bond between us. It was as if we had married twin sisters. It was one of the happiest days of my childhood.

Biking through Beaconsfield now, passing Yaapie's and the tailings hill, I felt reckless and slightly mad. A kind of furious resistance had built up in me. I tried to imagine what the handsome boy would try next. I imagined it would be something even more extreme. A barrage of stones. Dynamite.

I stopped seeing Bill Byerley, my best friend, and spent all my free time with Ralph, practicing with knives in a park on the main road to Kimberley. We worked out tactics for injuring the greatest number of Afrikaners in the shortest possible time. After our maneuvers, I rode home briskly, past Yaapie's house and the tailings hill, my eye pricked to every shadow in every ravine. Ralph helped me work out a slashing and stabbing routine to be followed by a whirling attack. "The whirling dervish attack," he called it. The aim was to go home bathed in blood, none of it your own.

One afternoon, as we were perfecting our moves in the botanical gardens, an Afrikaner man strolled up casually and asked our names and our school. He wrote down all we told him in a grubby little notebook with a pencil stub. He then informed us that we were in very serious trouble. We had ignored the ordinance posted on the front gate that forbade bicycles in the gardens. So we would now be prosecuted and punished. He felt he must warn us that only a month before, a boy from CBC had tried to sneak his bike into the gardens. The school principal had given the boy a beating he would never forget. "You boys are in for a good lesson," he said cheerfully. "Then maybe you'll read what it says on signs, eh?"

I expected him to end his little lecture by confiscating our knives and calling the police to arrest us. But apparently there was no ordinance against flick knives. So we rolled out of the park badly shaken, but in full possession of our weapons.

We realized too late, as always, that we should have given him false names. We knew perfectly well that we junior boys lived in a fool's paradise—that punishment in the upper school made Brother Ellif's little taps with the leather strap look like caresses. We would have to deal with Brother Reedee, who resembled a Hollywood gangster, and Brother Keene, whose furious severity and hands like hams inspired little hope for the future. Brother McManus, the principal, represented ultimate authority, like Winston Churchill or the Pope. He had always been a distant, magisterial figure, heard from only when he addressed the assembled student body once a year and read the names of the "old boys" killed in Germany that season. His office, everyone said, was equipped with a rackful of flexible canes and whips of every size and shape.

It was not easy to concentrate in class. Whenever footsteps sounded on the loggia outside and passing figures disturbed the light on my desk, I tensed up. It was only a question of time before someone in a black cassock arrived to summon me to the principal's office. There, I would learn at last what a real whipping was all about.

The days dragged on, and still no one flung open the classroom door to point a furious finger at me. I began very hesitantly to hope that the Afrikaner park attendant had lied about contacting Brother McManus. Ralph no longer worried at all. He said Afrikaners never did anything right. And even if we were beaten, we would not be beaten senseless, as Ian Hogben insisted. Ralph even began to toy with the notion we might not be beaten at all. And just as my gloom was lifting, Kenneth Boxall stopped me on the way home from school to say the handsome boy was dead.

It was simply too good to be true. Surely, reality is made of sterner stuff! But no, Kenneth was sure. Jan, if that was his name, had been killed in a car accident. He had been wonderfully, magically erased.

There was no way to check the facts. The chasm between my English-speaking world and the shadowy existence of the Afrikaners was so deep that it never occurred to me to stop and ask Yaapie Hendricks about his friend. Yaapie and I no longer existed for each other. Had he called out to me, I would have ignored him with the same cold contempt he had practiced on me when I first arrived in Kimberley.

The death of the handsome boy left a great deal unresolved. I still felt the burden of my old shame every time I saw Yaapie's mother. The incident with the Siamese dogs had put a permanent crimp in my sense of how the Afrikaners saw me. I would be forever ridiculous in their eyes, a degraded figure. They would always think, "There he goes, the boy who likes to watch dogs stuck together." It was painful to reflect that no matter how much I felt at home in their language, they would never listen to anything I said. I was sure that emigrating to America was the solution to all my problems.

The death of the handsome boy bothered me for other reasons. I felt there was something vulgar in my new freedom. Unadorned good luck had given me the advantage. While I lived in glorious sunshine, the handsome boy was rotting underground. I imagined him decaying and stinking in his horrible, dark coffin. The justice of it all was slightly overwhelming. Hitler, too, we all knew, would end badly. But the handsome boy had been removed so quickly from the world that I'd not even had a chance to redeem my self-respect with a switchblade.

The handsome boy's death raised me to theology. Was it possible that I lived in a state of grace? I was forced to consider that possibility. Brother Ellif had described grace, and I felt I now lived near, if not smack in the middle, of that exalted state. The nagging anxiety I'd lived with for months had been lifted so suddenly that I pondered the possibility of angels. My new state changed the way the city appeared. The light in the fields was . . . lighter. Mornings and twilights were celestial in their peacefulness. If the handsome boy (whose whole existence, it seemed to me, was dedicated to making me miserable), if this petty demon could be so easily removed from my path, there was a good chance I had friends in very high places indeed. I sang on my way to school.

I was involved just then in the sort of religious instruction my mother had always tried to steer me away from. She had never forgiven the Catholic Church, in the person of her parish priest, for advising her mother to boycott her marriage in a Protestant church. At CBC, she had me put down as Church of England (Anglican). She had never mentioned religion before, and I had no idea how or why I was now Church of England. With my genius for avoiding work, I got myself excused from the Church of England instruction periods (in the gym) as soon as it became clear that intellectual effort might be involved.

I asked Brother Ellif for permission to attend the Catholic Mass instead. He immediately put a catechism in my hands and escorted me himself to my first Mass. I rather enjoyed turning the thin pages of the plump little catechism, and it was pleasant to read the sonorous prose. Nothing could have been more remote to a boy raised in the sensual and pitiless world of Greek and Norse mythology than the rich affectations of Roman Catholicism. I liked the vestments of the priest, the incense (which I figured had been introduced to cover the stink of rotting corpses), and I liked the richly dressed chapel with its stern saints and sad statue of Mary. I liked all the standing and kneeling. I liked the Latin language that gave God a remote but comprehensible tongue. And most of all I liked the twelve stations of the cross, which involved a kind of guided tour past twelve paintings whose agonies were bloody enough to satisfy even a ten year old's religious requirements.

In short, I absorbed Catholicism without suffering the responsibility of being a Catholic. I was free to imbibe the sensation of religion without having to bother with the metaphysics or suffer the guilt. Catholicism for me was like a visit to a health spa where they pack you in mud—after which, for an hour or so, you feel much better.

So I was feeling wonderful, was in fact approaching an apotheosis of self-satisfaction when I heard a rumor that brought terror back into my life. The word came down that our classes had been rescheduled. Instead of Brother Reedee, who was merely neurotic and bestial, we were getting Brother Keene, who was mad and murderous. In fact, Brother Keene was everything terrifying about a Catholic education compressed into one enormous man. This bad news was particularly unfair to a person like myself, who imagined himself living in something like a state of grace.

Brother Keene was presumably a man devoted to the Church, but I could no more imagine him kneeling down to God than I could see myself kissing a stone idol. He was more like a scourge sent by Jehovah, an Avenging Angel with an Irish accent. Tall, rawboned, a pale, white-haired man in his late fifties, our new teacher was filled with a cold, apocalyptic energy. He never smiled because nothing amused him. When he wrote on the blackboard, the chalk splintered and flew into fragments. He seemed to me a creature dredged up from the depths of a frozen lake in some Hans Christian Andersen tale— the North Wind who freezes little Kai and blows the Snow Queen's sled out past the pole star.

Brother Keene's furies were, like life itself, disorderly and unpredictable. He carried a long cane and, when we came up with a wrong answer, would strike it against the blackboard. The sound rang out like a gunshot, and this kept us in such a state of collective tension that we probably bore more resemblance to tombstones than ten year olds.

It was no use trying to hide in a back row, because Brother Keene paced restlessly, like a puma, circling and twitching at his black skirts. He toured up the aisles as he dictated, pausing to check what we were scribbling in our notebooks. In Brother Ellif's benign presence, I used to draw little faces in the margins of my notes. It would have been insane to doodle in Brother Keene's class. When our handwriting was sloppy, he slapped the pens from our hands, and if we didn't improve, knocked us bodily into the aisles. Our handwriting improved overnight.

We stood at attention to recite and spoke in loud, clear voices in complete sentences. Soon we were all spouting long pages of verse and memorizing arcane dates associated with conflicts in Prussia and the Venetian Republic. Only precision could redeem us from violence.

Aware that flinching might set him off into a sharkish fury, we learned to relax when he came near. Boys who twitched inspired his attack. He would sometimes delay his pounce until long after the offense was past. Like some dark recording angel, he added up our transgressions in a moral ledger of his own devising. And when the time was ripe, he came down like the sky falling.

Tender boys with pink cheeks and plump bottoms were hit hardest. Their hate for him hardened them. Even our best rugby player, the rat-faced Mighty Fredericks with fists like stones, put on a respectful expression when Brother Keene passed. Duma's murmuring recitation and St. Clair's stutter worried us all. Brother Keene would begin to hitch at his sash, his mouth working. He would stop behind some pour soul and demand to know what the trouble might be. He loathed our fear, our girlish quivering. And because he could read our thoughts, we tried to fix our trembling, butterfly minds on Shakespeare or the Punic Wars.

Brother Keene's pounce was too rapid for the eye to follow and it came always when it was least expected. Assume there had been some incredible exhibition of stupidity. Assume that Driver had no idea what large animal Hannibal led over the Alps, or that Brown had confused Wordsworth with Goldsmith, or that Hogben had dropped a hard-boiled egg on the floor just as Brother Keene passed. Brother Keene might not even glance at Hogben or the egg. The bell would ring for lunch. We would all hope and pray that Hogben had, *mirabile dictu*, got away with it. But after lunch it was Hogben who was gently asked to respond to Brother Keene's first question. Naturally, he made a total mess of it. Brother Keene's second question would be served up even more gently. And we would lower our heads, having anticipated in Brother Keene's twitching lip the horror that was coming. There would come a rustle (the swoop) and a thud (the slap), and there was Hogben lying flat in the aisle.

So we learned how to recite while maintaining a hair-trigger alertness to every movement around us. The danger of being stupid had never been more real. It was Darwin's world in action, though Darwin was unlikely to be mentioned at CBC back then. Because we all had to suffer on account of the slow and the stupid, we were ready to kill them at first. This proving impossible, we were stuck with trying to help them because when Brother Keene lost his temper no one was safe.

When he didn't lose his temper it seemed even more astonishing. Byerley was reciting one day when Waddington, a fat, nervous boy loudly farted. We assumed Waddington, and Byerley too, were done for. But Brother Keene circled the class and made no sign. And Waddington, having lost all control, farted again even more loudly. Gradually, we simply could not stop ourselves; we all began to squeak and hiss with laughter. And still Brother Keene circled without pausing, and Byerley recited. It took perhaps five minutes for the class to completely disintegrate. Even the pallid Bartram, who never laughed, turned blood red. The class sounded like a badly constructed steam engine coming apart. We held our noses, we grabbed our throats—no use. The laughter was more painful and more delicious than any laughter I have experienced since. It broke our will, and the sensation of being broken was wonderful.

Byerley could not go on and sat helpless in his seat. Brother Keene moved to the back of the room and stood there without speaking. Of course, no one looked at him. "Go to lunch," he said. We were being turned loose seven minutes early. Something miraculous had happened, but we could not say what.

Once he had us in good order, a whole week might pass without Brother Keene landing a blow. As souls in hell grow used even to fire and pitchforks, we grew used to him. We even began to calculate the amount of punishment we were willing to absorb and tried to adjust our study habits to that degree. As we toughened, we relaxed. Our weary bodies slumped, our pens, all by themselves, began to doodle in margins again. The names of convent girls appeared on desk tops. Then suddenly one or the other among us would lie sprawling in the aisle.

In my case, terror worked wonders. I shot up in class standing from thirteenth to third. Bill Byerley, also much improved by terror, still came in ahead of me. And, of course, there was Bartram, the thinking animal, whom nobody could beat, who was always first.

Byerley possessed a feverish imagination. We both had younger sisters. His was a small, frail girl with a cloud of red hair. The Byerley family lived off the Dutoitspan Road in Belgravia, a neighborhood I thought magical. I could never get enough of city suburbs, where the houses were copied from English models with tudor peaks and cut stone copings and cornices. These gardens unfolded like ideas with brick walls and statues and complicated spaces defined by gazebos, poplar trees, or spiraling cypress. The shrubs were shaped into spheres or pyramids. There were stairways with carved newels and goosenecks. From every window there were views of rooftops and trees that looked like spires.

Down from Byerley's house, the girls' Convent School ran for a quarter mile along the boulevard. And sauntering up the sidewalk every afternoon with her leather book bag, pausing to pull up a droopy blue stocking, was Betty Beck, the most elegant girl I had ever laid eyes on. Tall and slender, she had chestnut hair cut to a point on her cheeks and so low across her eyebrows that she would repeatedly toss her head like a little horse, a gesture that fascinated me.

Her parents often showed up at our garden parties and sometimes Betty came with her small sister, Chloe. My father filmed Betty at one of my sister's birthday parties, and she appears in a bright red sweater four inches short in the sleeves, delicately licking cake frosting from her fingertips. I imagine her grown now, wonderfully elegant and perfectly ordinary, but she was my ideal then, and I absorbed her image the way a boa constrictor digests a small deer. For long days, she inhabited my thoughts—the curve of her long legs, which she tossed around so carelessly, the straight bangs, the narrow wrists and spidery hands.

How many conversations did we have? Two or three at most. Our chitchat was pointless and dull. If she knew she obsessed me, she gave no sign. Had she shown any interest in me, I would have been too stunned to respond. It was impossible to tell her that while my days were sacked and pillaged by Brother Keene, my nights were redeemed by her brown eyes, her sharp elbows, her offhand gestures. I had read *Tom Sawyer* and carefully studied Tom's affair with Becky Thatcher. But I lacked Tom's cold blood. And I guessed that Becky Thatcher was a lot easier to deal with than Betty Beck, who looked at me (when she looked at me) as though she were viewing something very distant through binoculars.

It was Betty Beck's name I was ever so carefully working into the wood of my desk with the dry point of my dip pen the day Brother Keene knocked me flying. I imagined myself sitting with her in Bill Byerley's garden speaking in flowing sentences. She sat with her hand quietly settled in mine while I told her how addicted I was to that sidelong glance of hers, how I could not take my eyes off her as she worked her way through a large slice of cake, how I wondered whether I could lay a little kiss on the corner of her mouth—and then there was a tremendous explosion, the world filled with red light, and I lay flat in the aisle between two rows of school desks, my cheek paralyzed, and what sounded like a drum full of wasps buzzing in my ear. Towering over me stood Brother Keene, his face pale with fury. "Expound on the point I have just now clarified," he hissed. I had no idea whether we were doing history, mathematics, or Afrikaans grammar. I opened my mouth, but no sound emerged.

His skirts seething over his polished black boots, he whipped furiously to the front of the room. He demanded to know what I was doing in this class. He wanted to know exactly what went on in the mind of a creature like me. Then he came pitching up to me again and, seizing me by both ears, placed his nose a half inch from mine. He smelled of cigarettes and stale sweat. He shaved carelessly. I was obliged to return his basilisk stare.

"What are you thinking? What is going on in that brain of yours?" he hissed.

Usually one of the class survivors, bright boys like Bart or Byerley, would try to save those at sea by some sign, some word. But I was too far gone; I would never make it back. Scratching my beloved's name in CBC property, I'd heard no muted coughs and felt no flying spitball. I'd been lounging in some Muslim paradise with Betty Beck and Catholicism had every right to its revenge. I said I had been thinking about a girl.

"A girl," said Brother Keene. "A girl? Why?"

"Because," I said, "I love her."

My mind blank, I was reduced to the truth. I expected the class to howl with laughter. I expected Brother Keene to fly into a frothing rage and tear me to bits. But there was no sound. His cold, blue eyes stared into mine. An absent look came over him. He had the look of a man remembering something he'd forgotten to do. Turning abruptly, he stalked out of the classroom.

We saw him pass the window, moving rapidly along the loggia porch in the direction of the principal's office. The class was dead silent. No one spoke to me. People don't jeer a condemned man. I had a fleeting image of Brother Keene and Brother McManus flinging me over the loggia parapet, my body lying broken in the stone gutter that ran around the base of the chapel. I could not make my arms and legs stop shaking.

When Brother Keene dashed back into the class a few minutes later, he said nothing. None of us could read his expression. I should have had the courage to look more intently into his face, but I was afraid. There was no use trying to interpret Brother Keene; you could only fear him. I don't recall a single thing he taught us, but I will never forget him.

28

Poor Boys

LATE IN 1943, WHILE WAR RAGED OVER THE PLANET, SIR ERNEST Oppenheimer sent Lute Parkinson on a mission to the United States. Whatever Park was supposed to do for De Beers, the details were too secret to divulge in letters mailed casually across the Atlantic, so my mother's remarks give no details. Park was, she confides to Bess "gathering confidential information" vital to De Beers's future sales in America. There had been a gradual decline in the proportion of American income spent on diamonds. It was young Harry Oppenheimer who pushed for a publicity campaign in 1938. Sir Ernest had spent his career protecting the world diamond market for De Beers, and doubtless Park's trip involved assessing and perhaps assuring South Africa its American sales. Whatever the case, the chairman wanted everything kept hush-hush. The information Park sought was so hot it could only be reported back to Sir Ernest in person.

The war was at its height when Park and Margaret booked their passage across the Atlantic. (My father had been unable to buy us a berth for any price.) De Beers lavished a salary of $1,500 a month on Park, an enormous sum at the time. As a member of the board who had spent his best years playing Mercury to Jupiter, Park assumed he was in the catbird's seat, doing vital work for one of the most powerful men in the world. (Today Sir Ernest's heirs control nearly half of the entire capitalization of the Johannesburg stock exchange.)

The amassing of great wealth is always mysterious, like a talent for tightrope walking or locating water with a wand. When, in 1903, Sir Ernest had first arrived in Kimberley, the town was distinguished by a single original feature, the Kimberley Mine, known as the Big Hole. Begun in 1870, the Big Hole was, at first, a disorganized mass of ditches dug by hundreds of frantic men, each with his own tiny claim, collectively burrowing until they had opened a chasm hundreds of feet down under the open sky. An insane network of cables connected each claim to the surface. Heavy buckets rose and descended from dawn to dusk. The sides of the Big Hole began to cave in, killing many. But they endured, digging straight down to the water table, hundreds of feet below the surface. There a deep pool of glittering green water forced a halt.

Mud rushes finally forced the closure of the mine in 1914, but by then underground tunnels were being drilled into volcanic veins that appeared to have no bottom. Giant pumps forced the water out and pushed air in. What the engineers achieved with their heavy machinery was the technological equivalent of a moon landing, but the world hardly noticed. Writers and journalists were not stirred by the spectacle of a thousand human moles digging miles under the earth.

Anthony Trollope, the English novelist, had visited Kimberley in the 1880s and describes the place as "foul with dust and flies," reeking "with bad brandy . . . fed upon potted meats; it has not a tree near it." But its library, built in 1882, was the best in South Africa, outside of Cape Town. That same year Kimberley became the first city in the world with electric streetlights. By the 1940s, the town had five film theaters, a stage where Noel Coward and Gertrude Law-rence appeared, and impressive schools dispensing a remarkably pure Oxford English. Big Capital had created order, and the town famous only for its Big Hole was transformed. And this was Sir Ernest Op-penheimer's world. He was from Germany, but English civilization dominated. My Mrs. Lloyd never lacked for piano students. The dance studios were packed with students struggling to achieve grace. And in 1948 King George VI, the Queen Mother, and the two prin-cesses were photographed in the company of Sir Ernest, standing on the edge of the Big Hole.

By the time he hired Park and my father in the thirties, Sir Er-nest's corporate kingdom included the Anglo American group, cen-tered in Johannesburg, and the Kimberley group with its handful of expert Americans. The Anglo American group was American in name only. The Anglo American managers exhibited the arrogance of underdogs. Their entire education had taken place underground and they were a closed group who promoted family and friends. My father's early experience with Coe and Fleisher had exposed him to their peculiar competence.

In August of 1943, my father was offered the management of the Iscor Metal Mine in the North Transvaal with a five-year contract and "an enormous hike in pay." He turned it down because, my mother wrote, Sir Ernest let him know through McHardy (the gen-eral manager), that "Gus would be the successor to Park." Despite the broken promises in Oranjemund, my father found himself be-lieving the enthusiastic sounds emanating from Sir Ernest's office. McHardy reported that the great man was mightily pleased by his performance, and as day followed night, surely my father must rise like the sun to a director's seat after first taking over Park's vacated post. My mother adds, "Everyone thinks the world of him in these parts. It would do your heart good to hear what his workmen say about him. He is terribly busy these days with the new Dutoitspan mine opening. He loves having lots to do."

So my father once again was contemplating a future in Africa. He wrote Bess that nothing was settled, but no matter what happened, the outcome would be a happy one. If he did not succeed, then he would gladly return home. My mother was less happy. Her days and weeks in Africa had passed with excruciating slowness; nevertheless, the best years of her life had been whisked away in what felt like no time at all.

For the sake of my mother's mental health, my parents kept in constant contact with Cook's Travel. My mother made friends with the American consul in Johannesburg, who kept her advised about ships and planes crossing the sea. But nothing was sailing or flying, unless it sailed or flew for Sir Ernest. Park and Margaret had traveled first class.

On Christmas morning of 1943 Park received a telegram from the chairman. It ordered him to return immediately to Kimberley. Two reasons were given. One: Sir Ernest had decided he must hear at once whatever information Park had unearthed. And two: Sir Ernest had decided that one Hughie Hodgson from Anglo American would be general manager (the assignment promised Park), so Park was to come home and instruct Hodgson on how to do the job.

Sir Ernest with good reason had always set great store by secrecy. He was master of the unexpected lunge, the sudden lurch. Unfortunately, silence does not guarantee cunning, and this move completely backfired. Park spent his Christmas in a white-hot fury. He assumed first that this was Oppenheimer's way of giving him the sack. But no, another telegram arrived, making the same earnest request. Parkinson could not eat his Christmas dinner. Years of attempting to convert Sir Ernest's vague pronouncements into sensible policy, years of putting the company first, years of separation from his children, years of surviving in "the Oppenheimer atmosphere," all apparently counted for nothing. Park telegramed he was resigning.

Now it was Sir Ernest's turn to fly into a rage, his turn to feel betrayed. My mother wrote Bess, "We had dinner last night with the Morrisons and John M. was telling us of a long-distance conversation

Sir Ernest had with him anent Park's resignation. [Sir Ernest] said it was 'the shabbiest thing ever done to him.' He'll never forgive Park for letting him down. Park was doing investigations that could only be transmitted by word of mouth. After the war the information will be valueless to the company, so they wanted him back badly."

Dickinson, the American director, on hearing that Park was by-passed, resigned too. He refused to see a "third-rater" placed over one of the best managers in Africa. The chairman's reasons for put-ting Hodgson over Park would remain a mystery. But Park's resigna-tion made Sir Ernest so furious that the great man decreed that henceforth no top official then present in Kimberley would ever be promoted so long as he (Sir Ernest) drew breath. The top people in Kimberley were my father and McHardy, just about to retire. So much for my father's brilliant future.

Park wrote my father, "I would be very glad to hear the various criticisms leveled at me, but only because I am curious and not that I really give a damn. I know I should have given three months no-tice, and should probably have returned to Kimberley to give it. But I decided that, after having always thought first of the company in the past, it was about time I put myself and the family in the first place for once, particularly as they didn't appear to be falling over themselves in grateful acknowledgment of all my past sloppy efforts. So there we are.

"My job for De Beers in the U.S. was extremely interesting, but rather strenuous. At the time the good news [from Oppenheimer] came through I was getting up at 3:30 A.M. to catch trains to nearby cities, returning about 11:00 at night and then working up my notes. I had to put on a burst of speed with the report and was able to finish it on the second of February, the same day I left New York for Rio where I am now."

Park (always the cat) had landed on his feet with a new job. My father (always the dog) was left to face Sir Ernest's wrath in Kimber-ley. Donald McHardy came for dinner that New Year's day and brought with him the news. My father reported to Bess, "Dear Mother, a bit of company politics and the rage of the chairman at Park leaving the way he did has resulted in this innocent bystander taking it on the chin . . . or backside. The chairman has decided that all senior vacancies in this company will hereafter be filled by men sent down from the Johannesburg group [Anglo American]. The men now employed by De Beers may stay where they are till they die, but no senior promotion. This decision appears to be based on the pique felt on account of a De Beers man [Park] quitting. Can you tie such queer reasoning? Just because one person in a group lets him down the rest are no good!

"The new appointee for the job I had been promised [one Odgers by name] is a friend of the man [Hodgson] whose appointment caused Park to leave. The old, old saying on the Rand is 'Jobs for pals.' So, no matter that on all of the mines I managed over the seven years I have been with the group I improved mining methods, increased labor and machine efficiencies from 25 to 60 percent, found unsuspected sources of diamonds, and kept excellent labor relations throughout—all that can be swept aside and not even considered in making the new appointment. And what makes the whole business worse is the fact that I had been told that I was definitely a certainty for the job. . . . So it has not worked out very well after all."

Park replied to a letter from my father, "I am sorry to hear that old Dickie (the American director) resigned after all the years he has been with the outfit and the great service he has rendered it. Oppenheimer's criticisms were so ridiculous that there is no need to try to answer them. It all goes back to the fact that the group has *no* policy for more than a couple of weeks at a time, and this is the fault of the otherwise brilliant chairman.

"Yes, I had thought that some day you and I might make a team, but there was a slip between the cup and the lip, or the egg broke, or something of the sort. No use weeping.

"Normally, I should have been pleased to learn of your improvement in efficiencies at Bultfontein, but in the circumstances my feelings are mixed. You will get no credit for it. It will be interpreted as the result of introducing Rand management into the picture. And if you are not only running the Pan two shifts, but also in charge of Bultfontein, then you are a damned fool, my fine young friend.

"I have given up hope of convincing any of my African friends that I quit without having previously arranged another job. At the time, the way I felt, I would have gone on to a jackhammer in some western mine rather than return."

My mother wrote home, "Well, the blow has fallen. . . . the new man was shown over the place today. Gus is pretty despondent and bitter about the whole thing, as he worked his heart and soul out, all to no purpose.

"Furthermore, he has to grin and bear it as we have been informed by the shipping company there are no ships available for Argentina now. . . . Nothing doing now until the end of 1944. That cuts off our chance of getting home and making another start while the boom is on.

"Which only proves the copy book maxims are all wet. It doesn't pay to be honest, industrious, and pious unless you have the right boot behind you. Since Park left, we are washed up high and dry. I feel so darned sorry for Gus. This is the second time he's been cheated out of his due."

Odgers's appointment completed my father's denigration, since Odgers knew nothing about diamond mining and it was my father's job to train him. Odgers was a dim, lopsided little man, whose balding pate was festooned with tufts of pale hair. His eyes were darting and unsure, and his shoes always looked a size too large. I remember him in my father's office (now Odgers's office) quietly picking his pulpy nose.

It was about this time that my father's hens suffered an infestation of fleas and stopped laying. "I wouldn't be a poultry farmer for love or money," my mother squawked. "Now that eggs are over a dollar a dozen we don't get a solitary egg. I'm all for beheading the lot of them. But Patsy makes pets of them all, and she won't allow us to kill them. So I ask you, what's the use of keeping chickens?"

That same month, my father, for the first time in his life, was attacked underground by an African. A miner he had never seen before, came out of a side tunnel swinging a rock hammer. My father dodged the blow and went over on his back with the man on top of him. The rock ceiling was low, and he got his attacker wedged against the stone, squeezing the man until he howled. Released, the man ran off and vanished. My father refused to level any charge or have the man ferreted out. Like Sir Ernest's incomprehensible behavior, the miner's attack on him made no sense, so it was not worth brooding over.

My father now found himself working under a manager who had to come to him for instruction. For my parents the most demeaning moment arrived when corporate etiquette demanded they make a formal call on the new general manager who had moved into Park's house, and his job. Describing the visit to Bess, my mother cannot bring herself to mention Hodgson's name. "We are going out to make our call on the former Parkinson residence," she says. "This has been sticking in our craw for a long time, so we have put it off as long as we possibly could. But it's best to get it over with. Like pulling a bad tooth. They are quite harmless people, but they are in the wrong place."

My father's job was intolerable now; days felt like weeks, weeks like years. Under the new management, he watched production figures flatten, then slope gently downhill. My father couldn't help blaming himself for everything that had happened. If only, he argued furiously with himself, he had been better than he was—more persuasive, more gregarious, more witty at those cocktail parties. If only he had made a better impression on Sir Ernest. He couldn't help thinking less of himself. He condemned himself for being narrow, only an engineer.

Years later, when a university vice president (an English professor) informed my father that he wrote "like a plumber," my father thought the man might be right. I vehemently disagreed. In fact, my father wrote with great clarity. The English professor was probably objecting to his lack of jargon, an insufficient deployment of the important-sounding passive tense.

I once wrote a letter to my father accusing him of being distant, unfeeling, unemotional. He wrote back saying that when he had opened himself up someone usually inserted a knife in the chink. By then, he was well into his second marriage and learning not to hope for too much. In Kimberley, he had been foolish enough to hope. Sir Ernest taught him that the best laid plans always contain a flaw. The deviousness of the human heart would always take him by surprise.

Some demigod might come up with a reasonable explanation for Sir Ernest's behavior. I can only suppose that the great man assumed that his managerial pawns should behave like pawns, and not as if they had wills and fates of their own. Park and my father were American, and they had American ideals. Sir Ernest was a creature of the colonial world. And a colonial creature is like a mule driver who keeps his beast slogging by dangling a carrot in front of the animal all day, only to put the vegetable in his own pot at night.

My father and I often argued about the nature of people who rise to positions of power. He believed that such people must have ability and intelligence. But I could detect very little intelligence or ability in the administrators he admired. So I shouted him down, not pausing to reflect that he had grown up poor and disinherited. His mother had brought nothing with her from Charleston but stories from the past. Those stories were his only inheritance. When he was grown, he had set out, like the prince in the fairy tale, to recover everything she had lost. His success would redeem her brave independence and prove her right. His expedition to Africa was more than just looking for a job. It was a fantastic demonstration that Bess's son was not going to sit on his hands and rot like his lop-eared old man back in South Carolina.

He had grown up poor, but full of ideas, plans, hope. I had grown up as son of the man in charge. The people who ran Kimberley showed up at my mother's garden parties as a matter of course. I was handed the freedom to make of myself whatever I liked. So I questioned the meaning of success, and my lack of common sense perplexed him. He was an American living out the American story. I was some kind of hybrid—exotic, stalled among crosscurrents and forces it would take a lifetime to unravel.

My father had a practical man's impatience with metaphysics, metaphors, metapsychology. Did he ever ask himself what kind of European it took to make a success in Africa? He figured a man's worth in his "efficiencies." He was an engineer and an idealist, and Africa overwhelms idealists the way the jungle swallows a filigreed French administration building. My father pressed American solutions onto African complexities. They worked wonders, but he was simply not equipped with that combination of ruthless good manners and instinct for the jugular that made for European success in Africa.

It seems to me that Park and my father, no less than my uncle Nick, were fooled by Africa. In the American imagination, tribe, caste, and class are cobwebs—diaphanous constructs we must learn to brush aside. But the spider that spins the cobweb of history is real, and so is his poison. By the end of their lives, both Nick and Park had swallowed the poison. The symptoms were clear—a suppurating racism. They railed against "the black man." As their eyes dimmed, they could see only the superiority of their own technology, which they confused with whiteness. Did the series of heart attacks he suffered late in life coarsen Park's mind, leading him to fear the dark races? He was a brilliant man and a great friend, yet my father drew away from him in the last years of his life.

In Africa, they'd been poor boys who fashioned themselves into rather elegant articles, convinced as only Americans can be that they had every right to move on any level, in any society. Observing his American managers making themselves at home in the Kimberley

Club, it is possible that Sir Ernest suffered the squeamish sensation a general may feel when he sees a couple of master sergeants quaffing beer in the officer's mess as if they belonged there. The same American qualities that made them successful left them open to attack. Breaking production records was all very well. But it was no less important for a man to know his place, his fixed spot in the world. Perhaps Hodgson and Odgers knew better how to deport themselves under the long, cool porticoes of the Kimberley Club.

29

The Golden Age

DURING OUR LAST EIGHTEEN MONTHS IN AFRICA, MY MOTHER SUF-
fered from increasingly severe eye infections. "It's got the doctor
beat. He thinks I must have picked up a special bug in Oranjemund.
This is the windy, dusty month here [August] and that may have
something to do with it. I feel if I could only get back to a dull, rainy
climate I'd be OK again. It's only the cussed infection on the lids,
not my eyesight. And right now it's the left eye, all the blood vessels
on the eyeball red and angry. Really, it's a nuisance. As for my hair
[it was falling out], I'm taking ultraviolet ray treatments. Might do
some good. Outside of these minor complaints, we are all A-1, Gus
and I too much so. His latest suits are getting too tight around the
middle."

In addition to suffering from blepharitis, she was bothered by a
host of allergies that kept her from sleeping. She writes that in one
day she used up forty handkerchiefs. "I'm running like a faucet. I

look two hundred years old. But at least my hair is growing back in. Or so the doctor claims."

She went to a specialist in Johannesburg who cut dozens of tiny slits in her back where he inserted different types of pollen. Another doctor suggested she have her tonsils removed. So she did that, too, but it made no difference. The infections and allergies came in waves. But because she was essentially cheerful and uncomplaining, we hardly knew how sick she often felt. I remember her blowing her nose while she peered at a mirror and complained that she looked like Rumpelstiltskin's mother. (During the Atlantic crossing and after we arrived in the United States, the allergies cleared up and her eyes stopped bothering her. But over the years her immune system had been undermined. The anxiety of her final years in Africa may have encouraged the cancer that, in my family, always waits breathlessly in the wings.)

My mother used to say that our little setbacks in Africa were really a kind of luxury, because while we lived safe lives and ate cake and ice cream, people elsewhere were being starved and shot. The deaths of sons and husbands are sprinkled through my mother's letters. The wife of Captain Halse, the De Beers pilot, was lost at sea while steaming back from London, where she'd had a successful eye operation that saved her sight. The newsreels showed Europe turning itself into a massive death trap. And shortly before we left Kimberley, the local newspaper published a photograph of two South African beau-fighters sinking the *Julio Cesare*, the same ship that ferried us to Genoa nine years earlier—when the Italian count fell in love with my mother and loaded me up with toys.

My sister and I were blissfully unaware of our parents' frustrations. We led the uncomplicated lives of the perfectly ignorant and looked forward to our beatification in America. I assumed America would be a great improvement over my present anxiety. But my identity had been shaped along a different axis, and it would take me a decade to adapt myself to the exotic "American way of life." American children, with their fluid, inscrutable behavior, would long remain mysterious to me. On my first day in an American classroom, I would break into tears at their inexplicably bad manners. But in Kimberley, I imagined America as the remedy for the hellish future that already threatened me—trigonometry, Latin, Brother Reedee, the sonatas of Beethoven.

In America there were no bullies. No one there bothered with Latin. Americans were large, easygoing people, reasonable and humorous the way Park and my parents were. In America, there were no terrifying teachers with hands like granite blocks. In America, everyone was happy and unaffected—like the American flag, like an American film.

It didn't occur to me that I would never again see Bill Byerley or George McDonald, or Ian Hogben, or Ralph, Kenneth, Vaughn, Betty, or Chloe. My sister and I had been guided by our parents' unstable existence to live like those mythical birds born without legs that never touch down to earth. We were accustomed to a life where nothing lasts and no attachment—aside from family love—runs deep. I was ready to leave neighbors, ready to abandon gardens, horizons, languages, ready for strangers. Despite my clippy public school accent and easy Afrikaans, I was no South African. As Mecca is to the Muslim, so America was to my mother our spiritual home, and every uprooting was a move in the right direction.

So we loved travel. We were always ready to pick up a favorite doll and put another hot and dusty town behind us. Every move brought improvement, if only the pleasure of being older, stronger, and having a bigger garden to play in. It meant nothing to me to leave friends and walk away from the houses that never belonged to us. It was great to leave the wind, or the sand and the dark black sea, for . . . it didn't matter what. These were stage sets. America was real.

It was ecstasy to lean out the train window and watch the illusory landscape skid past, blue mountains tucked into the horizon, clouds with friendly faces. Every morning that we woke up in another town, I started another life. Only the Africans were the same—the same men in dusty, cast-off suit pants, or torn khaki shorts; the same patient women with great loads on their heads—water, wood, cassavas.

We had learned the secret of disengagement, the secret of feeling as little as possible for people who would soon be replaced by other people. We had learned that nothing was permanent except each other. And to start life you had to go to America.

My last months in Kimberley were euphoric. The handsome boy was dead, and how happy his death made me! The squat tin houses and grubby streets of Beaconsfield were no longer full of menace. I could bike anywhere. I sped down the hill from school with my arms magisterially folded, singing to myself. Here in Kimberley, I was living a kind of half life, joyful because it lacked the weight of the future. Soon brown Kansas would be technicolor Oz. Sometimes I felt nostalgic about Kimberley; it was fading so quickly, becoming transparent, a facade—these peppertrees with their tiny leaves and red pods; the low tailings dumps; the passing miners wrapped in blankets, carrying cooking pots; the white sky. Even Brother Keene appeared more benign as he strode past in his black boots. He, too, was fading, and only the future was solid.

Those last months in Kimberley my irresponsible nature found its ideal moment. Best of all, I was escaping from the dread of the following year at CBC. Ahead loomed the abstractions of algebra, a lot of turgid Latin, and a great thick book stuffed to its gills with the history of England. Brother Reedee with his disagreeable Jimmy Cagney face was preparing his straps and canes for our backsides. I was dead sure that Latin would show me up for the lazy fraud I was. Only in America might the lazy leopard keep his spots.

I now look back on my sloth with wonder and dismay. It was a great power, a drive, an appetite—this secret desire to let my brain quietly rot. I had studied *Life Magazine* and the few American comic

books that squeezed through the Nazi blockade to Africa. I had im-
bibed two or three dozen Hollywood films. And to judge by American
books, films, and the lacy valentine cards sent by my grandmother, I
felt sure America would be more my style—benign, easygoing, ready
to accept a chap with a good line and a quick smile.

Meanwhile, my parents sold off the things they had so carefully
accumulated during the long years in Africa. The inflation had
driven prices so high that everything was worth two or three times its
original price. Each month they received letters from Cooks Travel
announcing that another carrier had suspended services, another
ship had been lost at sea. Two or three times it was settled and we
were ready to leave for Cape Town. Then it was settled we would
leave by air from Léopoldville in the Congo. But after the Pan
Am clipper crashed in Trinidad, all air travel from Africa was suspended.

My parents' packing dragged on for months. After each packing,
we would unpack. I remember sitting among the trunks in my father's
small study, leafing through a new copy of *Life Magazine*. It contained
photos of the latest American sensation, an emaciated little man surrounded by young girls. They were trying to tear off his clothes.
Their mouths gaped open like helpless, feeding birds. He was Frank
Sinatra, and these were American women. I could hardly wait to join
the fun.

The number of permits required for ordinary people to move across
national borders increased every year. The war had induced a kind of
bureaucratic paranoia that reached its height when officials were
asked to clear a man traveling with wife and children. We needed
permits to cross borders, permits to withdraw small amounts of money
(large amounts were frozen), permits to carry cash, permits to buy
passage, permits to take personal goods. All of my father's papers and
books were shipped to Cape Town and read by the police. Satisfied,
after plowing through hundreds of pages of mining manuals and jour-

nals, that he was not shipping out the blueprints for a secret weapon, the censors requested the American consul to file an affidavit, which was then countersigned by a South African government represen-tative.

Certificates attesting to yellow fever and small pox inoculations were necessary, of course, as well as statements from the consul re-questing permission for Americans to pass through Argentina and any other nations where we might find ourselves if Pan Am ever decided to resume its flights from the Congo. It took my father six months to secure all of these documents. Then another six months passed, and, because we didn't find a way out of the country, he had to do it all over again.

The war, meanwhile, was blowing itself out. Its passing was as palpable as the first warm breeze after a bad winter. Some of Hitler's generals finally tried to murder him. The unthinkable was beginning to happen. I had lived with ugly Adolf as long as I could remember. He was the great celebrity of our infancy. His brave opposition con-sisted of American bombers filmed at forty thousand feet, British air-men in Spitfires, and certain Hollywood stars—the spellbinding face of Greer Garson in Mrs. Miniver; the bluff, brave face of Spencer Tracy in The Seventh Cross; the enormous, bruised eyes of the child star, Margaret O'Brien.

Aged eleven, I had a clear picture of Europe—black-and-white cities with jagged walls standing against a gray sky full of Messer-schmidts, sodden fields with leafless trees where the strafed corpses of old women and children lay in ditches. After seeing The Seventh Cross, I had a recurring vision of the souls of the dead rising into the sky, mixing with gray smoke from factory chimneys. Perhaps because my mother always knew it, we always knew the Nazis were murdering the Jews. Our understanding of the destruction was accurate and de-tailed. I remember sitting out in the summer heat on our front ve-randa reading an account of the first B-29 raid on Tokyo (God Is My Co-Pilot). And even now I still see what I saw then—the white line of the breakers off the China coast glimpsed through the windshield as the plane goes down in dark water. I felt the shock of the airman's broken legs in my own body. I felt a twinge of the pain he felt when the broad-faced Chinese peasant hauled him out through the cold surf.

We were set to leave Africa in the fall of 1944. The date was moved up to winter, then put off to the summer of 1945. In the dog days of December and January, when the temperature declined a little toward 110 degrees, my father would take us all up to the company reservoir on top of a high hill. Having given up on his future at De Beers, he used to quit work at four or five and spend the late afternoons with us.

Ascending the steep line of the hill to the reservoir on a long, straight road, I would pretend we were taking off in an airplane. The car rose above the plain, and there was nothing below but a bowl of yellow air, shimmering with heat, and a toy train dragging a line of V-shaped dumpsters along a shiny track.

The pool had steeply sloping sides, and a little spillway at one end created a white curtain of water, a mechanical waterfall. The color of the water was a deep green, shading off into blue at the deep center. Floating on your back, you saw only the pale sky and an airplane droning overhead. My father swam from sloping wall to sloping wall with my sister clinging to his back. She was still nervous about water.

The reservoir was reserved for managers, but we were the only family that bothered to use it. My mother, never satisfied with her figure, preferred privacy when she pulled on a swim suit—especially now that she'd begun to feel middle-aged.

The signs that her beauty was passing seemed a double burden. Her youth had been America; age was Africa. As soon as I was old enough to notice, I grew aware of her sharp self-scrutiny, her awareness of time and her body.

A photo of her at the age of five shows a very solemn, round-faced child with hair as violently abundant as that of a young woman. A studio portrait of her, shot when she first arrived in South Africa, shows her with bobbed hair. A soft sidelight picks out the line of her cheek and she appears the image of youth. The Rand and Fleisher, childbearing, and four years passing removed the bloom. In Oranjemund, anguish over her mother's madness [she wrote Bess] had caused her hair to fall out "in handfuls." A year later, in Kimberley, it began to grow back, but it would never be so full again. Silver strands appeared at her temples, though she was only in her midthirties. And by the time she managed to leave Africa, she had exchanged the face of a hopeful young actress for that of a matron from Middle Europe with sharp cheekbones and experienced eyes.

She liked risk. She jumped at the chance to gallop a horse across the desert, to ride a camel, to ride with Captain Halse in a biplane, performing acrobatics over the black Atlantic. She beat my father at tennis. His awkward serve across the net was just like him, a combination of practiced efficiency and innate vulnerability. Given her natural coordination, she easily whipped the ball by him.

Her medium was air, not water. She preferred easing into a pool, slipping beneath the surface with a neat, gliding motion that reminded me of a seal. This was impossible at the reservoir where the sloping sides forced her to dive. She would first pull on a rubber cap, then position herself carefully on the edge, with her arms held straight out, thumbs together. Rising on her toes, she leaped out cleanly, always hitting the surface at precisely the same, flat angle. That dive, so elegant and so inept, was her water signature, and I would never have wanted her to improve on it.

She swam always on her right side, reaching out ahead with the right arm and looking backward each time she pulled herself forward through the water. It was a style of water travel I've never seen duplicated. She called it her dog paddle, prompting my empirical sister to ask (at the age of two), "Do dogs look 'ahind 'em when they swim?"

The month the Allies invaded France was the coldest June on record in Kimberley—"twenty-two degrees below freezing most of the time." There was no central heating in our schools. In class we wore two sweaters, a hat, a muffler, and gloves. My sister's institution had a fireplace in every classroom and the girls took turns sitting by the fire to thaw out.

We were leaving for America as soon as we could find a boat or plane that would have us. Sir Ernest had managed what no one else could do—he inspired my father to get out of the mines. My mother must have been greatly relieved at his failure, no matter how much she sympathized. As for the dark spots in my life, they were all self-inflicted.

Knocking down wasp nests in the backyard one sunny afternoon after the cold had abated, I glanced through the open window of our servant Stephen's little house and saw the gleam of silver. A half crown piece lay on his table, and something feeble and greedy in my nature prompted me to reach in and seize the coin. The false logic of the thief told me he would never miss it. I buried it in the far corner of the backyard. Stephen missed it immediately. Within two hours, I was summoned into the house by my mother and asked what I knew about the missing money.

Lying to my mother was no more possible than leaping out the window and flying across the horizon. Lying would have been even more shameful than stealing. I admitted at once that I was the thief.

She asked me to fetch the money. Squatting to dig it up, I had an image of a dog digging up a stolen bone. But I felt worse than any dog. My mother told me to place the half crown on the kitchen table. So there it was and we both looked at it. She asked me some questions, speaking sweetly, without emphasis or anger, as if she were merely very curious about who I might be. I felt our estrangement like a knife in my chest. Her words were direct. "What did you need this money for?" But they felt more like hammer blows than words. When I started to blubber, she suggested I go to my room. "Go and think about yourself. And come back when you have something to say."

I spent the afternoon and evening in my room, too ashamed to show myself for dinner. I was quite sure I would never be hungry again. Remorse was far more filling than meat and potatoes. My small sister looked in once with a worried face. When she saw my face, she closed the door at once, as if she'd discovered a corpse. Later, she found the courage to come back and eased herself into the chair near me. She asked no questions—just sat for a time in quiet contemplation beside the body. No matter how evil I had been, she wanted me to know she was with me. I don't think we exchanged a word. I had sunk too low for language.

Around bedtime, I showed my face, although I would rather have scraped it off. I said I thought I now had a pretty good idea of what I was. My mother didn't ask me what that might be. She only looked at me for a moment with that same sad, sweet expression, then asked, "Will you give this back then?"

The half crown still lay on the table where I had placed it that afternoon. Evidently, I was the only one in the house who would touch it. It felt absolutely different to me. Cold and heavy. The sun had set. Stephen was sitting in his little house sewing, peering through reading glasses under a small light on his table. He had a wonderfully kind, ugly face. I had never noticed before how kind, how rich. How could anyone take something from such a man? I had become inconceivable to myself.

Because he didn't put out his hand, I laid the coin on the table where I had found it and said I was sorry. He looked embarrassed and patted my arm. This little tap of complete forgiveness was more than I could bear, so I went outside and sat in the bamboo grove. Looking up at the stars gave me an odd kind of solace, if only because they were so far away and knew nothing about me. On the other hand, maybe they did. I felt the remorse turn into weeping that burned like acid.

My father once told me the only thing that finally counts in a person is character. Everything else is window dressing. He might have added, "Show me a clever man and I'll show you a frail vessel." What clever self-deception had led me to steal from a man so much poorer than myself, a man who would never have any of the rights or privileges handed me by history and my white skin?

Stealing Stephen's half crown was among the most useful choices I made as a child. My weakness forced my mother to ask that question with her eyes: "Who are you? Is this what you have decided to be?" And then ask me, "What did you think you needed this money for?" with the slight emphasis on "this."

Her low, sweet voice threw a brilliant spotlight on my hidden self, the fool who fools only himself. Of course I would go on fooling myself for years. But she'd got my worst self out in the open, naked and ashamed, and I had been obliged to take him with me to my room and smell him for hours. It was a stink not easily forgotten.

My sister and I celebrated our final birthdays in Africa that September. Because I was born July 15, in the dead of winter, my mother decided to postpone the celebration and throw a big party for both of us. Nine months before the event, as soon as she had put Christmas behind her, my sister began to look forward to the party. It grew on her, and by September she had reached such a pitch of excitement that my mother had to put her to work mixing cake batter, washing pots, sweeping floors—anything to keep her occupied. The day before the party everyone was busy in the kitchen until late at night. Gallons of ice cream were prepared, and two three-layer cakes baked. Each layer was dyed a different color (yellow, red, green). This was part of our family tradition, and we simply had to have a tricolor cake. We were as rigid in our demand for this rainbow concoction on birthdays as we were for her braided Viennese bread with smiling egg faces every Easter.

On the afternoon of the twenty-sixth, children began to show up in the garden, which was in full bloom. There were eighteen children and half a dozen mothers (my mother reported) but I recall only a few names. Pretty Jill Hayston had come straight from school in her dark blue school uniform. Bill Byerley arrived in flannel shorts and scholarly glasses. At some point, he drew a mustache and goatee on his face with black grease paint, I forget why. His tiny, pale-legged sister, with her corona of red hair specially fluffed up for the party, would not stop jumping up and down. The day achieved its full measure when the Beck girls showed up—Chloe and Betty in her bright red sweater, too short in the sleeves.

We pushed eggs across the lawn with our noses (the sort of intensely silly game that amused my father), and we ran in a circle around the tennis court until Bill's little sister slipped and skinned her knee. My father made a film of Betty Beck sitting on the front veranda with her white socks bunched up around her ankles, and women in blue hats and white hats under the gazebo with their tiny children, and a crush of small girls pulling at my green-and-gold school sweater, which I favored because it was old and familiar and had holes at the elbows.

The camera keys other memories: my flat failure to tell Betty Beck that I loved her. The irritation I felt when Ruthie Morrison remarked that Betty's sister Chloe was the really beautiful one. Betty licking white icing off those elegant fingers that I had never had the courage to touch. The sun setting on the blue garden that became suddenly silent as the last child bounced out the front gate.

Without foreboding, my sister and I waved good-bye to the departing children. We didn't mind at all that this garden and these children were about to dissolve. The chirpy conversation; the carefully dressed mothers, faces shaded under hats; the fishpond with its bright orange carp and single gold water lily; the lawn under the syringa trees—all would dissolve. My sister led one child and then another by the hand. She had no idea where she was leading them. She dragged them here and there. She wanted to touch them all.

She wanted to belong to them all; she wanted them all to be here on her birthday, the day that had taken forever to arrive and was already being carried away by the long shadows—the one bright afternoon when the joy she had imagined came so close she could almost take it by the hand.

30

The Congo

On the morning of April 7, 1945, we were scheduled to leave Kimberley at 9:20. Through Warner Shelley, the American consul in Johannesburg, my parents had arranged a loose agreement to board a Norwegian ship in the port of Matadi at the mouth of the Congo River. They were told they had a good chance because the consul either knew the captain or knew about him or knew someone who knew him. In any event, my parents had neither tickets nor a firm commitment from anyone. The ship would certainly be there, the consul said, provided it was not sunk crossing the Atlantic. With the European war winding down, it was no time for ironclad assurances. Africans take obstacles for granted, and my parents by then were, to that degree at least, African. My sister and I felt no anxiety whatever. We were headed for Oz and a bright, new life—no doubt about it.

Stephen saw us off at the front gate that April morning. I can see him still, wrapped in his white work apron, his feet formally placed side by side. Was it possible that the sadness in his face was directed into a void, that never again would we see each other, that this separation was no less than a death in the family? Where was my fabulous talent for discarding friends without a second thought? Leaving for America just then felt like sailing to the moon.

We left the house early because my parents wanted to arrive at the station well before the farewell party began. We got there at half past eight. Already, a small crowd was clustered together on the concrete slab, greeting us gaily, as if this were merely one more social event under the syringa trees by our tennis court. Soon, forty people were gathered around us.

The day before, my mother had rushed off to the doctor to have a pair of moles removed from her nose and cheek. She wanted to look her best when she arrived in the States, although she knew that she bore little resemblance to the young woman who had driven away in March 1932 and signed her first letters home "The kids."

Time had mysteriously turned her America into a kind of Africa— alien and vaguely hostile. Louis Newman, who had underwritten their voyage out, was five years dead. My mother's college friend, Haroldine, had a boy at the university and a girl engaged to marry. Her youngest brother, Emil, twelve when she'd seen him last in Sarajevo, was a paratrooper in the Pacific war. Her oldest brother, John, was off the Japanese coast in a submarine. Her mother was in a madhouse. Only Bess remained firmly fixed at the same 1705 Belmont Avenue address, embedded like a steel rivet in the rickety bridge to the past.

She felt comfortable showing up among her Kimberley friends with tape plastered across her nose and cheek. These were the people she knew and trusted. But they would vanish before lunchtime, like Stephen at the front gate. Meanwhile, conversation was animated. Subjects dropped a week or a month before were picked up and worked over, as if soon, next week or next month, we would certainly see each other again. The human mind cannot admit total absence, the notion of never. So we speculated on when we would see each other again and on the weather and the war.

We knew that soon, in a half hour, this jovial, damp-eyed crowd would vanish just as the faces in Nigel, Kleinzee, and Oranjemund had vanished—Donald McHardy with his matter-of-fact grin, the Seculls, the Becks (Betty was at school), and Ruthie Morrison, who kept coming around to hug my sister and me, throwing her arms around us, leaving a light trail of face powder on my blue sleeveless sweater.

Molly Ziervogel had laid on a big farewell dinner the night before and she stuck close to my mother. A few months earlier, Sir Ernest had phoned up my father and asked him to inform Molly that her husband was missing in Italy. For a week or two thereafter Molly had more or less lived in our house with her children.

Old Mr. Gray was there, emaciated and kindly. I forget his precise function in the mines. Beside him stood his double, my father's private secretary, equally thin and kindly. They were quite unrelated, and I was probably the only person in the world who thought they were identical. I could distinguish Mr. Gray from his twin only because the secretary had lost an arm in the mines. He was easily identifiable by the empty sleeve, and I thought of him as the Second Mr. Gray, because there was less of him.

There were many others: the Marises, the Hays, the O'Brians, the Knights—the faces and voices that attach to these names have blown away like dust over the desert. The McKenzies, the Lawrences, the Cawoods—all are recorded by my mother in her travel diary. She knew that soon even their names would be lost unless she wrote them down. So I write them down here for the last time.

Brother Ellif showed up, wearing black trousers and a crisp, clerical collar. He shook my hand, looked at me with his direct, green eyes, and said he always hated to lose a rugby player. Then he patted me on the shoulder so hard that I was knocked forward a step. By the time I recovered, he was walking briskly away, the stiff white clerical collar riding up his bright red neck.

The day was warm and clear. The train was late. We glanced over the track at the veld, where the light intensified as the sun lifted higher. We were loaded down with roses and carnations. Our train compartment would smell like a funeral parlor. I obsessively checked my pocket to make sure I had not lost my fountain pen. In a world where such things no longer existed, my mother had somehow found one our last week in town. "So you can keep a journal," she said.

The train was already well over an hour late. Our friends were reluctant to go before they saw us safely on board. It didn't seem quite right to leave the four of us standing there alone on the platform. Another hour dragged by. It was ten-thirty, and the locomotive was nowhere in sight. Conversation began to peter out. Those who had appointments completed their good-byes and went back to their lives. Another hour passed—eleven-thirty. Only the passionate talkers and the seriously upset remained. Gradually even those broke away—Molly Ziervogel, Ruthie, the tiny woman with the blonde child and the narrow hips whose pretty face remains unattached to a name.

By noon, we were alone. My mother broke out the sandwiches. Much to my sister's dismay, we had slaughtered our entire chicken population during the last weeks in Kimberley. At first we had killed them secretly, as the children of a deposed potentate are assassinated behind stone walls. But murder on such a scale could not be hidden for long from Patsy's sharp eye. She had to adjust herself to the decapitation of her darlings. Night after night we had chicken—broiled chicken, roast chicken, fried chicken, chicken soup, chicken in aspic. Packed the night before in waxed paper, the chicken sandwiches were now most welcome.

The train stumbled in well past noon and stretched out the length of the station for forty minutes while the engineer did surgery on her with a sledgehammer. We settled ourselves in our compartment and stared at the empty platform. It was 12:45 when the machine worked its way cautiously out of Kimberley, as was sloppily recorded in my diary with the new pen.

Because there were four of us, we always had a compartment to ourselves and we knew how to make it feel like home. At night, two recessed shelves became bunk beds that hung on chains over the seat-beds below. Between the two windows, a polished wall panel pulled down and became a table. There we wrote, or played "battleship," or spread out our snacks. Through the open windows, the familiar veld glided respectfully past. The slum houses of board and rusting corrugated iron outside Kimberley were replaced a few hours later by conicular grass huts with peaked roofs. The light was brilliant, the plateau immense, but we took Africa for granted. We concentrated on sibling squabbles, dry biscuits and tea, or a card game of our invention that involved a lot of shuffling and noisy slapping down of kings and queens.

Our locomotive was obviously ill and streamed black plumes of foul smoke full of hot cinders. Years before, a cinder had flown through a train window into my mother's eye, and she claimed that all her eye problems had started then. Even so, we traveled with the window open to catch the breeze, fastening the frame with a leather strap that pulled up over a brass node. We loved leaning far out with our noses to the wind. If the train swung left, its smoke came roiling into our compartment, and we sprang to yank the window shut.

Climbing the escarpment north of Kimberley, the train barely crawled. I ventured onto the platform between cars and stood on the steps, a few inches above the rail bed. Tall grasses brushed my feet. With a delicious sense of doing something illegal and dangerous, I prepared to hop to the ground and walk alongside the train. I was on the lowest step when I sensed someone watching me. A shadowy passenger stood on the platform above. Under his broad-brimmed hat, I made out a leathery, impassive Afrikaner face. His expression was not unlike the unperturbed, sleepy look of a lion at ease, digesting the innards of a springbok. "So what do you think you are doing, my boy?" he said in Afrikaans.

"*Niks*" (Nothing), I said.

"If you get off this train," he said, "they will not allow you to get back on it. That is the rule. You will stay out there." He pointed at the landscape.

"*Ek het daardie nie geweet nie*" (I didn't know that), I said.

"Now you know it," he said, never taking his eye off me.

I excused myself and went back into the corridor, inclining my head at precisely the angle an Afrikaner boy would use to indicate respect toward an adult. I found my sister looking for me.

"What's wrong?" she asked.

"There's a lady down there who is giving away slices of cake with strawberry jam on it," I said.

"*Ag*, come on!" she said, not believing a word. But she went to investigate, just in case.

It was delightful to reflect that in America I would no longer have to worry about Afrikaners popping up to threaten me. I didn't know that I had just had my last conversation in my second language— and I would later consider the uselessness of all those Afrikaner words bumping about pointlessly in my memory.

That April, as it happened, our family's euphoria over leaving Africa was matched by universal joy. All over the planet, chains were being thrown off, prison camps opened. Fascism, with its passion for social control, had created global chaos. Our trip though Africa reflected the disorders of that year. To get from Kimberley to New York in 1945 on a small Norwegian freighter, we had first to travel over a thousand miles through tropical Africa (by road, river, and rail) on the chance that the captain of a ship that might not be there would find room for us on the strength of a telegram from the consul in Jo'burg.

Our parents never told us that all we really had going for us was Warner Shelley's cablegram to a Norwegian captain at sea. The captain had not bothered to radiogram back. But that, according to the consul, was the captain's style. The consul was sure the captain would have room for the four of us. Why? Because the captain liked to travel with people who could liven up the conversation at dinner. The captain had a great sense of humor. So we were traveling through the middle of Africa because a Norwegian captain had a good sense of humor and might like us.

Thorn trees and tall grass gave way to patches of viny jungle in damp ravines. My mother's hay fever grew intense and the stitches in her face ached. But she didn't give a damn. After thirteen years we were finally headed in the right direction, traveling six miles an hour uphill, with six suitcases and a big straw basket full of chicken sandwiches. We were working our way through the last of the white meat when we pulled into Victoria Falls, where my mother lost a filling.

We took rooms in the palatial Falls Hotel, and my parents drove off with a friend to his dentist. (By then, it seemed they had friends in every town in Africa.) The hotel was almost empty, but my mother quickly picked up a Swiss student, who had just come down the Congo, and pumped him for information. He was "doing" Africa before starting his graduate studies. He had found the Congo trip easy and comfortable. Comfort was high on his priority list. He approved of the Belgians, who provided decent service and passable food. He was quite upset about the film situation. He had run out and there was none in Africa. He was far more concerned about his own future (a career in banking), than the outcome of the war, which, he said, bored him. If Europe was peopled by maniacs whose only pleasure was hating and killing each other, what could Switzerland do about it? "He has the soul of a mayfly," said my mother, and she didn't invite him to dinner.

Prodigious rains had raised the falls to their highest level since 1904. We rode a little railcar down to the riverside and stood a foot or two from the edge of the falls, which raised such clouds of mist that the river below was obscured and all we could see was a rainbow. The baobab trees were swarming with monkeys. They seemed full of fun and, at the same time, profoundly sad, their tiny faces crushed with anxiety and disappointment. Bad luck to find yourself stalled on the evolutionary ladder somewhere between a squirrel and a Swiss banker. "Like never making it onto the De Beers board of directors," said my father.

Across the Zambezi, European engineers had constructed a bridge that I tried to sketch in my diary. The feeble results distressed me. Even then I felt that I must develop some way to order my perceptions, or the world would always rush past me—unreal, a disheveled dream.

Passing through Africa, with its well-dressed Europeans and half-naked Africans, I was conscious of the dislocation between their world and mine, but I accepted the disjunction without strain. Extreme poverty cheek by jowl with colonial splendor was simply the way things were. But looking back through the eyes of my eleven-year-old self, I can detect in that complacent small person the mental embryo of the skepticism that later formed me. My generation, like every other, had been handed *a* world as if it were *the* world. Aged eleven, I sensed dimly that I would have to somehow master what had already been seen before I could start to see for myself. It was my mother's example that aroused in me the instinct to question the placid, fixed world that children are assured is the last word. My attempt to draw the bridge over the Zambezi was a first faltering effort to seize conventional perspective by the ears. My mother made plain how skepticism is really love in a mental guise—not to doubt is not to give a damn. But to avoid mastering a convention is to succumb to it.

Leaving Victoria Falls, we traveled up the line to Ndola, a town as indolent as the name suggests. At every stop, the train was besieged by mobs of begging children. Clever boys a year or two older than I made little airplanes and lorries of aloe wood, toy bicycles of bamboo, and tiny sports cars with steering wheels and running boards neatly pegged together without glue. Hawkers in tiny loincloths sold bananas a foot long, giant papaw fruit, and curios. The platforms were lined with wood and ivory beasts, crocodiles carved into paper knives, wildebeest trays—the sorts of things that excite traveling Europeans. In my diary, I list ivory "elephants, lions, deer, and buck bookends." No one in 1945 was anxious about the extinction of the elephant.

We crossed the border of Northern Rhodesia where the people wore very little or simply went naked. The women moved elegantly with great loads on their heads, their long, breasts swinging free. The official language was French, and the mosquitoes were even more ambitious than their cousins in Kimberley. The train crouched comatose for hours in nameless sidings. Occasionally the engineer would beat the engine with his sledgehammer, whether to knock some stubborn bolt into place or simply to relieve his own frustration was never clear. We strolled about in the twilight heat, listening to a perpetual African conversation, for the people never stopped chattering. The night was full of shouts and cries, followed by laughter and singing, as if minor disasters were forever being succeeded by great celebrations. Like the Irish, the Africans north of Ndola loved language and poured themselves into it. And language, as it always will, released their spirits as it raised them to eloquence.

Ignoring the all-night party in full swing outside the window of our compartment, my mother unfolded our pajamas from the suitcase and, after brushing our teeth and washing our bodies, we climbed into our bunks. An early bedtime was the unswerving principle of our childhood. Like the British who dress in dinner jackets in the desert or in the jungle, we observed a rigid order of conduct. Our rules, however, were prescribed by American civilization. Whenever a question arose, my parents resorted to U.S. Government health pamphlets. Soon after landing in South Africa, my mother had discovered more good information to be had from these booklets for pennies than could be bought at any price from most doctors in the country.

As for children who didn't have a "decent" bedtime, in her view they were simply being neglected. Children should be fed lots of fresh vegetables, required to imbibe as much milk as they could gurgle down, and put to bed at eight sharp. If the car broke down or trains stalled or didn't appear or if we found ourselves without a hotel room, without dinner, without a foreseeable future, we could still count on a glass of milk, an eight o'clock bedtime, and all the legumes she could lay her hands on.

It was soothing to nod off with your head hanging half out the window over a crowd of people arguing passionately. It was thrilling to stir to consciousness when the train at last moved off with a terrific bump, and the all-night party outside was replaced by jungle foliage lit by the compartment light, and the ticky-tack, clickity-clack of the rolling metal and the bellow of thunder that arrives often around midnight. Motion was satisfaction because ahead, just beyond the impenetrable tangle of the Congo, lay America—bright, bright, bright.

The locomotive suffered a serious breakdown in Bukama, and no amount of sledgehammering would bring it around. While the engineer telephoned for another engine, we wandered around the town. Bukama is where the Congo River has its source. The river runs north in a great, insane circle, sweeping across the equator before dropping south again down the rapids over Matadi, door to the Atlantic. It was our plan to bisect that circle by taking the train to Port Francqui (now Iliebo) and a riverboat down the Kasai. The Kasai joins the Congo one hundred and twenty miles above Kinshasa (then Léopoldville).

Beyond the town in a jungle clearing, we discovered a Catholic mission. My mother walked out into a field where nuns in white sun helmets were bent over furrows full of melon plants. Working alongside the sisters were African women in full-length dashikis of orange-

and-gold cloth. My sister offered a piece of white candy to a little boy her age, who mistook it for chalk and tried to write with it. A naked teenager outside the mission sold us a dozen oranges and a pineapple the size of a football.

On the station platform African women were boiling pots of manioc, a bubbling, evil-smelling gruel that only a porridge-besotted Scotsman might find palatable. We tried it, as we tried most everything, and it tasted like the food poor people eat everywhere—a grayish sludge that filled the stomach without enriching the blood.

Around midnight, the train abruptly clanked into motion, and after "the worst night I ever had" (to quote my diary), we arrived in Elisabethville about breakfast time.

The town looked like a French village transplanted onto a Hollywood jungle set. There were surreal sidewalk cafés and good French pastry served under palm and banana trees. It seemed perfectly normal to us, but if a dinosaur had walked out of the jungle, we would probably have made the proper mental adjustment to include that as well. We had grown up among the juxtapositions of impossible things.

Most odd in Elisabethville were the multitude of American flags. They hung outside every shop and from every flagpole. "Someone must have told them we were coming," said my father, and we groaned, as we always did when he attempted a joke. A policeman in a blue coat with gold buttons and bare feet explained the phenomenon. President Roosevelt was dead. The Congo, no less than California and Idaho, was in shock. And now we could understand why no one smiled, why all the faces in the cafés were somber.

Back at the station, our new locomotive had developed boiler trouble, so we were going nowhere that night. We slept fitfully, suspended a few feet above another raucous party on the platform outside. Around dawn, I woke and saw the jungle slipping slowly by. Women covered from head to toe with red clay were lined up on an embankment.

We had entered the region of Africa that Park had "opened up" in 1923, soon after he graduated from the University of Colorado. Given a two year contract to explore the boggy, fly-infested Luana and Luembe rivers that run north to the Kasai, he found himself tramping south from the wretched outpost of Djokopunda, to the Angola border. He was then carried on the shoulders of African porters through the elephant grass on a *tshipoya*. Raised above the foliage on this platform, he was able to take sitings and map the country. He used a bicycle wheel attached to an RPM counter for triangulating distances.

Port Francqui, where we headed the day after the President's death, was upriver from Djokopunda. There Park had brought Margaret and her piano twenty years before. The piano, purchased from the English consul in Léopoldville, had been lashed into a double crate and trundled into the interior by truck and riverboat—cartwheeled, dropped, hauled up rapids, and carried by groaning Africans down muddy sloughs through driving rain, then bounced from Djokopunda to Luaco on a flatbed truck. It took Park a week to tune the strings. After Margaret pronounced it fit to play, he raised it on concrete blocks and kept the soundboard dry in the wet season by burning a bed of charcoal below the instrument night and day.

The railway line went no farther than Port Francqui. It had taken us only nine days to reach the heart of Africa where we were to meet the boat to Léopoldville. Rubbish littered the streets. I saw a litter of dead kittens at the bottom of a garden wall. My mother found the heat overpowering. My sister and I felt fine; it was the damp cold of Seattle that would make us miserable.

The cafés of Port Francqui were inhabited by sleazy European males. My mother thought they resembled the cast of a Peter Lorre film. Sydney Greenstreet doubles in soiled white suits sipped aperitifs at sidewalk tables.

The Hotel de Palms [sic] was the only decent place to sleep in town, but it was booked solid. So we hauled our suitcases down to the docks and sat there looking at the river and staving off native porters who wanted to take us somewhere, anywhere, though there was nowhere to go. A clerk at the hotel had said the boat would arrive that evening. My father hoped we might sleep on board. "But what if it doesn't come?" we asked.

"Why are you worrying about something that might not happen?" said my mother.

"But what if it really doesn't come?"

"If it doesn't show up, then we get to do something else. Now come along. We'll find some fruit for dinner."

31

Euphoria

THE BOAT ARRIVED AT DUSK—AN ENORMOUS GHOST-WHITE PADDLE-wheeler sailing straight out of *Huckleberry Finn*, the wrong boat beating its way up the wrong river in the wrong century. My parents marched on board while my sister and I sat on the suitcases. Twenty minutes later we were summoned into the best two cabins on board—noble affairs with the windows removed to help the air circulate. But no breeze came off the black river.

My diary complains a lot: "Had a very bad night of sleep. 6 mosquitoes in my net. Got up very early and had a bad day. By night I had a headache and I just about fell to sleep at dinner. After, I went straight to bed and slept like a log. Left at 9 P.M. [I meant A.M.] First time I've been on a river boat. Coffee mighty terrible. Saw no crocs, hypos [sic] or elephants."

The Kasai was wide, but quick flowing, boiling along like dark chocolate as it describes an arc within the arms of its mother Congo.

The weather was cool on the river. Every afternoon, black-and-silver squalls swept in, attended by lightning. Steam rose from the jungle as thick as smoke. And every evening at dusk the paddle-wheeler tied up and took on a load of wood for fuel. My sister and I roamed the lower deck where the African party never flagged. Families camped out and bartered with the river dwellers, who came swarming out in pirogues, which they tied to the boat. They sold manioc and bananas and smoked monkeys—crushed, black little faces tied in bunches by the neck.

Whenever the boat stopped, we bartered with children our age who sold aloe wood toys. When the boat took on fuel, we went ashore and wandered about in the twilight, my sister in her white frock and straw hat, me in my rugby shirt with the school colors. When darkness fell, the paddle-wheeler picked its way along the shore with a great spotlight, searching out its landing.

The captain, outfitted in spotless whites, maintained an African mistress. Her beauty was classic, her expression severe, her back very straight. She might have been carved by a master sculptor and set up in a museum. She lived in his cabin and appeared at dinner, no questions asked. There were two or three other African women registered among the top deck passengers. "We have definitely left South Africa," my mother wrote in her diary.

The crowd at table began to thin out as passengers were picked off by malaria. We stuffed ourselves with quinine and Atabrine tablets. If you could stave off the fever, the food was all right—a little heavy on the leeks, in my mother's opinion. Leeks showed up in everything including the morning omelet.

I was reading Robert Graves's I, Claudius in an old Penguin paperback, and my mind was full of Roman images. After reading all day, I felt stiff and limbered up by leaping repeatedly from a bench to an overhead pipe, missed, turned my ankle, and remembered a long green snake I had seen the day before swimming out of a dark tributary like a portent. Lying on the deck in pain, I thought, *The snake got me.*

When we entered the enormous body of water (Pool Malebo) that backs up behind the rapids below Léopoldville, I found I could barely walk. On shore, I made my way painfully hobbling behind my father and just ahead of an enterprising rickshaw man, who kept nudging his vehicle closer as I fell behind. Finally, my father, with a weary gesture, motioned the man to give me a lift, and I rode into the city like an emperor.

Léopoldville in 1945 belied its past and its future. While Europe lay in ruins, the Congo capital offered a picture of peace and prosperity. The gleaming buildings were surrounded by airy arcades where men sat at sewing machines ready to mend your trousers or shirts for a few centimes. My parents were surprised to find the banks run by Africans. It was an African teller who corrected the mistake made in their currency conversion by a European manager. My parents had the impression that Africans in Léopoldville were much better off than any native South Africans. I note in my diary that the Congolese children were not dressed in rags nor covered with a mantle of flies. They did not have mucus running over their upper lips (the universal sign of neglect in Africa).

Only fifty years before, King Leopold's Congo overseers had hacked off the right hands of Africans to promote social control. By 1945, this history had been largely forgotten or suppressed. The only memorial we passed was Prince Albert's statue in the main square. I had no idea who Prince Albert might be. My thoughts revolved around Augustan Rome and the stuttering emperor Claudius, not the modern monarch whose overseers had bloodied the river flowing below our windows at the Hotel ABC.

My diary entry for April 24 says: "Started out on a boring day but my mom and dad brought some English mags along and saved my situation for 3 hours, after which I was bored again, because I couldn't go out for walks or anything because of my foot. Found Hotel ABC very dirty and the food worse than the boat." My mother was inclined on more than one occasion to tell me that I was turning into a little British snob. But I was only imitating my parents, who complained that the ABC coffee was wretched (loaded with chicory) and breakfast a dead loss (a plate of greasy, cold meat served with two-day-old bread). The town that year was jammed with refugees— German, Hungarian, French, Russian—all eating badly and all eager to tell their stories.

On board the riverboat, my mother had been appropriated by a gabby Belgian woman. "Mrs. Siefert, long-winded," she notes curtly in her diary. But in Léopoldville, she came across the delightful M. Mikhailov, who'd fled Russia, and M. Leferts who had lost a leg in the French resistance. We joined Mikhailov and Leferts on a palm-oil plantation where the two men lived in a hut. Leferts broke out some prewar wine for the occasion, and the grown-ups, like most people who loved to read, found they had a lot in common. They knew the same books; they had come to similar conclusions; similar patterns snaked through their lives. Mikhailov and Leferts, too, found themselves imprisoned in Africa. They talked for eight hours without pause, realized they were exhausted, exchanged addresses, threw their arms around each other, said good-bye, and never saw each other again.

Kinshasa (later Léopoldville, and now Kinshasa again) was built on Stanley Pool (now Pool Malebo), where the Congo creates an enormous lake before rushing down thirty-two rapids over some two hundred miles of gorge between hills of granite. The railway, hacked through cliffs of stone above the river, is infamous. Africans called it "The Road of Death." Park wrote that the hundreds who died during its construction are traditionally accounted for in this way: one white man dead for every kilometer of track; one Chinese dead for every span of track; and one African dead for every tie laid beneath the track.

We left Léopoldville by train at six in the morning, armed with bottles of carbonated water, Atabrine, and quinine. The carriage was a pleasant contraption, with wicker seats to keep European bottoms cool. The train was manned entirely by Africans, and the stations along the Matadi-Kinshasa line were little works of art where African stationmasters competed with each other. Neatly painted buildings were nestled among clipped shrubs with brilliantly colored leaves. We children played the card game we had invented and drank warm fizz water with American cream-filled cookies. Overhearing our parents talking about the river rapids on the gorge below, my sister wanted to know what distinguished bunny rabbits from river rabbits. We pulled into Matadi just in time for dinner.

The Métropole Hotel in Matadi is an impressive six-story Moorish castle constructed around a courtyard. It was built to last by men who intended to stay in Africa forever and surely it is still there today. I recall palm trees in a courtyard, the watery arch of fountains . . . but it may be that my imagination is improving on memory. The hotel was constructed from the same gray granite that underpins the town of Matadi.

Matadi looked to me as if it were taking off, soaring skyward on tall hills. The main square below our hotel window was a steeply tilting field of stone. Like the cathedrals in El Greco's *Toledo*, the buildings outraced each other toward the sky. Unstable as a dream, Matadi's spirals of stone matched our spirits. We, too, were escaping upward, rising to another level.

We had pink papaw for breakfast and fresh eggs—a sign that things were looking up. The cook at the Métropole had escaped occupied Paris. I made the mistake of ordering an "American hamburger" and was brought a slab of raw ground beef covered with slices of fresh onion. Raw hamburger aside, he was, my mother said, the best cook in Africa.

The guests at table had assembled from all over Europe and could hardly wait to unload their stories—a French officer, a Jewish jeweler from Hong Kong, a gaggle of missionaries, a blond woman who wore stockings. All had survived disasters. All had lost husbands, brothers, children, legs, arms. All were trying to get out of the Congo. Those who had been trying for a long time thought it impossible. "Well, we certainly expect to do it," said my mother.

"Ah, you are American, of course," said the French officer, and whether he meant we were cockeyed optimists, or generically dim-witted my mother could not make out.

Our first morning in Matadi, my father headed for the shipping office to confirm our connections with the Norwegian freighter. No one there had heard of us. No Pan Am flights were leaving for many weeks, and those had been booked months in advance. Every European who could bribe his way to a visa was apparently headed for America. "We may have to stay here awhile," said my father.

"Then we can learn French!" said my mother.

They didn't seem very worried, so neither were we. My father fired off a telegram to the American consul in Johannesburg. Shelley said he would send another cable to the captain, whose name was Jensen. A lot seemed to hinge on the captain's good humor, and my mother was doubtful that a man called Jensen would have a sense of humor. Shelley cabled us again, advising my parents to meet the ship, if possible, and to twist Captain Jensen's arm.

On the morning the *Tarn* arrived, my parents went down to the docks with a bottle of wine. The African guards, lounging on some oil drums, said the quay was a restricted area. My father said he'd been sent by the American consul and it was vital he get through. My mother, who was translating, improved somewhat on his version and said he was an American consul. The guards wanted to see papers. My parents produced their passports and some insurance forms. The guards said they had no authority to let anyone through. My father said he was going anyway and pushed past them. My mother said, "He's very important" and followed.

On board ship, they found Jensen, in undershirt and boxer shorts, in his cabin. He was a man immediately bored by explanations and, pulling on his trousers, said, "Yes, yes, I know all about you. You're the ones Shelley is pushing off on me. He knows very well I have no room on board. So there's no use asking. Waste of time."

"We can sleep on the deck," my mother said.

"Have you slept on the deck of a small ship in an Atlantic storm?"

"Have you tried to get out of Africa for thirteen years?" asked my mother. "I'd rather sleep on your deck. I'll bring my own rope."

Jensen began to laugh. "Is that a bottle of wine you've got there? Did you come here to bribe me?" he said.

"Yes, but the moment I saw you I could see it was no use," my mother said. "A man like you. We'll have to drink it alone."

Jensen accepted her invitation to lunch. My diary records: "All fears at rest because captain of boat said he was going to take us when he came here at 12 today. Had a walk and saw our ship. Quite a nice Norwegian one."

Jensen was the kind of man women and children like. My father felt a little awkward with him, as he always did around men who make it a rule to ignore rules. But Jensen, like my mother, lived by his own rules. And he ferried two sorts of passengers—missionaries and people who amused him. The American consul had been right about him.

We were entering a season of miracles, one of those lovely moments in human existence when all anxiety ceases and the soul drifts in delicious free-fall toward the object of its desire. Eventually, of course, you must pull the rip cord and hope your parachute opens. But with everything settled, all forms filled out, all visas stamped and signed, we found ourselves free to enjoy the illusion that absolute tranquillity exists, after all, somewhere between earth and heaven.

On the hillsides the African children performed a singing and clapping game—jump and kick the rump with both feet, jump and kick forward with one foot, jump and kick the rump with the other foot, then turn, and repeat. My father records the sequence in his notes, adding, "Object? Speculative." Was this the same dance the children did when Joseph Conrad had stopped in Matadi fifty years before us? Are they doing that same dance now, a half a century later? Or is it rock music from London they now skip to?

Across from the Métropole stood the Catholic church, crowded each Sunday with throngs of Africans. At seven A.M., an American car disgorged two European priests with long beards and robes, followed by two African priests, identically clad but without beards. They proceeded into the church at a steep angle. Sloping streets delivered barefoot policemen in red fezzes and short blue capes. The shops sold everything from American canned peaches to ugly little ivory saints crossing to heaven on a Venetian bridge carved into elephant tusks. Enormous trees soared above the French architecture with trunks that resembled the muscled legs of weight lifters, and their branches were perfectly horizontal, supported by ungainly, triangular brackets that looked like deformed shoulders. These trees were objects children might fashion from Play-Doh or Silly Putty, the sort of thing inexperienced nature would have devised at the beginning of the world.

But strangest among all this strangeness was the day-old news that arrived each morning in Matadi. On the first of May, the papers reported that Mussolini had been strung up with his mistress in an Italian square. On the fourth of May, we heard unrestrained singing. People poured down the steep, angled streets. Men embraced. Children danced with policemen. What was it? What were they singing? Hitler was dead.

His name was being chanted over and over, as if his corpse were running for political office. Nazi Germany had collapsed. Europeans staying at the hotel thought it must be gossip. But the air was more filled with light. Evil had been lifted from the world. Even the flies and mosquitoes were gone.

We felt that our real lives were beginning at long last. We were going to America, and Hitler had thoughtfully shot himself to improve on the occasion.

Plugged in among all the happy memories are images of Batman and Robin, because, somewhere among the dog-eared magazines in the Métropole lobby, I found a comic book and studied it like a catechism. The little line drawings, the dramatic shifts in perspective, the city of Gotham with its spiny buildings and black shadows affected me profoundly. Batman's Gotham, I knew, was the city where I was headed—glittering and artificial. I must have read that comic book fifty times, seeing New York as Batman saw it—a series of wildly disparate perspectives, from a rat's-eye view in an alley to a skyscraper rooftop where my alter ego, Batman's Robin, crouched before leaping into the American brightness. Those pictures reinforced my own irrational desire to draw, to entertain the mystery of space by reducing it to scratches on a sheet of paper. I had acquired a fatal itch to get to the bottom of things, although I had no idea then how serious was the disease.

My sister and I had days to waste and invent. We discovered a stream that ran like molten crystal along a bed of granite near our hotel. In an adjacent field, Africans in prison pajamas with yellow-and-black stripes swung machetes in a whiplike motion, cutting down the tall grass. On our way home each day, we passed a man who sold tempting, lukewarm custard from a metal cabinet baking in the sun.

We spent hours each day dabbling in the water, creating our own world, as we had all through childhood. It didn't occur to us that this journey out of Africa was the last time we would find ourselves together and happy, day after day, perfectly matched in our nonstop prattle and familiar love. The trip we took through America four years later was very different. I was sixteen and brutally self-absorbed. Patsy was thirteen and plunged into a disgruntled adolescence. Our mother was recovering from cancer surgery. We believed she would be fine because we believed in science. But it would be the last journey our family made. My sister, whether out of brooding foreknowledge or instinctive need, clung, hand in hand, to her mother, who would die three months later.

On May seventh at 3:28 in the afternoon—as my father noted with his usual precision—sirens began to wail from the port and continued without letup. Church bells joined in. Cars careened around the square below our room. Big guns boomed salutes from the hillside above the town. Infected by the growing bedlam, my sister and I began to scream "Hip-hip-hoorah!" from our perch on a window ledge. Every flag in town was hauled out and hoisted aloft. The whistles and bells rang out for over an hour.

Various new acquaintances came running in to shake our hands and dance around the room—a pretty Argentine woman, who lived in the hotel without visible means of support; a French officer with a bottle of champagne; an American missionary woman, who refused the champagne but jumped up and down with my father on the bed.

A Belgian colonel, very drunk, invited everyone to the Portuguese Hotel for a long night of celebration. My sister and I ran out into the street, where a children's band, directed by a grinning priest, ground out lopsided marches. The band danced around the square, followed by a throng of bouncing school children.

The victory celebration continued into the next day with parades of Africans from nearby missions. The cook and Antoine, the maître d', were too drunk to stand up, much less prepare meals. Guests wandered through the kitchen to find what they could—odd bananas, oranges sliced for drinks that no one was sober enough to serve, anchovy sandwiches and red wine, white wine, sparkling wine.

On the second night, there were torch processions and fireworks from the roof of the post-office building next to the cathedral. We all rushed off to someone's farm, but soon left, driven away by the stench of overripe manure. On the way home, my father insisted on knocking on the door of a house where the American flag was being displayed upside down. The resident was not a fascist, but Georgette

Le Brun, who'd fought with the resistance. She apologized about the flag and invited us for dinner.

We stayed past midnight, listening to tales of the German occupation in France. Songs were sung in three languages until two in the morning. I sang "Sarie Marais" without a vestige of the self-consciousness that would soon turn me into a social basket case. My father carried my sister home in his arms.

32

Full Circle

THE *TARN* WAS A HAPPY SHIP. WHAT ELSE COULD SHE BE? SHE HAD crossed and recrossed a submarine-infested Atlantic for five years without being sunk. Her flanks were still painted a dark, wartime gray when we went on board. Every porthole was blacked out in case a sour German captain decided to fire a last torpedo. Anti-sub guns remained bolted fore and aft. At night, the crew took care to show no light, and the passengers were asked to light no matches and smoke no cigarettes above decks. But the war was over. We had to keep reminding ourselves that the war was over.

Sloshing through muddy Congo water, we dropped a river pilot at Banana, an island so narrow you could see past the bamboo and tin shacks of fishermen to the sea beyond. Banana is the oldest white settlement on the African west coast, the spot where slaves were herded onto the ships that carried them to New Orleans, Savannah,

and Charleston. The green coast of Africa slipped back over the horizon, but the sea remained brown with river water.

We were sailing down to Lobito Bay in Portuguese Angola to fill
the empty holds with sisal and copper. So our trip to America began
with a 500 mile tack straight south, back toward the same Namaqualand we had escaped three years earlier. But Lobito Bay is 1,200 miles
north of those wind-crazed dunes off Kleinzee and Oranjemund,
where my mother had stood so often, staring out across the black
Atlantic toward home. Now we were out on the big waves that rode
in to shore, and pressing her hand to her chest, she repeated, "Can
you believe it? Can you believe it?"

My father's diary records that I disgraced myself after our first
lunch at sea by vomiting at the feet of the four missionary women.
A day later, we docked in Lobito Bay. The water was calm and crystal clear. The depths were alive with great schools of fish. My parents
were greeted by the British consul and his wife and whisked away for
lunch and a game of golf. They were dying to talk with anyone who
could speak English.

My sister and I strolled around the curving lagoon to the western
side of the bay and lounged on a deserted beach. That night, we
joined the grown-ups at the Lobito theater, where we sat for the first
time surrounded by Africans. In South Africa, the rigorous separation
of European and African had seemed no less inflexible than the law
of gravity. It was exhilarating to find ourselves abruptly "ensconced
in the forbidden crowd," as my mother said. (She would cause a
small uproar a few weeks later in South Carolina when she sat us all
down in the back of a bus in a crowd of African Americans. Pre-
tending to be nonplussed when the driver refused to drive on unless
we moved, she objected, "But we're from Africa, too.")

On board the *Tarn*, my sister was soon in tight with the cook and
steward. She insisted on setting the captain's table for every meal
and laid out the silverware in her impeccable way. There were about
a dozen passengers on board. They all ate with Captain Jensen, blue-

eyed, rubicund, blond. Beside the four missionary ladies, I remember only a sad-eyed Portuguese businessman and a young Egyptian woman with brown-orange hair and golden skin. She pulled her hair back and piled it high to show off her pretty ears, and her blouse was filled with a lovely wobble. Her approach was always signaled by the click-click of strapless high heels. Her days she spent tanning on a tiny deck just behind the bridge, and her nights, with the captain. This seemed only proper, since they were the two most fascinating people on board. She was, she claimed, on her way to meet an American fiancé in New York.

I liked to lean on the rail above her and chat while she tanned every square inch of herself, save for the portions strategically covered by tiny swatches of bright green playsuit. She asked if I liked to smoke and gave me a half pack of her cigarettes, which I puffed on deck in the dead of night, lounging on the fantail, where I could be alone, staring down into the boiling wake.

On the day before we quit Africa for good, my father came down with a fever. He was in his bunk sweating when the lines were cast off. The continent disappeared over the horizon on May nineteenth, and my mother wrote in her diary, "THE GREAT DAY!" adding: "Departure marred by malaria. Quinine and Atabrine don't seem to do much good."

The weather was burning hot, the sea glassy calm. On the second day, my father's fever rose to 104 degrees, and Captain Jensen made hourly visits to his cabin to see how he was doing. He affected not to be worried. My mother was. My father passed out and had moments of delirium. He seemed to think he was still working under Fleisher in Nigel and shouted angrily. My mother wrapped him in wet sheets and tried to cool his burning skin.

The fever broke on the third day, and on the fourth he tottered on deck, white as a ghost, his eyes tinged light yellow. For two days, he sat in a chair thoughtfully communing with the horizon. His illness never worried my sister and me. We took the immortality of our parents for granted and never doubted his recovery. Now that we were headed for Oz, nothing could go wrong.

We taught our card game to the missionaries, and they taught us how to sing "Rock of Ages" and "That Old Rugged Cross." We had never been exposed to hymns before and sang them with gusto. Our mother quietly removed herself and the novel she was reading to another part of the deck.

We crossed the equator on May twenty-third, and on the twenty-fifth the captain got word from London that the blackout could be lifted. Our Norwegian crew, that same morning, dropped scaffolding over the side and began painting the ship white. Light flooded the cabins as the black film over the portholes was scraped off. My mother had developed cysts in both eyes but said she didn't care.

We were the first children the crew had ever had on board, and they gave us the run of the ship. The war was over, and everyone was sick of rules and restrictions. A new age was beginning. Even the stars overhead were changing. My familiar Southern Cross had disappeared. Orion was rising. We hung about the crew's quarters, reading American magazines and picking out favorite sailors to bother. I made a model replica of the *Tarn* in the carpenter's shop, and it was packed in the trunk that got lost on the journey to Seattle.

Somewhere in the mid-Atlantic, we sailed into a tropical storm. I was thrown out of my bunk before breakfast. The walls of my cabin had exchanged roles with the ceiling. The sea no longer showed any horizon. Steep hillsides composed of green water came rolling across the *Tarn*, and the sky had degenerated into white spray. Passengers made their way up and down the ship's passages by hanging onto ropes or crawling. The ship pointed its prow steeply up, then fell forward with a shudder and plunged down the side of a waterfall, racing toward the sea floor until another mountain of water heaved her back on high, only to fling her down again. The deck disappeared under five, then ten feet of solid water until the ship shook herself free. I stood most of that day staring at our chaotic world, watching sailors struggle from the bridge to their quarters below decks, grasping guidelines while their feet were swept out from beneath them.

Passengers were forbidden to venture out. I sneaked out, anyway, and got a nose full of water. The storm calmed a little toward dinner, but our family and the Egyptian beauty in her strapless high heels were the only takers at the captain's table that night. By morning, the horizon had reestablished itself, but the sky and the air were as cold and gray as an English admiral's eyes. Our tropical world had vanished.

My sister and I reveled in the smooth, yellow American pound cake and the slick vanilla ice cream that came in rockhard bricks. It was the gustatory equivalent of Montovani's predigested music, but we knew nothing of that. In the United States, we would briefly adore the fluffy white bread, the spearmint gum obtainable in subway stations for a nickel, and spongy pancakes served with burned bacon and eggs over easy, the whole mess floating in a brown lake of supersweet syrup. The perfect bodies and ideal teeth of American women would soon absorb me, their nubile outlines fusing with Firestone tires, Studebaker cars, General Electric light bulbs, whiskey, brandy, biscuits, beer.

On the night of June fourth, we saw a glow in the western sky. Across the horizon, a hundred miles away, New York City was rising like the sun. I rose very early, not wishing to miss the *Tarn*'s approach to New York harbor. But we were already sailing between headlands and buildings. Manhattan's skyline was half erased by mist, so the skyscrapers looked like designs in lace. Only the Statue of Liberty was starkly visible, moving in on the portside with her torch pushing up through a cloud. As we crept closer, I tried to read her expression. It remained inscrutable, neither welcoming nor threatening—the face of reason.

My sister and mother joined me at the rail, and, laying her hands on our shoulders as she always did, my mother pulled us closer. We all gazed at the goddess approaching, and my mother addressed her, saying, "Well, *you're* still here, at least."

In her account of our landing, my mother wrote, "It was time we came home and made Americans of our two South Africans. In New York harbor, when they looked down into the hold of the ship being unloaded by stevedores, Patsy exclaimed incredulously, 'Why look! White men are working!' "

The ship was at rest. It had taken my parents thirteen years to come full circle. What surprised me most about the New World was its extreme old age. The waters in Lobito Bay had been crystal clear and packed with brilliant fish. New York harbor was crepuscular, opaque with grayish sludge. The filthy waters of the bay slopped greasily against the black piers. The buildings looked ancient, decayed. The windows of the warehouses were boarded over, nailed shut. I could never have imagined an America so dilapidated.

A taxi whipped us downtown and out across the Brooklyn Bridge to a hotel across the river. A feverish energy flew off the bright surfaces and poured into these streets from the mechanical angles of signs and buildings. The city was a wild animal with its skeleton on the outside, scuttling rapidly in every direction at once, and I felt this frightening apparition would never have any use for the likes of me.

33

After

THE FIRST EUROPEAN GIVEN PERMISSION TO ENTER THE AFRICAN CITY of Harar (circa 1855) was Richard Burton, the English writer and orientalist. Once in, he found the ruling emir in no hurry to let him out. Burton cooled his heels for a fortnight awaiting the potentate's nod. "All these African cities," he grumbled, "are prisons on a large scale . . . you enter by your own will, . . . and . . . you leave by another's."

Burton's experience was my parents' experience. Of course it was no African emir who allowed them in and then kicked them out, but Burton would have understood. Held hostage by ambition, debt, and war, my mother felt her life wearing out in a world where, no matter how slowly the years dragged by, too much time had passed. This, I know, is the reason I have never felt the least urge to go back. It is the reason I cannot understand intelligent people who long for remote deserts that resemble the landscapes of other planets.

My Africa was narrow, limited, primitive, because I was primitive, limited, a child. I absorbed Africa with all the inattention and cloudy self-centeredness of a child. I was, in rapid succession, an Afrikaner, a miniature Nazi, an English boy, an American by default. Arriving in the States at last, I would imagine that Africa had no influence on me whatever.

My sister and I saw our grandmother Bess for the first time in the King Street Station in Seattle. For as long as we could remember, she had sent us books, strange American clothes, valentines swathed in lace. Seeing her in the flesh was like arriving in heaven and meeting Saint Elizabeth. But our Elizabeth appeared in sensible black shoes and a boxy hat, too filled with emotion to speak. A few weeks later, America dropped the bomb on Hiroshima.

Our mother died four and a half years after our return. Later, in her last illness, she told her friend, Estelle Parsons, that "it was the desert that killed her." In Kimberley, I remember her saying she felt like a young woman in an old body. She died in December, Pearl Harbor day, and Bess died in the same month fifteen years later. My father sat by both bedsides.

After my mother's death, my father said he could not marry again. But eighteen months later he flew off to Hawaii on his honeymoon while my sister went to summer school, and I worked in a copper mine. Unable to adapt to the atmospherics of our father's new household, Patsy and I moved out as soon as we had the means. My sister was soon married, bore three sons, took advanced degrees in psychology, and, among other things, now works with people dying of AIDs. I diverted into naval aviation.

Park and my father wound up their careers as the deans of mining schools—Park at the University of Colorado in Golden, my father at the University of Washington in Seattle. Park and I had music in common, and the year my father remarried, Park got me a fellowship at Aspen with a composer. But my father sent me to that copper mine in Eastern Washington instead. The last letter I ever got from

Park urges me to phone up a clarinetist friend of his who plays in the Seattle Symphony. She was looking for a pianist. I needn't be afraid, he adds, because she is ten years older than me and married.

As Park grew older, he began to fear that a tide of tropical humanity was advancing north from the equator to sweep away European civilization. Like my uncle Nick and Joseph Conrad's Kurtz, he somehow came to see dark skins as the sign of chaos. My father believed that a series of heart attacks had affected his old friend's mind. Once, when I was enthusing over Park's sardonic view of things, he told me that they were no longer friends. The race issue had divided them. And soon after that we got news that Park had died in Mexico in the early sixties.

Years before, I had sat with Stephen in the backyard of our house in Kimberley, plucking the feathers from a chicken, and he began to speak about the eyes of white men. "They look at you," he said, "but they don't see you."

"I see you," I objected.

"Yes, now you see me," he said and laughed.

I tried to convince him that I would always be able to see him; he patted my arm sympathetically. He had put in me the fear of going blind.

In 1886, the African king Ahmadu concluded a trade agreement with Europeans and said, "We like the French, but do not trust them; while they trust us, but do not like us." The remark contains a brief moral history of the relations between Europe and Africa. I have tried to imagine how Africans saw those first Europeans who suddenly appeared in the Congo with their pale blue eyes and bushy beards. They stopped for fruit and fresh water and were soon shipping men and women to the New World in chains, with plenty of help from other Africans, whose prejudice lay strictly along tribal lines.

Africa, so vast and diverse, should disturb the European's faith in his own formulations. It seldom does. Joseph Conrad is attacked in some quarters as a racist, but he was among the first to tell how the

European in Africa enters the desert of his own dead reckoning and ends by slaughtering the Hottentot. Conrad saw how Europe fused Christ with technology to excuse its own rapacity. By calling Africa "the dark continent," the West covered, with a journalist's cliché, its own failure of imagination and placed its own savagery outside the realm of moral judgment.

I know that morality was the last thing on my father's mind when he dropped toward the middle of the earth in a cage or buttoned up his dinner jacket to drive through a sandstorm to a company soiree in Walvis Bay or Lüderitz. He and Park were part of the last colonial wave, men who saw Africa as the gateway to a respectable profession, an international career. After thirteen years of it, my father left with a few diamonds, an interesting resume, and a sick wife.

Faced with unreasonable Africa, the idealizing European mind feels an irresistible desire either to destroy ("Exterminate the beasts!" cries Kurtz) or to write poetry. Cecil Rhodes, sickly son of a clergyman, goes to South Africa to dry out his diseased lungs and ends by trying to attach the entire continent of Africa to tiny Britain. Isak Dinesen grows coffee in Kenya, falls in love with the African people, and sings their praises in *Out of Africa*. It's Cecil Rhodes or Isak Dinesen—make your choice.

How many books have been written, and will continue to be written, on the beauty of the African landscape where space has mysteriously acquired another dimension? How many lavish descriptions of a generous, happy, simple people, of touching good-byes as the author clasps their hands in warm friendship before heading back to London or Copenhagen? Standing always with a cannon behind him, the European is able to bring to Africa the most exquisite shades of subtle arrogance. He ponders the plethora of cultures as Richard Burton did; he maps the landscape as Park did; he tries to change something as my father did. Nothing quite works out. So he decides to learn something. He lives among the Ovambo or Dinka and takes copious notes. He translates his raw data into the abstract truth of his science or the elegiac constructions of his poetry and translates himself right out of Africa.

My Africa was Africa at a great distance. There was a sort of reality in the hatred of the Afrikaner boys that left me banged up and bleeding, but the train whistle sounding across the Kimberley plain is more faithful to the spirit of my childhood. I was not African. I sometimes think I was hardly there at all. I never slept in a rondavel covered with flies. I never covered five hundred miles in broken shoes. My mother insisted I was an American, so I trusted that my world lay across the black Atlantic. From the doorway of our house in Oranjemund, I saw men singing boisterously to my father in words I could only half make out. Drummers under the peppertrees slyly invited me to dance. So I danced, and they laughed. No, African I was not.

I was the manager's boy riding his horse along the Orange river; the English boy with a face bloodied by the children of Boers; a public-school boy assuming his place somewhere near the top of the social heap. Years later in London, I would feel instantly at home. The manners, the polite distance between people, the complexities of British syntax were as comfortably familiar as an old family friend. Put me tomorrow in a Zulu tribe and the freedom of their gestures and their unrestrained laughter would rekindle memories that predate memory. But their words would be familiar only as music is familiar.

Still . . . in Oranjemund, my mother let me escape from Mynheer Meyer's classroom at just the moment when my imagination was being crystalized. She allowed the desert to instruct me. And when she wandered out into the garden, leaving me to ponder one of her cunningly ambiguous questions, or when I heard voices whispering out of the hot wind, or when I observed the sun rise four or five times on that single unforgettable morning, an alternate reality crept into my consciousness and lodged there like a second sun. I see that my fabulous sloth was my way of resisting too much certitude. By dragging my feet and dreaming, I bought time to advance at my own slow African pace, picking my confused way through a world where there existed not one, but two sources of light. My perception is still confused by double shadows from these twin suns. I would never say that my perception is African. But Africa is lodged in my perception all the same.

As our Norwegian freighter wallowed out of the Congo on its way to America, I never dreamed that I would always be a stranger over there—or, at least, be somewhat strange. Earnestly trying to adapt myself to the American way, I would feel like a skeptic in a clown suit. It would take me half a lifetime to understand how Africa had shored up this skepticism of mine against the West, saving me from the bitter certainty that our sun is only a dying star passing over futile lives on a fading planet.